MW01055614

STEPHEN DODSON RAMSEUR

LEE'S GALLANT GENERAL

STEPHEN DODSON

RAMSEUR

LEE'S GALLANT GENERAL

GARY W. GALLAGHER

The University of North Carolina Press

Chapel Hill and London

98 97 96 95 94   9 8 7 6 5

Library of Congress Cataloging in Publication Data

Gallagher, Gary W.

Stephen Dodson Ramseur: Lee's gallant general.

Bibliography: p.

Includes index.

1. Ramseur, Stephen Dodson. 2. Generals—United States
—Biography. 3. Confederate States of America. Army—
Biography. 4. Virginia—History—Civil War, 1861–1865—
Campaigns. I. Title

E467.1.R2G35   1985   973.7′56   84-13035

ISBN 0-8078-1627-2

ISBN 0-8078-4522-1 (pbk.)

Portions of this book have appeared in somewhat different form in "A North
Carolinian at West Point: Stephen Dodson Ramseur, 1855–1860," *North
Carolina Historical Review* 62 (January 1985).

FOR GI,
who made the long march with me,
with love

CONTENTS

ILLUSTRATIONS

MAPS

Biographical literature on Confederate military figures is extensive. Most of the top-level officers have been the subject of at least one adequate biography, and many, such as Robert E. Lee, Stonewall Jackson, and Nathan Bedford Forrest, have attracted the attention of several talented writers. Of divisional and brigade commanders few studies exist. Inescapable questions confront anyone who would examine a figure of the second echelon. Did the individual make a sufficiently important contribution to warrant a biography? Would the work go beyond a mere retracing of familiar campaigns? Did the man leave enough personal papers to ensure that he would be more than a shadowy presence in the background, known only through official reports, newspaper accounts, and the writings of others? In the absence of affirmative answers to these questions, a subject might best be left alone.

Stephen Dodson Ramseur of North Carolina is a leader in the second echelon who successfully meets these tests. Among the best of the younger Confederates who lacked prewar exposure to combat but who rose rapidly through excellent performance, Ramseur's career constitutes a case study in the development of general officers in the Army of Northern Virginia. He compiled an enviable record as a brigadier, enjoying great days at Chancellorsville and Spotsylvania and winning plaudits from Lee, Jackson, and other prominent southern soldiers. Commissioned major general the day after his twenty-seventh birthday, he was the youngest West Pointer to achieve that rank in the Confederate army. As a divisional leader he showed considerable ability in the maneuvering and fighting in the Shenandoah Valley in fall 1864. His death, coming at a point when talent and experience had equipped him to assume a larger role, was symptomatic of the collapse of the high command of Lee's army in 1864–65.

Ramseur left a large and revealing body of papers extending from boyhood through his final days, letters rich with frank opinions and observations on a wide range of topics. This correspondence, which includes a set of beautiful love letters to the woman he married during the war, offers insights into the formation and development of Ramseur's character and helps to explain his motivations. Together with other sources, Ramseur's letters shed light on his growth as a soldier and the process by which he molded the men entrusted to him into effective fighting units. His perspective was that of a man in the middle tier of command—one who carried out the orders given by more famous captains whose reputations often owed much to the competence of their lieutenants. Apart from its historical significance, Ramseur's story has much drama and tragedy. An understanding of his life brings into sharper focus some of the crosscurrents of the turbulent era of the American Civil War.

Many people gave generously of their time in the course of my work on Dodson Ramseur. I am deeply grateful to Barnes F. Lathrop, my mentor and dear friend, whose contribution went well beyond what I had any reasonable right to expect. Robert K. Krick made available materials on Ramseur's later career, improved my understanding of the ground at Chancellorsville and Spotsylvania, and painstakingly criticized the manuscript. George B. Forgie, Lewis L. Gould, John E. McDaniel, Jr., and Norman D. Brown were steadfast in their support and made many helpful suggestions. To Allan Purcell I owe a special debt. He first brought the Ramseur materials to my attention and urged me to write this biography.

Paul W. Schenck, Jr., and John R. Schenck, Jr., kindly gave permission to quote freely from the Ramseur letters. The Ramseur family in Lincolnton, North Carolina, and Mrs. L. B. Satterfield of Milton, North Carolina, graciously provided genealogical information and shared with me local traditions regarding Dodson and Ellen Richmond Ramseur. Edmund J. Raus guided me around the battlefields at Fisher's Hill and Cedar Creek; Michael Gore performed a similar courtesy at Belle Grove and tracked down an early photograph of the monument to Ramseur on the field at Cedar Creek. Stephen D. and Saralind Mings prepared the maps, retaining their sense of humor while working against a cruel deadline.

Archivists and librarians were without exception helpful and tolerant of my many requests. Richard A. Shrader of the Southern Historical Collection received most of my queries; his cheerful professionalism was matched by the staffs of the North Carolina Collection at the University of North Carolina, the William R. Perkins Library at Duke University, the North Carolina Department of Archives and History, the United States Military Academy Library, the Barker Texas History Center at the University of Texas, and the Western Reserve Historical Society.

To my wife, Mary Ann, and to my son, Will, I can only say that their patience was beyond reckoning. In effect, they welcomed Ramseur into our family for a period of several years. "Big Bill" and I could not have made our journey without their encouragement and understanding.

Austin, Texas   *Gary W. Gallagher*
February 1984

STEPHEN DODSON RAMSEUR

LEE'S GALLANT GENERAL

PROLOGUE

O n 20 May 1861, 122 men filed into the southern wing of the state capitol in Raleigh to de- cide whether North Carolina would join ten sister states that had already severed their ties with the Union. A crowd that spilled out of the gallery and occupied every available space elsewhere in the chamber listened as delegates argued the relative merits of leaving the Union through secession or through invocation of the right of revolution. The need to act was not at issue. North Carolina had been reluctant to renounce the Constitution in the wake of the election of Abraham Lincoln, but the attack on Fort Sumter, the president's call for troops, and the secession of Virginia caused even staunch unionists to accept the inevitability of a break with the national government. Debate ended about six o'clock, when, by unanimous vote, the convention adopted an ordinance of secession written and presented by Burton Craige of Salis- bury.[1] Secessionists in the hall responded to the vote with wild rejoicing while unionists viewed their handiwork soberly and with foreboding, a divi- sion of sentiment that one participant said gave the body a look of "a sea partly in storm, partly calm."[2]

Immediately upon passage of the ordinance, Major Graham Davee, pri- vate secretary to the governor, threw open a window on the west side of the hall and related the news to a young captain of artillery who waited with six guns of his battery on the lawn below.[3] North Carolina had ceased to be one of the United States, and a salute must mark the occasion. By prearrange- ment, Stephen Dodson Ramseur, twenty-four years old and scarcely eleven months out of West Point, had the honor of ordering the cannons to fire. The measured cadence of one hundred discharges alerted the city that North Carolina was a sovereign state. As the cannons boomed, citizens from all parts of Raleigh gathered at the statehouse. The capitol bell joined the celebration, and church bells across the city pealed their support. Ram- seur and his men rested a few minutes after the sound of the hundredth gun died away, then fired ten shots for the other seceded states; the crowd gave three cheers for each of them. Another rest, and a battery and nine cheers rang out for North Carolina. Next came news from within the building that the convention had adopted the constitution of the Confederate States of

America, and Ramseur and his Ellis Light Artillery responded with a salute of twenty guns. A newspaperman who groped to characterize the atmosphere in the crowd during all of this could only say that the excitement was "beyond our power of description."[4]

It was a heady moment for Ramseur, this opening scene in the drama of the Confederate experiment. Before leaving the stage three and one-half years hence, mortally wounded, he would rise to the rank of major general and be a conspicuous actor in great battles of the Army of Northern Virginia.

CHAPTER 1

WHO KNOWS BUT THAT I MAY

WRITE MY HISTORY WITH

MY SWORD?

One hundred and fifty miles west of Raleigh, North Carolina, across the Catawba River on the edge of the Piedmont, lies a fertile, rolling country, rich in minerals and traversed by many streams. The land beyond the Catawba knew few European settlers before the arrival of a German from Pennsylvania named Henry Weidner, who entered the area about 1745. Weidner returned to tell of what he had seen, and soon a steady flow of Germans from southern Pennsylvania followed him back to what would become Lincoln County.

Among these pioneers was Diedrich Ramsour, who migrated from Pennsylvania in 1750 and became a successful farmer. He erected on Clark's Creek near Lincolnton a gristmill that passed after his death in 1780 to his son Jacob.[1] Near Ramsour's mill, shortly after Diedrich died, Loyalists and Patriots fought one of the sharpest engagements of the War for Independence in North Carolina. This contest between neighbors and kinsmen pitted about 1,300 Tories, who had gathered to await the advance of Lord Cornwallis from the east, against about 400 Patriots, and produced 300 casualties. The Patriots won, thereby denying Great Britain support it had hoped for. An important preliminary to Kings Mountain, the battle of Ramsour's Mill scarred Lincoln County in a way that a much greater civil conflict would in the next century; it also supplied martial lore to be absorbed by future generations of Lincolnton's youth.[2]

One of Jacob Ramsour's sons, David, established himself as a merchant in Lincolnton. In 1805 he married Sarah Wilfong, daughter of a wealthy veteran of the battles at Kings Mountain and Eutaw Springs. David and Sarah Ramsour reared a large family and figured prominently in the social and economic life of Lincolnton. Unlike his father-in-law, John Wilfong, who was a Jacksonian Democrat and a Van Buren elector in 1836, David was a Clay man and a Whig elector in 1840. David Ramsour was an organizer and longtime pillar of the first Presbyterian church in Lincolnton and also a founding trustee of Pleasant Retreat Academy, chartered in 1813 and available to the children of the more affluent families in Lincoln County.[3]

Stephen Dodson Ramseur's father was Jacob A. Ramseur, son of David Ramsour.[4] Like David, Jacob was a leading merchant in Lincolnton. He married, in 1833, Lucy Mayfield Dodson of Milton, Caswell County, North Carolina. The town of Milton, on the Dan River southeast of Danville, Virginia, lay in a fertile area known for its fine tobacco, which had brought enough wealth to smooth the rough edges of the frontier still present in most towns across the Catawba River. Lucy's father, Stephen Dodson, stood among the first citizens of Milton. Farmer, owner of a flour mill, and partner in a company that manufactured yarns, he was a Mason, sat on the board of the Milton Male Academy, and was three times elected to the legislature.[5]

The Lincolnton to which Jacob Ramseur took his bride was a small town —a village, really—in which the streets remained unnamed for years to come.[6] Set amid the rolling hills of the Piedmont some forty miles northwest of Charlotte, it had been established in 1785. Town and county were named after General Benjamin Lincoln, a hero of the Revolution. Diverse economic elements in the area allowed merchants such as David Ramsour and Jacob A. Ramseur to prosper. Lincoln County contained deposits of iron ore that supplied several furnaces in the half-century prior to the Civil War. The first cotton mill south of the Potomac River was built a mile and a half east of Lincolnton in 1816, and others began operation in the ensuing decades. There were corn and flour mills, a paper mill, and small gold mines. Tobacco and cotton were the principal cash crops. Lincolnton, though small, boasted several churches and two schools, Pleasant Retreat Academy for boys and Lincolnton Female Academy. A few fine homes testified to good fortune among local planters. Thus, Lincolnton offered Jacob's young wife and family more gentility than was typical in a town of its size and location.[7]

The first son of Jacob and Lucy Ramseur, second of their nine children, was born 31 May 1837, and christened Stephen Dodson.[8] The boy, known throughout his life as Dodson or, to his intimates, Dod, was raised in a stable, comfortable household. Both parents were active Presbyterians, and Lucy instructed Dodson from his early youth in the teachings of the Westminster catechism. Dodson's childhood letters reveal genuine affection for his brothers and sisters and love and respect for his parents. While both mother and father shaped his personality, his closest friend observed that it was to Lucy Ramseur that Dodson "owed the mental and moral foundations of his character." Together with "great force of character" and "judgment clear and firm" she possessed "gentleness, tenderness and sympathy." Those who knew Ramseur in his maturity often described him in very similar terms. She also instilled into her son a profound devotion to duty both Christian and civic.[9]

From an early age, Dodson impressed his friends and comrades with an unlikely combination of personal gentleness and reckless daring in dangerous circumstances. The Reverend E. H. Harding, an intimate companion during the last two years of Ramseur's life, saw developed in him "in a remarkable manner two elements necessary to the highest type of man, viz: a womanly tenderness of feeling, united with the most manly courage and self reliance."[10] Colonel E. A. Osborne, who served under Ramseur through much of the war, thought his commander "blended in his nature all those qualities which fascinate by their loveliness, with those which, by authority and force, command admiration and applause."[11] Playmates knew that Dodson's small stature and mild demeanor belied his willingness to confront bullies. One of those playmates, in reflecting on Dodson as a boy, thought "with loving regret of the little arm, which was ever strong to shield or uphold those whose weakness claimed its protection; for that heart was as brave and chivalric then on that childish field of action, as since in the terrible contest through which it has passed."[12] Ramseur seemed something of an enigma because he fused sensitivity with utter fearlessness in crisis. Even as a child, he felt confident enough of his strength in traditionally male roles to reveal his more sensitive side.

Many diversions beckoned Dodson to the woods and fields around Lincolnton. He and David Schenck, Robert F. Hoke, and other boys stalked rabbits and squirrels, pigeons and woodchucks, doves and partridges, hawks and swallows. Nearly every day in fall they pursued ducks along the Catawba River and the local creeks and rarely came home empty-handed. They hunted on horseback with dogs, or tramped miles on foot, or occasionally drifted down the river in a boat. Bats and other hard-to-hit targets presented a special challenge. David Schenck, Dodson's dearest friend in childhood and later his brother-in-law, recorded in his diary that Dod "shot two bats and some swallows on the wing . . . [he] is an excellent shot."[13]

Besides hunting, the boys had other pastimes. The rivers and creeks invited swimming and fishing. An old stillhouse on the Catawba was a favorite swimming haunt, and on one hot summer day four of the boys took a bateau out on the river, got stuck on a mud bar, stripped and jumped into the water to free their small craft, then rode for about a mile in the boat "naked as Cupid's statue." One August morning Dod and David Schenck "rode down to Mr. Kistler's plantation and revelled long in the luxury of the melon patch." On other days, they simply roamed about the country.[14] A fine horseman as well as a keen sportsman, Dod was in his element in the environment of Lincoln County.[15]

In town, the boys played draughts, attended court, practiced marksmanship with pistols in a back street, or lolled about Johnson's Hotel watching people. An icehouse behind Pleasant Retreat Academy attracted them because its steep embankment formed a natural slide and nearby chestnut trees supplied the frolickers with nuts.[16] Muster days in Lincoln County offered the spectacle of military drills and, perchance, opportunity to purchase ginger cakes from Hiram Revels, a free black barber who eventually would represent Mississippi in the U.S. Senate.[17] Circuses with their exotic freak shows came to Lincolnton, but, as David Schenck noted ruefully in his diary, children from pious families were not allowed to attend.[18]

As teenagers, Dod and his cohorts devoted much of their attention to young ladies. With banjo and flute they might make their way around the town serenading different girls. One late December night in 1852 found them drinking lemonade and smoking cigars until ten o'clock, when they set out to enliven Lincolnton with music. Nine days later Dod and David attended "tableaux vi-vants" and had a "joyously merry" time.[19] Girls found Dod attractive, a fact not lost on him, and he in turn was "fervently fond of ladies' society."[20] Nearly 30 years after Dod's death his friend Schenck in effect explained Dod's popularity among young people of both sexes: "marked by an open, generous, frank bearing, he was free from envy, devoted affectionately to his friends and family . . . happy and cheerful in disposition . . . handsome, bright and companionable . . . and was a model of politeness." "Brave to a fault," Dod rarely "indulged in petty mischief, so common to boys, but enjoyed an innocent joke even at his own expense. He had a merry, earnest laugh and a joyous face."[21]

Dod's parents, coming from families who knew the worth of education, paid close attention to the instruction of their children.[22] Dod attended school in Milton briefly, but received most of his formal education in Lincolnton. At Pleasant Retreat Academy he took the usual curriculum of Latin and Greek, algebra, chemistry, grammar, and logic. The academy, housed in a two-story brick building on a hill, earned an enviable reputation in the western part of the state before the Civil War.[23]

The evening debating society at Pleasant Retreat counted among its membership current and former students up to age twenty-one. In 1852, Ramseur, though only fifteen, was elected president of the society. He and Schenck often participated as a team in debates, successfully arguing in one match that George Washington was greater as a statesman than as a warrior, in another, that law rather than moral persuasion was the way to stop the liquor traffic. David Schenck's diary shows that the boys spent many nights preparing for their debates. They made use of Dod's small library and David's much larger one, trading volumes and reviewing their contents during long walks in late afternoon or quiet evenings in their rooms. On one occasion Dod and David strayed from their work at hand to contemplate "boyhood and lascivious habits"; the latter they "severely condemned."[24]

Dod especially loved to read about battles and the lives of great captains.[25] As a child he must have heard many stories of the Revolution and the service of his great grandfathers at Kings Mountain, Guilford Courthouse, and Eutaw Springs. He also must have played many times on the battlefield of Ramsour's Mill, perhaps imagining himself one of the Patriot soldiers. Whether or not he appreciated as a child the fratricidal character of that fight, he must have sensed the ghosts of his people around the mill. By his fifteenth year Dod's passionate admiration for the military figures he called the "World's renowned Heroes" set his eye on West Point. Failing to secure an appointment to the Academy in 1853, he turned to college to prepare for another attempt to gain admission.[26]

On the last day of September 1853, sixteen-year-old Dod left Lincolnton on a twenty-five-mile journey eastward, across the Catawba River, to enroll as a freshman at Davidson College.[27] He found a small Presbyterian school struggling for financial survival, its faculty and inept administration in disarray. The only buildings of note were a pair of two-story Greek Revival halls with outsized porticoes that faced each other across a space of but a few yards. The other one-story brick structures were hardly calculated to impress a student from even so small a place as Lincolnton. Tuition at the college was thirty-two dollars per year. The student body numbered fewer than one hundred.[28]

Settling quickly into the classroom routine, Ramseur discovered that his preparation at Pleasant Retreat Academy had been more than adequate. To his sister he reported in mid-October that his studies were quite easy except for Greek, and by diligence he could keep up in it. Overall, Davidson disappointed him. He considered only one member of the faculty fit to teach. Several upperclassmen spoke incorrectly, yet, unbelievably, did well in class. Bad as things were, Dod predicted further decline unless Daniel Harvey Hill, a West Pointer who was to arrive in the spring 1854 term to teach mathematics, could turn the school around. In sum, because Davidson did not offer a first-rate education, Dod did not wish to become a graduate, and would spend at most two years there. He implored his sister to have their father ask Congressman Burton Craige to get him into West Point as soon as possible.[29]

Untoward events somewhat marred Dod's first year at Davidson. In February 1854 an epidemic of scarlet fever closed the school for the remainder of the winter term. Then came a major faculty–student clash occasioned by the North Carolina gubernatorial contest of 1854. During the campaign Democrat Thomas Bragg and Whig Alfred Dockery scheduled speeches about three miles from Davidson. A number of students, instructed to stay on campus, went to the rallies anyway. This action threatened to terminate Ramseur's career at Davidson sooner than he wished. Three offenders were suspended, and the other thirty-eight, including Dod, were made to pledge strict obedience in future to all laws of the school. Influenced perhaps by this episode, the faculty refused to allow Dod to visit home at the end of the spring session.[30]

Disappointing as Davidson was to Ramseur, its religious atmosphere suited him well. He reported home that, though a few wicked boys attended the school, fully two-thirds of his classmates were members of the church. They held prayer meetings on Saturday nights; they went to church on the Sabbath; and many planned to take up the ministry. A typical Sunday for Dod began with sunrise prayers in chapel. After breakfast came Sabbath school, then a sermon by one of the faculty. In the early afternoon he read on a religious topic in his room. At three o'clock he joined other students to recite Bible lessons before the faculty. An evening sermon brought the day to a close. Dod assured his sister that he tried "to spend the Sabbath in such a way I think will please my Father in Heaven, and will be beneficial to my never dying soul."[31]

The strict religious regimen encouraged in Ramseur a deep personal commitment to God, a commitment obvious throughout his entire correspondence. His devout behavior at all stages of his life evoked comments from those who knew him. Deriving a genuine happiness from his faith, he tried to perform what he deemed his Christian duty. His friend David Schenck, on the other hand, also lived in a pious household but agonized over his faith. Noting in his diary in June 1854 that his brother thought of joining the church, David remarked: "What friends he and Dod will be. I love Dod but 'My ways are not his ways.' "[32]

In a lengthy letter to his mother from Davidson in July 1854, Ramseur discussed the demands and rewards of Christianity. He was hard at work on his studies and marveled at how quickly time passed. "Happy is he who, when almost done with this world, and is about entering an unknown eternity, can review a well-spent life . . . a life passed in usefulness—a life, which has been devoted to *labor*, noble, manly, Christian labor." Childhood and its innocent pleasures were now behind him; soon he would be finished with the tasks of a schoolboy. Manhood approached with its "more arduous duties—so we go on—with our cares and duties increasing by degrees, until we are 'armed and equipped' ready for the warfare of life." In that battle he would depend on God for shield and protection, and in so doing find eternal happiness. Having made his decision to give all to God, Ramseur felt a *"peace* now that the world 'can neither give nor take away.'" He would "never, no never, no never forsake" the Lord.[33] A month earlier Dod had assured his mother that he did not grieve for a sister who had died. She was now "an Angel worshipping in the presence of that Jesus she loved so fondly and served so faithfully while she was with us in this world of sin and sorrow."[34] On 22 April 1855, five weeks short of his eighteenth birthday, Dod was received into the communion of the Presbyterian church of Lincolnton.[35]

Increasingly during his time at Davidson, Ramseur came to believe that service to his country was part of his duty in life, and that attendance at West Point was the best way to undertake it. Most of his letters home during 1854–55—to his mother, to his sisters, and to David Schenck—included mention of the military academy. When Dod was in Lincolnton he and David discussed their futures, sometimes on walks that lasted hours. Schenck, who favored the law, tried to dissuade Dod from the military, but Dod, a "frank, free and independent spirit," would not be deterred.[36]

The key figure in Dod's effort to gain entrance to West Point was Daniel Harvey Hill, whom Dod had mentioned earlier as the potential savior of Davidson College. A graduate of West Point with brevets for gallantry in the Mexican War, Hill had a nimble mind and a caustic tongue that caused trouble with his superiors whether military or civilian. The trustees at Davidson recruited him for their chair in mathematics specifically to raise academic standards and tighten discipline. He quickly became the dominant figure on the small faculty and instituted a system of demerits reminiscent of that at West Point. The president of the school, whose tenure had been plagued by student riots, offered resistance, and many students bridled at the plethora of rules. But Hill overcame both and emerged triumphant when the trustees dismissed the president. Ramseur advised his mother of the changes Hill wrought, adding dolefully that permission to go home would be granted henceforth only under extraordinary circumstances. The new mathematics professor had made it clear, said Dod, that one's duty lay with one's books and lessons.[37]

When in due course Hill learned of Ramseur's interest in West Point, and formed a high opinion of his abilities, he encouraged the would-be cadet to concentrate on the subjects that received emphasis at the Academy. What was more important, he mentioned Dod to Francis Burton Craige, member of Congress from the Seventh District of North Carolina. Craige thought enough of Professor Hill and his student to make the appointment, which called for Dod to take his place in the class that began its service in June 1855.[38]

Though neither he nor Harvey Hill can then have imagined that both would take up arms against the United States and become generals in a rebel army, Dod Ramseur did dream of glory. "Who knows," he asked his friend David, who scoffed at a life in the military, "but that 'I may write my history with my sword'?"[39]

CHAPTER 2

FOR MYSELF, I BELIEVE

AN AWFUL CRISIS IS APPROACHING

West Point in the 1850s was an institution of great reputation. Controlled by army engineers to such a degree that many officers believed it produced better civil engineers than soldiers, the Academy was the outstanding scientific school in the United States. A rigorous course of study compelled cadets to work harder than their counterparts in civilian colleges. A decidedly eastern orientation permeated West Point; nearly the entire faculty, from professors down through assistants and instructors, hailed from the East, and the leading students in each class usually were easterners who had profited from the superior schooling available in that region. Students from the South and West, unless very able, labored to keep up with them. Although prior work at a college or university improved chances for success, even cadets from Harvard and Princeton felt unprepared for the Academy. Weakness in mathematics, the subject that dominated the curriculum, meant almost certain failure.[1]

The Academy was a national institution, however, and Congress kept standards of admission low to ensure a republican equality of opportunity. Ten at-large presidential appointments and one man from each congressional district and the District of Columbia made up the Battalion of Cadets. During the 1850s, fewer than half of those admitted managed to graduate. Most who failed were cadets from the South and West who passed the easy entrance examination but simply could not carry the workload once classes began.[2] Ramseur's class of 1860 mustered at graduation just 41 of its original complement of 121.[3]

West Point graduates received praise for both their peacetime activities and their efforts on the battlefield. A congressional commission chaired by Senator Jefferson Davis of Mississippi, himself a graduate of West Point, observed that the construction of nearly all the great public works in the country—river and harbor improvements, lighthouses, and even public buildings—had been directed by graduates of the Academy. West Pointers were pioneers in the construction of railroads and had conducted most of the scientific projects of the federal government. The military services of graduates, according to this report, were even more conspicuous than their achievements in engineering and science. In short, West Pointers had been found "to possess in an eminent degree . . . all the best qualities of the soldier."[4]

On 15 May 1855, Dodson Ramseur left home to begin his career as a soldier. His leave-taking was difficult, especially for Lucy Ramseur, who implored him to write often. From Milton, where he stopped to visit relatives, Dodson wrote a letter to his mother that betrayed homesickness and prompted a reassuring answer from her.[5] In the ensuing weeks Ramseur saw impressive sights, including New York and other cities, celebrated his eighteenth birthday, passed the academic and physical examinations for entrance to the Academy, and mingled with his fellows.

The new arrivals became "fifth classmen," that is, cadets in the first year of a five-year program. The traditional four years had been recently extended at the urging of Superintendent Robert E. Lee to accommodate more English, Spanish, military law, and field instruction. Ramseur and the other plebes would stand two sets of comprehensive examinations each academic year, in January and in June. Success in January 1856 would bestow full cadetship. They would spend the summer of 1855, and each succeeding summer, in an encampment devoted to practical soldiering. The challenges there were physical, and few cadets would fail to perform adequately.[6]

Several weeks into his first encampment, Ramseur wrote to David Schenck about his initial impressions of the Academy. "You know that I thought long and considered well on the probabilities of my success at West Point. I imagined all the difficulties and hardships which I expected to encounter." But no one, he continued, could ever "*i m a g i n e* the severity of the West Point course." Seemingly exaggerated stories about the hard life of the plebe turned out to be accurate. He now understood why so few Americans chose the army as their career, for most balked at subjecting themselves in peacetime to the "severe and almost tyrannical laws which are necessary for the preservation of order and discipline in a standing army."[7]

Tired of the physical labor and tedium of the encampment, Dodson complained to his mother that he was ready to get on with the higher work of cultivating his mind.[8] Two concerns preoccupied him. The first was whether he would be able to compete with the northerners in his class. The twenty-five who came from Harvard, and those from Yale, Princeton, and Union College, began with a distinct advantage over cadets, like Ramseur, who knew only the "rudiments" of mathematics.[9] His second concern was to get a congenial roommate, someone "pious, careful and studious" and preferably from the South. He would be delighted if rumor were correct in pairing him with Wade Hampton Gibbes of South Carolina, a "fine fellow, a real southerner, frank, warm-hearted and generous to a fault."[10]

Apart from boredom compounded by these worries, Ramseur's first encampment went smoothly. His furniture, which consisted of a bed, table, washstand, and chair, was spare but adequate. He earned few demerits and rather coldly predicted that nine classmates who had accumulated more than fifty demerits would certainly "die of the 'January Fever.'" A visit from his father toward the end of August briefly buoyed his spirits, but Jacob Ramseur's departure left him once again homesick. He missed Lincolnton acutely, and the knowledge that he would get no furlough for two years produced in him "sadness deep, lasting, almost overwhelming." In his blackest moods, he despaired of ever seeing his parents or his town again. Mortified by this weakness in his character, he renewed his determination to excel at West Point, reported himself getting along well enough, and vowed to be zealous in the pursuit of duty and the cause of truth.[11]

Once regular classes began, Ramseur and his classmates worked hard, keeping constantly in mind the January examinations that would cut short many careers. Algebra, geography, and English grammar were the principal subjects, and Dodson had difficulty with both algebra and English. In late September he cautioned his mother that he might rank no higher than twenty-fifth, adding that she must remember that he competed against the chosen young men of the country. In January, thirty-four of the plebes failed, including Zachary Taylor's nephew.[12] Dodson performed below his expectations and apologized to his father for a poor report. Still, he had passed, and on 29 January 1856, took the oath of allegiance and received his warrant as a cadet at the U.S. Military Academy. "No longer a mere 'conditional thing,'" henceforth he was "a dignified, brass-buttoned cadet."[13]

These introductory months at West Point gave Ramseur his first prolonged exposure to people and places outside of the South. They did not impress him favorably. He told his mother that since leaving he had confronted the follies and vanities of the world—upon which he did not elaborate—and perceived that in Yankeeland everyone worshiped money.[14] The South knew little of the "cold distrust and mean deceit, which is inborn with the Yankees." Everything was too fast in the "scheming, cold-hearted North," including the women, who were "all the go." Southern ladies certainly were more admirable; with luck, they would never learn the "*bold lessons* of *immodest* Young America." Ramseur did admit that the Yankee girls were pleasant to be around. Their conduct excited in him passions and imaginings that were enjoyable, if not proper, and he intended to love "them to their *hearts content*."[15]

Among the cadets, Ramseur preferred the company of southerners like his roommate Wade Hampton Gibbes. He did have a few northern friends, notably Walter McFarland, and he conceded that northerners were usually good students. Trained from the cradle to apply themselves, Yankees arrived at West Point knowing how to study: "We have to learn after we get here." Ramseur took pride in the fact that only three southerners outperformed him on the January examinations.[16]

Dod scorned most northerners, especially New Englanders. As he explained to David Schenck, only the latter were called Yankees at West Point. They represented avarice and antislavery sentiment. Southerners shunned them. Ramseur looked forward to punishing severely any "miserable Abolitionist" in the next class of plebes. Men from the South excelled Yankees in everything except classwork, and made better officers. Reared to command, not to obey, they gravitated to positions of authority and occupied two-thirds of the officer slots within the Battalion. The other side of the coin, lamented Ramseur, was that southerners bridled at taking orders and often suffered dismissal because they had earned too many demerits.[17]

During the second half of his fifth-class year, Dodson improved his grades and demonstrated an ability to lead. Though perfectly disgusted with the intense drilling in math, he moved from the third to the second section in that subject and in English.[18] He ended the year ranked fourteenth in a class of sixty-one, a very good start.[19] Even more pleasing were recommendations by the captain of his company that he be made first corporal, and by the adjutant of the Battalion that he be second corporal of all the cadets. To be *"2nd out of a class of 60!"* was surprising and gratifying.[20]

Dodson looked forward to his second encampment. His parents would be coming to visit, and he, like other cadets, basked in the attention of the young ladies who watched the Battalion drill and seemed to love the "brass buttoned angels" of West Point. The hoped-for appointment as a corporal came on 12 June 1856, in time for Dodson to greet his parents as a noncommissioned officer.[21]

The encampment of 1856 took place in the midst of a heat wave described as "perfectly intolerable" by a plebe from Delaware, Henry A. du Pont, grandson of the founder of the du Pont Company. The arrival of Lieutenant Colonel William Joseph Hardee, a Georgian who had recently published a manual on light infantry tactics, to be commandant of cadets was the highlight of the encampment. Hardee, though a strict disciplinarian and drillmaster, won the admiration of the cadets and was a favorite of Ramseur's. He introduced the cadets to changes in tactics occasioned by the advent of rifled muskets, preparing them so well for a late summer review by Winfield Scott that the old Hero of Chapultepec likened them to seasoned veterans.[22]

The presidential election of 1856, contested against the background of troubles in Kansas, the assault on Charles Sumner in the U.S. Senate, and overblown rhetoric from both antislavery and proslavery extremists, caused Ramseur to examine and articulate his feelings about slavery and its spread, about compromise to save the Union, and about the future of the American nation. He was a staunch Democrat.[23] His grandfathers, uncles, and other relatives were substantial slaveholders, and his father, though a merchant, owned eight slaves in 1840 and twenty in 1850.[24] Such chattels surrounded Dodson as a boy in his house and those of his kin in Lincolnton and Milton. He shared the usual contempt for slave traders, but considered the institution itself a blessing.[25]

As early as mid-July, Ramseur fretted about the November elections. He implored David Schenck, who had just passed an important examination in his law studies, to "prepare *now* for struggles, which, I believe, are inevitable." He hoped Schenck would be a "Champion of the South." Thomas Bragg's reelection as governor of North Carolina delighted Ramseur, but he despaired the presidential nomination of John C. Frémont by the fledgling Republican party. Did Schenck think the nomination made dissolution of the Union necessary? What of Kansas? "For myself," Dod said, "I believe an awful crisis is approaching." Coming events would determine whether America advanced toward "a *perfect state* of civilization, as one great and united people; or, whether we shall be troubled with divisions & distressed with enemies without and traitors within and destroyed by civil wars." Antislavery men in Kansas should be punished for their outrages. Southerners must battle for their sacred rights against abolitionists and "Black Republican hell-hounds."[26]

When Frémont lost, Ramseur invited David to join with him in "huzzas for Buchanan & the indomitable Democracy." The victory was but a temporary palliative, however; any man of the smallest observation could see that "the Union of the States cannot exist harmoniously." Disunion would come peacefully, Ramseur prayed, "but *at whatever cost*, it must come." The manners and character of northern people ordained a split. Frémont was a renegade, a cheat, and a dissembler who had garnered his considerable vote solely because he opposed slavery, "the very source of our existence, the *greatest blessing* both for master & slave, that could have been bestowed upon us." The education and attitudes of the North and South differed so strikingly that the sections in effect constituted two nations. With abolitionists making great strides, the storm would be upon the South by 1860. Southerners should establish armories, collect stores, and otherwise prepare for the "most desperate of all calamities—civil war." Ramseur lamented that many of the southern men now at West Point would not receive all the training they should. Of four North Carolinians in his class, only he was doing well. Many southerners failed, not from lack of talent but because they were weary of the constant studying and refused to submit to the terrible discipline. Their failure constituted a wasted southern resource.[27]

Touching the lives of West Pointers more directly than the state of public affairs was the return of Major Richard Delafield to the superintendency of the Academy, a position he had held from 1838 to 1845. Delafield brought with him a reputation as the "best disciplinarian & most thorough soldier in the Army."[28] He had a habit of scurrying around the Academy looking for infractions of the rules, and enjoyed making sarcastic puns. Opposed to furloughs and leaves of absence, and dedicated to economy, he quickly alienated many cadets. Henry du Pont concluded that Delafield was insane.[29] Ramseur agreed that the regimen at West Point had become nearly intolerable, the "most *despotic in the world.*" He had never known a cadet voluntarily to resign; now eleven did so in a matter of six weeks. Deeply dissatisfied with the situation, Dodson worried about what lay ahead. Still, he resolved to graduate, grimly predicting that those who did would know that they had "endured an ordeal that none but *men* of the *true Stamp* could stand."[30]

Ramseur's first furlough would come his second year. As early as September 1856 he began anticipating the time nine months ahead when he could return to North Carolina; however, first he must perfect himself in calculus, analytical and descriptive geometry, and surveying. Ahead also lay "long and tedious hours spent in the close study of Rhetoric, History, French . . . of *painful* hours passed in the practice of Light Infantry, or Shanghai, and Artillery drills, Small Sword exercise, and worse than all, terrible 'Guard Duty.' " In breaks from study, Ramseur liked to explore old Fort Clinton, on the west side of campus near the bend in the Hudson River. There he felt the presence of Revolutionary heroes and of patriotism unencumbered by sectional loyalty. "As I climb around the falling battlements, or grope among its dusky dungeons, My heart fills," he wrote, "and I thank God that I am an American."[31]

The tranquillity of Fort Clinton could not shield Ramseur from events that brought sectional friction to the fore at the Academy. In early March 1857, James Buchanan's inauguration and the Supreme Court's decision in the Dred Scott case reminded antislavery advocates of their impotence in Washington. At the Academy, southerners increasingly evinced their contempt for the North, and northern cadets were loath to let slights go unanswered. Fights between cadets over political questions increased in number through 1857 and into 1858. Ramseur's roommate Gibbes acted as second for William McCreery of Virginia in a violent confrontation with James Harrison Wilson of Illinois; this clash, arranged and carried off as if it were a formal duel, attracted a large crowd.[32] Ramseur's fondness and high praise for Gibbes are instructive, for others regarded Gibbes as an extreme secessionist and agitator. Ramseur shared Gibbes's outlook without gaining a similar reputation.

The onset of spring in 1857 called forth a burst of enthusiasm from Dodson. He delighted in the magnificence of the fields and woods around West Point. And his furlough drew nearer. He calculated on 16 May that he had been from home two years and one day—he would start back in *"only thirty-eight days more!"* for a blissful visit with family and friends.[33] He finished his second year at West Point ranking fifteenth in a class of forty-five, one notch lower than the previous year. On 16 June he set off for North Carolina, a free man for ten weeks.[34]

Returning to West Point at the end of August, Ramseur again served as corporal during the academic year 1857–58.[35] No doubt he performed the duties of his position admirably, for he reported to David Schenck that he ranked first in all things military. Indeed, he confessed to David that he thought himself something of a military genius.[36] Even so, nonmilitary subjects took up most of his time. He and other third classmen labored over philosophy, French, Spanish, and drawing in the topography class. Drawing posed a special problem, but Dodson applied himself diligently and scored high marks.[37] By the end of February, however, he was complaining of the "same old monotony."[38]

Diversions did exist at West Point, and Ramseur sought out most of them. Smoking and chewing tobacco were prohibited by Academy rules, but Ramseur indulged in both and received a number of demerits when caught doing so.[39] Regulations also forbade the use of liquor; however, many generations of cadets frequented Benny Havens's tavern. As a cadet, Jefferson Davis, fleeing the place one night a few steps ahead of an instructor, had slipped off a bluff along the Hudson, dropped sixty feet, and ended up in the infirmary.[40] Though Dodson could claim no such thrilling escape, he too savored Havens's hospitality. There were also strolls with young ladies along "flirtation walk," a mile-long path that wound among boulders along the Hudson.[41] When Colonel Hardee instituted a series of cadet balls, Ramseur helped manage them. These "hops" attracted many young women and received detailed newspaper coverage.[42] All-cadet dances and concerts were less exciting but nonetheless popular events.[43]

The students always kept alert for opportunities to escape for a good meal or to smuggle food into quarters. Benny Havens's specialized in roast turkey and buckwheat cakes that tasted infinitely better than the fare at the cadet mess, which a congressional commission characterized as "neither nutritious nor wholesome, neither sufficient nor nicely dressed."[44] Seeking to avoid the "miserable, stringy, boiled beef & cold bread" they usually ate, Dodson and some friends purchased from a farmer a mixture of sauerkraut, potatoes, and bacon, and sneaked the contraband into their rooms for a feast. Even better were teas held at Colonel Hardee's home, to which selected cadets received invitations. Ramseur went often and reveled in the food and the company of the colonel's two "mighty nice Daughters."[45]

Religious activity also provided happy interludes. Throughout his time at West Point, Ramseur kept up Christian study and prayed that the Lord would sustain his efforts to resist temptations and pass through all trials.[46] Chapel was mandatory, but Ramseur was one of the few cadets who attended cheerfully. Emory Upton, another believer, wrote home in 1858 that the Academy was a "hard place to practice religion; though few scoff at it, yet a great majority totally disregard it." Thomas Rowland, a cadet from Virginia, singled Ramseur out as the "one professing Christian in the class." Dodson wrote David Schenck that time at West Point would change any man. One had to choose between two paths: he could join the hosts of the wicked who laughed and blasphemed things once holy, or he could withstand the attacks of the Devil and emerge a purer man and better Christian. So much human depravity had passed before him that Dod had changed his opinion of men. Too many lacked moral courage. On the other hand, when he saw a man struggling against the powers of earth and hell, supported only by his own moral courage, he rejoiced "exceedingly that there are *some* heroes left."[47]

A new chapter in the religious life of West Point began when Lieutenant Oliver Otis Howard arrived in the fall of 1857. So devout that he expected to leave the army for the ministry, Howard immediately secured permission from Colonel Hardee and the chaplain to organize a social meeting for prayer and conference to be held twice a week during the free half-hour between supper and the call to quarters. A cadet recalled that "Howard's little prayer meeting" usually included ten to fifteen cadets. All knelt while Howard conducted services consisting of a hymn, a passage from the Bible, and a prayer. Ramseur was one of the prayer leaders.[48]

Ramseur's correspondence with David Schenck during the first six months of 1858 abounded in thoughts about Christianity. Schenck, nearly finished with his law studies, wanted to marry Dodson's sister Sallie, and the prospect of this long-term commitment turned his mind to religion.

Ramseur welcomed David's interest in both his sister and the Lord. David needed faith and the grace of God—either alone was not enough. If David's faith were true, he would enjoy God's grace; this was the secret of salvation. Schenck worried that his desire to be a successful lawyer conflicted with his need to accept Jesus. Not so, Ramseur assured him; God commands His children to be "fervent in Spirit, diligent in Business, Serving the Lord!" Religion leads to happiness, not to the gloomy, sorrowful life that so many nonbelievers suppose.[49] Several months later, as Schenck still struggled with his problem, Ramseur implored him to give his "heart completely, unreservedly to God: this alone is peace; this alone is *true happiness*."[50]

In the fall of his third-class year came news that tested Ramseur. His father, long a merchant of considerable means, lost much of what he owned through the dishonesty of a partner. Most galling of all, that partner was a northerner. The thought that his family had been "robbed of all earthly goods by the damning treatchery [*sic*] of a miserable Yankee, a villain, a liar, a fiend of Hell—a—" tortured Ramseur, who vowed that if he ever met this man he would "certainly crush him to atoms." His bitterness over this episode never left him. Drawn even closer to his family by what happened, Dodson felt a duty to help relieve their financial distress. Part of his salary after graduation could underwrite his sisters' education. In order to do more than that, he determined to stay in the service only long enough to establish his credentials as an engineer. As a second lieutenant he would earn $600 a year; as an engineer, $5,000 or more. "Tho' it will be like cutting off my right arm, for me to leave the Army," he wrote Schenck, "still I will gladly do it, to perform a Duty, which I consider as the one object of my life."[51] His anxiety over the bad news brought on severe and prolonged headaches that rendered him temporarily unfit for duty. Even after four months he still fretted about his family and wished he could fly to their aid immediately.[52]

A combination of the troubles in Lincolnton and the failure of the pro-slavery Lecompton Constitution in Kansas provoked Ramseur to lash out at the North. "I am a *Secessionist* out and out," he insisted, "in favor of drawing the dividing line from the Atlantic to the Pacific." The balance of power so carefully constructed by John C. Calhoun would crumble if Kansas were admitted as a free state. Should this happen, the South had no recourse but to establish an independent nation, a confederacy whose foundation would be "*Liberté et Egalité*." Tar and feathers awaited any Yankee foolhardy enough to trespass on this southern territory; a second transgression asked for the hangman's rope.[53]

The promise of spring 1858 turned Dodson's thoughts to his next encampment. He looked forward to those summer exercises as a time for rest and reading, but especially as the "*beginning* of the FOURTH year of

my bondage. Yes, *two years more*, and I will be *uncaged*, and *then!*——"
Through March and April the cadets speculated about their chances of
becoming involved in the Mormon War. Ramseur expected the Mormons to
fight tenaciously and thought he and his classmates might see action in
Utah.[54] The Mormon War turned out to be brief, however, and Ramseur's
third year at the Academy came to a peaceful close. He stood seventeenth in
a class of forty-two, his lowest standing in five years at West Point.[55]

Outweighing Ramseur's small loss in class standing was the honor of his
appointment as sergeant of the Battalion for the summer encampment of
1858, a position in which he continued for the academic session 1858–59.[56]
This latest reward for exceptional military bearing set him apart as one of
the leaders among the cadets. A plebe in the encampment of 1858 reminisced years later about the glamour investing the officers of the Battalion
and how other cadets looked upon them as models. He recalled vividly the
"dark-eyed, stern, dignified Ramseur of North Carolina." James H. Wilson
thought him "as handsome and attractive a young man as could be found."[57]
Slender, erect, and graceful, Ramseur stood just over 5 feet, 8 inches tall,
his square features highlighted by a broad forehead and penetrating eyes.[58]

As first orderly sergeant, Ramseur rated larger quarters. He and Gibbes
had a bedroom and a study, the latter octagonal with three windows, rather
than the single cramped rooms occupied by most others in the Battalion. In
addition to more privacy and a better environment in which to prepare
lessons, the new quarters overlooked spectacular scenery. Out his north
window Dodson could see the Hudson River and the Catskills; to the east
were stately homes across the river; but it was to the south that he most
often looked, thinking of North Carolina.[59]

In September came news of great interest to every member of Ramseur's
class—the five-year course might be shortened to four, which would mean
condensing one and a half years' work into about nine months and moving
their graduation to June 1859.[60] The rumor proved true. Cadets happily
pitched into engineering, ethics, chemistry, drawing, and other subjects,
driven by the desire to cut a year off their stay.[61]

Ramseur guessed that he would graduate fifteenth in his class. Since
assignments followed this ranking, with the top men usually choosing engineering or ordnance, he counted on a choice between artillery and cavalry.
Cavalry paid better than artillery and brought faster promotion, but service
in the West limited opportunity for marriage. In artillery he would be stationed in the East, where society was better and he could reasonably count
on "taking a 'rib' unto himself." Perhaps more important, he would not be
impossibly far away from Lincolnton should his father need him. He hoped
to follow the example of Gustavus Woodson Smith, who had resigned from

Ramseur (left) and West Point classmate Frank Huger in 1860. "I know I am a fine looking youth," teased Ramseur in a letter to his sister at about the time this photograph was taken, "but . . . am somewhat surprised to see the girls all *after my picture." (Courtesy of the North Carolina Department of Archives and History.)*

the army to run three iron factories and then accepted the post of street commissioner of New York City at an annual salary of $15,000. One thing was certain, he must make money; "possessing no capital, my education must be my tool." Civil engineering or a professorship at a respected college headed his list of options.[62]

But that was in the future, and Ramseur needed money soon. Due a one-month furlough in the summer of 1859, he planned to return to Lincolnton and find a temporary job. In fall of 1858 he asked David Schenck to keep an eye out for openings. Engineering or practical instruction of some volunteer military organization were two possibilities: "What I want is *work that will pay*, the bolder and harder the better—I am young and strong!" Above all, he wanted to make "a little money & a big reputation in my short furlough."[63] In Ramseur's mind, this preoccupation with money was no doubt legitimate because of his father's misfortune. Yet it seems unlikely that any northern, or even Yankee, cadet devoted more thought to the subject. That Yankees could have comparable reasons for pursuing money probably did not occur to him.

Visits by David Schenck and other friends from North Carolina broke up the monotony of winter, as did a party in November to which twelve cadets were invited. At the party, Ramseur danced with two girls, including Superintendent Delafield's daughter. Though Dod found Miss Delafield quite ugly, he played the gallant and complimented her, or so he wrote his sister Luly. In the feast accompanying the dancing, Ramseur consumed a plate of stewed oysters, a plate of fried oysters, and sandwiches, salad, candies, cakes, nuts, and grapes. The hosts understood the horrors of the mess hall and gave the young men a meal to remember.[64]

In mid-January 1859, Colonel Hardee learned that Dodson and four other first sergeants had been excusing first classmen from sentry duty. For this they were charged with gross neglect of duty. The superintendent, after observing that they had been chosen first sergeants on account of their "high military bearing and capacity for command," regretfully returned them to the ranks.[65] Each had to perform ten extra tours of camp guard duty and was confined to post until those duties were discharged.[66]

Two weeks later a heavier blow fell: the secretary of war decided to reinstate the five-year course. Almost on the eve of graduation Ramseur and his classmates had been condemned to another year of imprisonment. Professing himself "completely prostrated," Ramseur blamed President Buchanan on the supposition that Buchanan wished to give his friends the commissions in the army that would have gone to the graduating West Pointers. The class complained to the president and to their congressmen, but Dodson expected no result—"selfishness not justice is the controlling principle." In Lincolnton the news cast a "gloom of melancholly [*sic*] and grief over the whole [Ramseur] family, who have calculated so much on his return."[67]

After the passage of twenty days Ramseur designated Secretary of War John B. Floyd instead of Buchanan as the culprit. Actually, Floyd had capitulated to arguments presented by the administrators of the Academy, who had consistently favored the five-year course. Observing that "Such is the *fortune* of war," Ramseur managed to reconcile himself to another year. With most of the prescribed work already done, Dodson thought he and his classmates should have an easy final year.[68] Meanwhile, the only bright spots were improvement in his class ranking to sixteenth of forty-two and the thirty-day furlough scheduled for July.[69]

Happily for Dodson, the summer of 1859 brought good fortune to help him forget the troubles of the spring term. Colonel Hardee, thinking highly of his military talent, forgave the incident of the previous January and appointed him a lieutenant in the Battalion of Cadets for his last encampment.[70] In August he journeyed to Lincolnton to attend David and Sallie's wedding and enjoyed the occasion "hugely."[71] Upon his return from Lincolnton he found himself promoted, at Hardee's recommendation, to cadet captain of Company B of the Battalion. This position, awarded primarily on the basis of military rather than academic ability, was the highest to which a cadet could aspire.[72] Ramseur was now very mature for his years, reserved with those whom he did not know well, always quiet, courteous, and dignified. Endowed with strong character and great good sense, he made a "most excellent soldier." He was also, as Illinoisan Wesley Merritt later recalled, one of the most universally beloved men in the class.[73]

Tensions at the Academy increased in the fall of 1859. Friction tinged with sectional feeling already existed, but it was John Brown's raid on the Federal armory at Harpers Ferry that provoked the first clash of a clearly political nature between northern and southern cadets. The principals were Dodson's roommate, Wade Hampton Gibbes, and Emory Upton, an avowed abolitionist who had attended Oberlin College before entering West Point. Oberlin admitted blacks, and Gibbes claimed that Upton slept with black women while there. The ensuing fight was a standoff, but it drew a crowd and the "national significance of the affair was interpreted at once."[74] For Ramseur, the lines had long been drawn. A week before the raid on Harpers Ferry he had revealed his distrust of northerners by advising his sister Luly, who attended school in Philadelphia, to seek out "some warm Southern hearts which will beat in unison with your own—I must confess that as a general thing I would much prefer your intimate friends to be Southerners."[75]

In early December, with Christmas near and snow blanketing the Academy, Ramseur received tragic news—his mother had died in late November.[76] The two had always been extremely close. Her letters to him at Davidson and West Point constantly urged him to be useful and good, and he in turn pledged to "walk straight forward in the path of duty," to be a man, and to be a Christian.[77] Their strongest bond had been religion. He considered his mother a wonderful influence whose love was his strength. His chief object in life was to be a good son to Lucy Ramseur.[78] In January 1860 Ramseur attempted to console his father on the terrible misfortune of losing so fine a wife, to let him know how his son's heart "ached as these thoughts filled my mind." Two months later Dod's grief was undiminished. He missed his mother and knowledge of her suffering tormented him. At least she had found eternal happiness, "Blessed hope! We too may join that precious band."[79]

At the Academy there remained engineering, ethics, and mineralogy with which to contend, but there were also artillery, cavalry tactics, and other military subjects at which Dodson excelled.[80] At last the cadets were studying campaigns of the great captains. He reminded Luly how fond he always had been of reading about famous generals: "Now that the subject is studied critically and scientifically investigated I am in ecstacies." To his cousin Ellen Richmond in Milton he confided that the workload was heavy but not burdensome. She could imagine what an absorbing interest the topics had for one "who has been from early boyhood, a great admirer of the World's renowned Heroes."[81]

As his time at West Point wound down, Ramseur also found opportunities to relax. There were concerts on Saturday nights and rare moments alone with young ladies. "I know I am a fine looking youth," he teased Luly in February, "but . . . am somewhat surprised to see the girls *all* after my *picture*." David Schenck visited again in February. As always, Ramseur relished the brief time with his brother-in-law.[82] In January 1860 he joined the Dialectic Society, one of two debating groups at the Academy. Modeled on similar societies at other colleges, the Dialectic and Amosophic societies served as a forum for the exploration of theoretical and political questions.[83]

The wildest adventure of Ramseur's last spring at West Point took place at Benny Havens's tavern. George Custer, a second classman from Michigan with a genius for acquiring demerits, arranged a farewell party for Ramseur, Gibbes, Wesley Merritt, and Alexander Pennington. Thomas Rosser, a Virginian appointed from Texas, John Pelham of Alabama, Adelbert Ames of Massachusetts, and several other second classmen joined Custer as hosts. Placing dummies in their beds to conceal their absence, the dozen cadets congregated at the tavern, where Havens had set out mugs of flip, a drink that combined egg, sugar, and rum. Ramseur and Gibbes raised their tankards and began to sing the first verse of a tribute to Havens written in 1838—"In the Army there's sobriety, promotion's very slow"—at which point the others chorused, "And we'll sing our reminiscences of Benny Havens, Oh!" Havens broke out his banjo and the cadets, two by two, rose to dance. Celebrating until past midnight, they drank a final toast to Ramseur and his classmates, members of what Custer called the finest class ever to go through West Point.[84]

Though not the most distinguished of West Point classes, Ramseur's was a special group, both because it had undergone the five-year course, and because it was the last full class to graduate before the Civil War. On 14 June 1860, the forty-one members marched to the Academy chapel for five o'clock commencement exercises.[85] Ramseur ranked fourteenth.[86] He had held every cadet rank from corporal through captain and earned 389 demerits. Northerners continued to dominate the top third of the class; indeed, only two southerners, Benjamin F. Sloan of South Carolina and William McCreery of Virginia, were ahead of Dodson. First in the class was his friend Walter McFarland of New York; Horace Porter of Pennsylvania, later a member of Grant's staff, was third; Illinoisan James H. Wilson, subsequently a Union major general of cavalry, was sixth. Wesley Merritt, also outstanding as a Union cavalryman, ranked twenty-second; Wade Hampton Gibbes, soon to direct mortar fire against Fort Sumter, graduated twenty-eighth. After the ceremony, the young men filed out through the front door of the chapel, under a massive pediment supported by large wooden columns, and descended broad steps onto the lawn. In the months to follow, thirty-two would stay with the Union and nine would resign to serve the Confederacy. A quarter of the class would not survive the war.[87]

Dodson left the Academy chapel that day a "respected, honored and loved" cadet.[88] Whatever course he might follow after graduation, he seemed destined for success. He had been a leader since boyhood, whether in the debating society at Pleasant Retreat Academy or on the parade ground above the Hudson. Introspective and reticent, he gave forthright opinions when asked, but never trumpeted his views. Leadership came to Ramseur naturally. Bright, athletic, and an accomplished horseman, he possessed the physical and intellectual attributes deemed desirable in an officer. Women admired him, and he was fond of their company. A practicing Christian comfortable with his religion, Ramseur held to his beliefs in the secular atmosphere of West Point. Because he smoked and chewed tobacco and ventured to Benny Havens's, his classmates did not scorn him as they did those cadets thought to be prudes. A firm believer in slavery, he disliked most northerners and despised abolitionists. His sense of duty, carefully cultivated over the years by his mother, was, first, to his family, second, to his state and section, and third, to his country. Before his twentieth birthday, and well in advance of most southerners outside the lower deep South, he had embraced the idea of secession, and of war if necessary, to free the South from the deleterious grasp of the North.

Almost immediately after graduation Dodson headed for Lincolnton and the "dearest spot of Earth Home sweet Home."[89] Stopping at the North Carolina Military Institute in Charlotte to visit with Harvey Hill, who had left Davidson College to join the faculty there, Ramseur observed drill and dress parade. A cadet who saw him that day remembered his face as having a "pensive, reflective cast, *not* austere, but grave and meditative."[90] Dodson's gravity may have been partly worry about his father, whom he would see shortly. In the wake of his financial disaster, fifty-two-year-old Jacob Ramseur worked as a clerk in a mill. In April Dodson had encouraged Luly to return to Lincolnton to help their father with the household;[91] for himself, the choice of artillery as his branch of the service ensured that he would be stationed initially at the Artillery School at Fort Monroe, Virginia, a short trip from Lincolnton. He would be in position to keep an eye on his family and lend assistance.

Commissioned a brevet second lieutenant in the Third Regiment of artillery, Ramseur found himself back at West Point at the end of July.[92] Jefferson Davis's commission was pursuing its investigation at the Academy and had called Dodson to testify. In response to queries, Ramseur suggested several changes in the curriculum and system of discipline at West Point. The ethics course was too long, particularly the study of moral science, a subject ridiculed by the cadets. Additional practical experience with astronomical and surveying instruments was needed. Military exercises such as riding and fencing did not interfere with other classes. Artillery tactics merited more attention, but infantry drills took up so much time that other arms suffered.

Ramseur questioned the assignment of graduates to a particular corps on the basis of class ranking. Why not rotate them among the several corps and then place each where his talents would show to best advantage? This idea went against the thinking of many cadets, who saw the privilege of selecting a branch of the service as the only incentive to hard study. Ramseur argued for stricter discipline; students who exceeded the number of demerits allowed by regulations should be dismissed with no possibility of reinstatement. As matters stood, feeling in the Battalion was "rather to the prejudice of a cadet who raises himself above others by avoiding demerit."[93] Ramseur's testimony, especially his preference for emphasizing aptitude in the assignment of graduates, anticipated the future direction of army policy. But in 1860 nothing came of his ideas.

The recently established Artillery School at Fort Monroe to which Ramseur reported as a brevet second lieutenant introduced artillerymen to the finer points of handling guns. Two companies from each of the four regiments of artillery attended at any given time, one company rotating out annually. Instruction touched on the gamut of topics, both theoretical and practical, considered necessary to the education of an officer of artillery.[94]

Before completing a year at Fort Monroe, Ramseur received orders to transfer to the District of Columbia for a stint with a battery of light artillery. Allen B. Magruder, later a major in the Confederate army, met Dodson in Washington, saw him at work on a daily basis, and entertained him frequently at night. Though only a beginning lieutenant, Ramseur impressed Magruder with his "great personal gifts and attractions." He moved easily in society, where his intelligence, graceful form, impeccable manners, and cultivated mind presented to friends and colleagues an admirably rounded personality.[95] While in Washington, Ramseur watched the headlines that traced the breakup of the Union. By 1 February 1861, the seven states of the lower South had seceded. The upper South and the Border states scrutinized president-elect Abraham Lincoln for clues as to what his response would be.[96]

For at least five years, Ramseur had considered secession a legitimate response to northern provocation. The question was, what constituted sufficient provocation? In the lower South, Lincoln's election alone was enough. Other slave states waited. The voters of North Carolina on 28 February narrowly defeated a proposition championed by Governor John W. Ellis for a convention to discuss secession.[97] After becoming president on 4 March, Lincoln let an entire month expire without a decisive move in relation to the departed states. As one of his routine duties Lincoln signed on 19 March a commission promoting Ramseur to second lieutenant in the Fourth Regiment of artillery.[98]

But Ramseur would never report to his new unit.[99] Unwilling to wait until his native state aligned itself with the newly formed Confederacy, he submitted the first week of April his resignation from the service of the U.S. government.[100] The crisis he had anticipated, had at times seemed almost to welcome, was now an actuality, and he meant to put his training to use. Immediately he set out for Montgomery, Alabama, capital of the Confederacy, to offer his sword in defense of the South.[101]

CHAPTER 3

I WANT TO GET UNDER

A MOVING MAN

Ramseur's journey from Washington to Montgomery, Alabama, away from an old allegiance and toward a new one, took him first to North Carolina and probably to Lincolnton for a reunion with his family. On 18 April, twelve days after his resignation, he met in Charlotte with his old professor from Davidson, Daniel Harvey Hill. Five years before, Hill had helped Ramseur into West Point; now he telegraphed Governor John W. Ellis of North Carolina that Ramseur wished to serve his native state.[1]

Since Dodson's departure from Washington, the Confederates, provoked by a Federal attempt to reinforce Fort Sumter, had fired upon and taken the fort, Lincoln had called for 75,000 volunteers to put down the insurrection, and Virginia had adopted an ordinance of secession. With Virginia out of the Union and the sections in open conflict, North Carolina must secede, and would need officers. Ramseur preferred service with the troops of his own state. Meanwhile, he would continue on to Montgomery to enlist in the Confederate army. On 22 April he received a commission as a first lieutenant of artillery and orders to proceed from Montgomery to Memphis.[2]

Almost simultaneously, however, Ramseur learned from Governor Ellis via telegraph that he had been elected captain of the Ellis Light Artillery of Raleigh. One day after his appointment as a Confederate lieutenant, he was on his way back east to Raleigh to assume a command in the service of North Carolina.[3] His selection had come about after B. C. Manly and others of the Ellis Light Artillery had gone to see Ellis.[4] Having known Ramseur before the war, and with Hill's telegram regarding Ramseur in hand, the governor immediately said he had the very man.[5] "You couldn't get a better. It is Lieutenant Ramseur."[6] By 1 May Ramseur was in Raleigh, encamped at the fairgrounds of the city with sixty-two men of the Ellis Light Artillery.[7]

The new company counted among its members numerous sons of leading families of Raleigh who had joined the artillery as twelve-month volunteers because they saw it as the most attractive branch of the service. These gentlemen considered it an affront to be asked to subordinate themselves to officers with whom they were social peers. Quickly sizing up his command, Ramseur saw that the men's esprit de corps was high and could be used to turn them into real soldiers. The first order of business was to reorganize the company for the duration of the war. Men who felt that this meant conversion from gentlemen volunteers into regular soldiers were allowed to withdraw. Those remaining were mustered in for three years or the duration at Raleigh on 8 May 1861, becoming Company A, Tenth Regiment North Carolina State Troops.[8] Ramseur himself received promotion to major of artillery in the North Carolina State Troops.[9] The war had in three weeks brought to him a rank that might have taken twenty years to reach in the U.S. army.

With his unit committed to serve for the entire war, Ramseur turned his attention to its training and outfitting. The company lacked nearly everything. From the arsenal at Fayetteville, Governor Ellis supplied two 12-pounder howitzers, three 6-pounder bronze smoothbore guns, one 3-inch rifle, two large battery wagons, and a pair of forges.[10] Ellis could not, however, procure enough horses, and the battery had to be worked by hand. In lieu of tents and a suitable parade ground, Ramseur accepted the offer of a country residence with many outbuildings. There, on the outskirts of Raleigh, he drilled his men twelve hours a day. Advertisements for volunteers to bring the battery up to strength emphasized that those who joined would have the "great advantage of being drilled and instructed by an experienced tactician, which is no small advantage in battle."[11] Ramseur was a martinet, and his battery, soon fully manned, began to take on the character of a polished military outfit.[12]

Twice during the period of drill the state called Ramseur and his men into ceremonial service. When on 20 May the North Carolina convention voted to go with the Confederacy, "Ramseur's Battery stationed outside [the hall] fired a Salute of a hundred Guns! This seemed a signal for men, women & children to flock to the State House."[13] Seven weeks later the company served as part of the military escort at the funeral of Governor Ellis, for whom it was named. On the day of interment, with the flag at the capitol at half-staff and the city in mourning, the Ellis Light Artillery fired guns on the half-hour from sunrise to sunset.[14]

Drilling continued through July at Camp Boylan. Ramseur had a "splendid Company numbering 112 men, officers and privates." Visiting artillery officers pronounced it "one of the very best drilled Artillery Companies in the Confederate Army."[15] The war now appeared to be erupting in earnest; North Carolinians had spilled their blood at Big Bethel, Virginia, and regiments from the state would fight with distinction at the first battle of Manassas. Troops from across the lower South passed through Raleigh on their way to the Virginia front, while Ramseur's crack battery drilled endlessly. A newspaper in the city snickered that the unit was a "Parlor Battery," looking pretty but seeming averse to fighting. Authorities in Richmond, now the Confederate capital, wished to know when the battery would be ready to move. Even friends of Ramseur questioned such protracted drilling and reviewing.[16]

The Raleigh *Register* came to the defense, however, asserting that any implication of reluctance to take the field was a *"low down slander."* When the battery received ammunition and other essentials, it would go forth to "aid in beating back our invaders and enemies."[17] Finally Ramseur was able to telegraph General Benjamin Huger in Norfolk that he would leave on 25 July for Suffolk, Virginia.[18] A last-minute problem with equipment and an accident in which Ramseur broke his collarbone when thrown from his horse in a severe storm brought delay, but on 29 July they were off. "A better drilled and equipped corps cannot be found in the army," said the *Register*.[19]

The Ellis Light Artillery stayed briefly in Suffolk, then moved to Smithfield, on the south side of the James River, to be attached to John Pemberton's brigade of Benjamin Huger's division. Ramseur's battery would help defend about twenty miles of the James River stretching from the upper part of Burwell's Bay, northwest of Smithfield, down the river to the mouth of the Nansemond River, some ten miles above Norfolk. Pemberton had 3,000 men spread along this front; the Confederates expected trouble here because the James provided a convenient route from the coast to Richmond. General John E. Wool's Union force at Fort Monroe appeared to threaten both Huger, at Norfolk, and John Bankhead Magruder, who was north of Fort Monroe on the Peninsula (between the York and James rivers). Rumors of impending northern activity kept the Confederates alert, but Ramseur and his men spent the balance of 1861 and the early months of 1862 with no duties more taxing than an occasional reconnaissance in the vicinity of Norfolk.[20]

In the absence of Union movement, Ramseur filled the days with drill. Though hateful to the men, who were impatient for action, this work brought attention to Ramseur. Invariably, the Ellis Light Artillery was the principal attraction at reviews, garnering for its commander encomiums from visiting generals. Basking in this praise, Ramseur wanted to know whether North Carolina newspapers were spreading the favorable reactions. Did Schenck "hear anything about 'Ramseur's battery'?"[21] In September Ramseur endured a bout of typhoid fever so serious that David Schenck came up from North Carolina to see him. Ramseur's cousin Dod Richmond had found him very ill and was "quite uneasy about him." A couple in

Smithfield cared for Ramseur during the fever and saw him through the crisis.[22] In late November, John Pemberton left to take command at Charleston, and after his departure Ramseur's company was reassigned to a predominantly North Carolina brigade commanded by Raleigh E. Colston, who had taught at the Virginia Military Institute.[23]

On Saturday morning, 8 March 1862, Ramseur was serving on a military court in Norfolk. As he left the courtroom he heard a shout: "The *Merrimac* is going out." Borrowing a horse from Frank Huger, a close friend from West Point now a captain of artillery, he hurried to a Confederate battery, where the officer in charge gave him command of two 32-pounder rifled guns. Ramseur watched the *Merrimac*, a scuttled Union vessel raised by the Confederates and outfitted with a ram and iron plating, steam toward the *Cumberland*, a Federal sloop of twenty-four guns, rake it with fire, and then ram it. In less than thirty minutes the *Cumberland* went down. The fifty-gun frigate *Congress* next faced the *Merrimac*, sustaining serious damage and running aground within an hour.

While the *Congress* and *Merrimac* were battling, Ramseur saw the forty-gun frigate *Minnesota* set out from Old Point, moving southwesterly to help the *Congress*. About the same time, guns at the Rip Raps, near the entrance to Hampton Roads, opened on Ramseur's position. Distracted by this fire, Ramseur's green gunners hesitated, but he "directed the guns at the [Batteries] to fire first over the *Minnesota*, then to diminish the elevation until we got their range, then to give it to them." After five shots the *Minnesota* moved out of range, eventually running aground. Presently another ship, the forty-gun Union frigate *Roanoke*, sailed into range. Ramseur's guns got off six shots at this vessel, the fifth of which, he claimed, struck its shaft and disabled it. The *Roanoke*, too, ran aground, whereupon two "tugboats carried her ingloriously back to Ft. Monroe." Nightfall halted the fight, with the *Merrimac* in control of Hampton Roads and four Union vessels destroyed or disabled.

A heavy fog on Sunday morning prevented a resumption of the struggle until ten o'clock, "then the famous Erricson [*sic*] iron battery [*Monitor*] entered the lists against the [*Merrimac* and] a formidable antagonist she proved to be." In two hours of pounding one another, the *Merrimac* and the *Monitor* both inflicted injury. Then the "Erricson drew off in a damaged condition" and left the *Merrimac* "the winner of the fight." In truth, this first contest between iron ships was a standoff in which each side thought it had bested the other. Ramseur seemed not to appreciate the larger implications for future naval history of what he witnessed off Hampton Roads. For him, the Federals' heavier loss in ships constituted a conventional victory for the southern navy.[24]

The Merrimac *passing a Confederate battery on its way to attack the Federal fleet.*
(Battles and Leaders of the Civil War.)

The success of the *Merrimac* did not blind Ramseur to Confederate misfortunes elsewhere. On 8 February 1862, General Ambrose E. Burnside captured Roanoke Island and its 2,000 Confederate defenders, thereby gaining an excellent base for Union attacks against Ramseur's home state. Eight days later Ulysses S. Grant forced the surrender of Fort Donelson, Tennessee, and more than 10,000 men. These setbacks, and particularly the surrender of troops, angered Ramseur, who though hardly a battle-tested veteran did not hesitate in private to excoriate the commanders who capitulated. He hoped North Carolinians would fasten "disgrace & condemnation on the cowardly *or* ignorant officers who had the command of *brave* men" at Roanoke Island. "We are fighting for *existence* as well as honor & right"; any general who surrenders should be hanged. The conduct of Generals John B. Floyd and Gideon Pillow in making their escape and leaving Simon Bolivar Buckner to surrender Fort Donelson marked them as scoundrels beyond redemption. Had "F. & P. possessed *moral* courage there would have been a different result." Southerners must sacrifice at home so that the armies might be clothed and fed. This war was no joust between two restrained opponents, it was an ugly business that would scar the South and demand total dedication if the Confederacy were to triumph. They must "show them we are terribly desperately in earnest—Let us lay waste our beautiful country & leave [the enemy] a wilderness to possess. Let us hang traitors as did our forefathers." Ramseur's motto was "victory or death."[25]

At the beginning of March 1862, Confederate leaders in Richmond considered Burnside's small army a serious threat to southeastern Virginia.

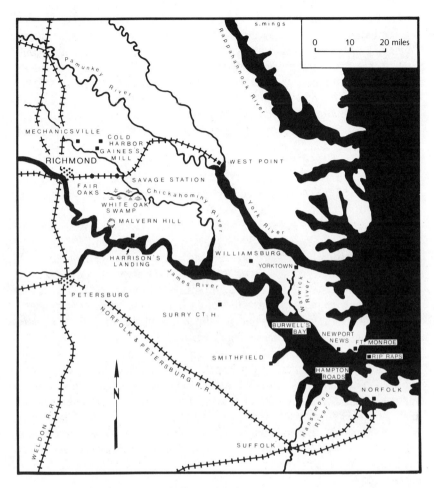

The Peninsula of Virginia

Should he move up the coast from his base in North Carolina, he could capture Norfolk. Anticipating such a movement, they ordered John B. Magruder to transfer 5,000 men from the lower Peninsula to Huger at Norfolk.[26] Ramseur's battery was preparing to move from Smithfield toward Suffolk. Huger planned to place his 15,000 men near railroads to await Burnside's move and then "to pitch into him & press him to the death." With two more weeks' preparation, Ramseur thought Huger would have little trouble handling anything Burnside might try. The Ellis Light Artillery was in fine condition, primed for a fight.[27]

When Burnside moved south along the Carolina coast against New Bern rather than north toward Virginia, attention shifted from Norfolk to the Peninsula. Magruder nervously eyed a Union buildup, estimated at 35,000 men, in the area between Fort Monroe and Newport News. These troops were, he soon learned, the advance elements of George McClellan's Army of the Potomac, a force of more than 100,000 marshaled for a quick strike up the Peninsula to Richmond. With barely 11,000 men at his disposal, Magruder warned the secretary of war that he needed reinforcements, and quickly.[28] Union dispatches captured on 4 April indicated that McClellan's immediate target was Yorktown. The next day Ramseur, receiving orders to prepare his battery for transfer to the Peninsula, rejoiced that he would be among the "15,000 who will have the honor of resisting . . . successfully or dying in the attempt."[29]

Crossing the James River just south of Williamsburg, Ramseur and his battery landed at King's Mill Wharf[30] and proceeded down the Peninsula to lines Magruder had constructed behind the Warwick River, a sluggish stream that meandered from near Yorktown south across the Peninsula to empty into the James.[31] The Ellis Light Artillery would now be attached to Paul Semmes's brigade of Lafayette McLaws's division.[32] One of Magruder's staff who met the battery when it landed commented on its "complete organization and equipment," "splendid appointments," and "skilled evolutions." Others who observed the battery on the Peninsula praised Ramseur for the fine job he had done. Before the transfer Ramseur had made a good impression in meetings with Magruder and been promised "the post of honor—which means the post of danger." Considering him too valuable an artillery officer to be restricted to command of a single battery, Magruder entrusted him with a battalion of artillery on his right wing and charged him with "the arduous duty of organizing the drill and evolutions in lines of batteries—the French system of artillery tactics—not generally known in our service."[33]

While he waited for reinforcements from Joseph Johnston's army at Manassas, Magruder perfected his defensive lines, damming the Warwick River in several places to flood lowlands, throwing up earthworks, and digging rifle pits. Believing his foe to be formidable, McClellan probed these lines for a month and brought up huge mortars to lay siege to Yorktown. Inclement weather delayed until 16 April the first Union attack, at Dam No. 1, between Lee's Mill and Wynne's Mill south of Yorktown.[34] In this sharp fight Ramseur and his men experienced their first combat and helped repel McClellan's attack. Another skirmish followed a few days later at Warwick Island. The Ellis Light Artillery suffered no casualties in these actions, which Ramseur considered a mere prelude to serious fighting.[35] He did not relish the prospect of attacking McClellan behind his breastworks, but thought that once Johnston's force arrived the Confederates would either launch an offensive on the Peninsula or force McClellan to withdraw by moving on Washington.[36]

In the midst of his activities during March and April word came to Ramseur that a new regiment was making up in counties near his home, and he traveled to Lincolnton to explore the possibility of his securing command of it.[37] He had declined the lieutenant colonelcy of an infantry regiment in May 1861 to accept a majority of artillery, but to be colonel of his own regiment would be different.[38] On 5 April he asked David Schenck, then a member of the North Carolina state convention, to see Daniel M. Barringer, former congressman and adviser to the governor, about the colonelcy of the new regiment. If it had not come through, "Tell him I am entitled to lt. col. of [Artillery]. He and Gen'l [James G.] Martin [adjutant general of North Carolina State Troops] can fix it." Shortly thereafter, the men of the regiment, mustered in as the Forty-Ninth North Carolina, elected Ramseur colonel. On 21 April Barringer sent his congratulations: "I felt great interest in the matter & exerted all the influence I had with the officers to give you this command."[39] Upon hearing of his election, Ramseur left the Peninsula for Raleigh, where Schenck met him on 27 April. The next day he received his commission as colonel of the Forty-Ninth. Schenck found Dod in good health and high spirits—and why not? His plan had succeeded and he had his own regiment.[40]

For a second time Ramseur began the task of turning raw recruits into a disciplined military unit. His adjutant, who would remain with him the rest of the war, was Caleb Richmond, brother of Ellen Richmond, the cousin with whom he had corresponded while at West Point. The Forty-Ninth consisted of volunteers, many of whom were said to have sought service earlier but had been compelled to wait until the state could arm and equip them.[41] Ramseur's first reaction to the regiment was disappointment. In camp near Goldsboro, some forty-five miles southeast of Raleigh, he complained to David Schenck on 21 May that the elected company officers were of poor quality. If he thought better replacements would be chosen, he would force seven of them to resign. But election of officers was a travesty, the fault of "miserable, foolish . . . men who recommended such a course to the convention of N.C." He feared his reputation as a soldier would suffer if it depended on the Forty-Ninth North Carolina. Officers and privates showed no pluck, no desire to meet the enemy. Instead, they were timid, forever making anxious enquiries about when they would have to go to the front. "I will leave nothing undone that I can do to make them effective troops," he assured David, but he was "little encouraged."[42]

While Ramseur struggled with his regiment in North Carolina, the situation in Virginia appeared ominous for the South. Norfolk had fallen on 9 May, necessitating the scuttling of the *Merrimac* and opening southside Virginia and upper North Carolina to the Federals. Stonewall Jackson faced several Union armies in the Shenandoah Valley; Joseph Johnston's 80,000 men confronted McClellan's larger force on the Peninsula; and Irvin McDowell waited above Fredericksburg with another 40,000 Federals. The disparity in numbers between Johnston and McClellan notwithstanding, Ramseur felt that the Confederates' only chance lay in a prompt action to insure that McDowell did not join McClellan; should that happen, Virginia would be lost.[43]

In this critical situation every available unit was needed. Ramseur's regiment, though not yet fully trained, was ordered to Petersburg. The first contingent arrived there on the evening of 1 June, just as reports of the battle of Seven Pines, or Fair Oaks, came across the wires. Johnston had attacked two of McClellan's corps east of Richmond, but achieved only a bloody draw. Johnston himself was wounded, and the command passed to Robert E. Lee. Ramseur expected to be called to Richmond soon. Bone-tired and pessimistic, he worried about the prospect of leading green troops in battle: "My *militia* give me a *heap* of work to do."[44]

The Forty-Ninth North Carolina went into camp near Petersburg, with Ramseur still worried that his men might fail him in a crucial test. The regiment, which carried on its rolls 900 men, had been in Petersburg only five days and already 109 of 641 present for duty had taken sick, "or *pretend* to be sick" sufficiently to fool the surgeon. Rain had fallen for two days, but conditions were not bad enough to produce such ill health. "What can I expect when they are required to make forced marches, sleep on the wet ground & fight battles after all of this," Ramseur exclaimed to David Schenck. Whenever he spoke to his men of the coming strife and what he would expect of them "they look scared and anxious." He labored hard "to cultivate a proper feeling," an eagerness to meet the enemy, but doubted that he was succeeding. If the regiment were to turn and run and he survived, he would denounce his men. These misgivings he confided to David (and David only) so that his name might, in case of disaster, be vindicated.

Although Ramseur's concerns were not only about the effect of the regiment's behavior on his own reputation, he did want desperately to make a name for himself. Alluding to George B. Anderson's Fourth North Carolina at Seven Pines, he proclaimed a willingness to "give my life to have my [regiment] behave with the same glorious gallantry as did Col. Anderson's 4th N.C. State troops." He thought his chance might come soon. General Lee had announced that there would be no more retreating, that the watchword

Stephen Dodson Ramseur. The only photograph of Ramseur during the Civil War. "He abhorred newspaper puffs, gotten up to make a false reputation for those not worthy of it," explained Ramseur's friend David Schenck. "To such an extreme did he carry his modesty . . . that he would not allow his picture to be taken during the war for fear it would be displayed in some artist's show window, and it was only after much persuasion . . . he consented to have a photograph taken while a Major of Artillery below Petersburg." A new beard, which he wore for the rest of his life, and closely cropped hair made Ramseur appear older than his twenty-four years. ("Personal Recollections of General Ramseur," in Schenck, Sketches, pp. 24–25.) (Courtesy of the North Carolina Department of Archives and History.)

of the army "must be and is 'Victory or death.' May God give us the victory is my earnest prayer."[45]

The elevation of Lee to command the Confederate army around Richmond, christened by him the Army of Northern Virginia, together with increasingly favorable reports of Stonewall Jackson's exploits in the Shenandoah Valley, helped to dispel Ramseur's pessimism. As a soldier, Dodson himself would be audacious and combative; accordingly he admired generals who pressed the offensive, and Jackson especially captured his imagination. Hearing a rumor that the brigade containing his regiment would be sent to the Valley, he hoped very much that was so. "I want to get under a *moving* man."

Meanwhile, an incident involving his own men augured well for the future. Responding to a Federal feint at City Point, twelve miles from the camps of the Forty-Ninth, Ramseur formed his men and delivered a speech. They were all North Carolinians; some of them were his neighbors. Would they follow where he led? Would they stay and fight as long as he did? He mentioned Benjamin Butler's notorious "Woman Order" in New Orleans and said that it was men like Butler whom they would oppose in battle. "They cheered for me," he wrote David Schenck, "said they would stick to me ... & to tell you the truth I feel that *we will* make a name for ourselves that the State may yet be proud of."[46]

On 23 June Ramseur received orders to be ready to march. He assumed the brigade would be crossing the James at Drewry's Bluff, there to find itself "in front of the enemy's left wing." Jackson, whose army was hurrying to Richmond from the Valley, would hit McClellan's right flank, while the rest of the Army of Northern Virginia struck his center and left. If successful they would drive McClellan in confusion back to the James, where he would be pinned down and annihilated. The victorious Confederates could then march north and whip whatever force was sent to stop them. "All of these bright prospects turn upon the defeat of McClellan *during the present week*," Ramseur concluded. "God grant that we may overthrow entirely our base and merciless invaders!"[47]

On the day Ramseur sketched this scenario, Lee met with Jackson and the other principal Confederate commanders in the Dabb house on Nine-Mile Road outside Richmond. There they formulated a similar plan. Two days later, on Wednesday, 25 June, the fighting since known as the Seven Days' Battles around Richmond opened when elements of Huger's division collided with two Federal divisions south of the Williamsburg Road on the western edge of White Oak Swamp. McClellan sought to move far enough west to include all of this swampy ground within his lines. Robert Ransom's Confederate brigade, arrived that morning from Petersburg, took part in the affair. Ramseur's regiment played a supporting role and sustained casualties.[48]

For the next five days, the Army of Northern Virginia attempted to deliver a telling blow to the Army of the Potomac. Most of the fighting occurred on the Confederate left, away from Huger's division, as Lee tried on 26 June at Mechanicsville and 27 June at Gaines's Mill to crush a portion of McClellan's army that lay north of the Chickahominy River. McClellan avoided a major defeat; nevertheless, he decided on 28 June to withdraw to the James River. A rear-guard action at Savage Station on 29 June, and a bitterly contested struggle amid the steaming thickets of White Oak Swamp on 30 June, marked the fifth and sixth days of continuous fighting. Throughout the week, poor coordination, piecemeal assaults, and missed opportunities hampered the Confederates. Several times decisive victory seemed near, only to slip away when someone—including Stonewall Jackson, who was completely exhausted—was late or hesitant.[49] The Forty-Ninth North Carolina acquitted itself well but remained on the periphery of the combat for the first six days. Robert Ransom, a West Pointer and fine soldier, reported that the regiment, "in the service only about two months," was several times under fire and "acted handsomely."[50]

The first of July, last of the Seven Days, dawned hot and clear. Lee's disappointment at the failure to cripple McClellan in the previous days' fighting was evident to his subordinates, as was his determination to strike a final blow before the Army of the Potomac escaped.[51] McClellan had selected an ideal position from which to cover his retreat to the James, an elevated plateau northwest of his supply base at Harrison's Landing called Malvern Hill. His front line stretched across the crest of the 150-foot-high hill from the Crew house, which sat on a bluff and marked the left flank, to Western Run, a creek bordered by marshes that delineated the right. Along this distance of about one and a half miles, the Union commander massed artillery that could sweep the ground over which an assault would come. In front of the Federal guns open fields provided a quarter-mile of cleared ground sloping gently down to a line of woods. Behind the batteries on the crest of the hill, McClellan had packed the better part of five corps of infantry, and further up the hill two more lines of cannon stood in reserve.[52] It was a position to impress the stoutest fighter.

Stonewall Jackson opposed a frontal assault, preferring instead to turn the Union right. Harvey Hill, a combat officer second to none in the Army of Northern Virginia, learned about the terrain from a resident and warned Lee that if the Federals were on Malvern Hill in force they had better be left alone. But Lee, his combative nature aroused, believed that McClellan's army was dispirited after a week of retreating and that southern batteries could soften the Union position enough to open the way for the infantry. The Confederates must not waste this last opportunity to destroy their adversary.[53]

As in the earlier battles of the Seven Days, delay, confusion, and a failure of coordination plagued Lee's army at Malvern Hill. The sun had climbed to its midafternoon point before the soldiers of Jackson, Magruder, Harvey Hill, and Huger were able to reach their positions in the wooded and swampy creek bottoms.[54] Union batteries, opening about one o'clock, almost immediately commanded the entire field. The few Confederate guns able to unlimber in the difficult terrain were quickly disabled. So unequal was this artillery contest that Harvey Hill complained to Jackson, his brother-in-law, that the southern efforts were almost farcical. Through the afternoon northern guns also pounded the waiting southern infantry, who could do nothing but grimly await the order to advance.[55]

At about five-thirty Magruder finally began the attack, sending three of Huger's brigades—those of William Mahone, Lewis Armistead, and Ambrose Wright—and two of his own against the guns near the Crew house. Seeing this advance to his right, Harvey Hill turned to his brigadiers and exclaimed, "That must be the general advance! Bring up your Brigades as soon as possible and join in it." Between six-thirty and seven o'clock, Hill's division moved against the center of McClellan's line.[56] Without artillery support, the Confederate infantry crossed open fields into the teeth of northern batteries. Harvey Hill had seen nothing "more grandly heroic" than this assault, but the attackers never had a chance: "It was not war—it was murder."[57]

Ramseur and the 500 men of the Forty-Ninth North Carolina had formed in line of battle between two and three o'clock. Situated about a mile and a quarter north of the Federal lines, they and the rest of Ransom's brigade waited in the woods along Western Run for more than two hours, listening to the rumble of cannon and musketry and exposed to Union artillery fire. At five o'clock, a message from Magruder asked Ransom to come to his support. Ransom sent word of the request to Huger and received orders to disregard it. Thirty minutes passed, and another plea came from Magruder. Huger was present when this second courier rode up, and he instructed Ransom to decline with the explanation that orders to Ransom must come through Huger. A third rider spurred up to Ransom at seven o'clock. Magruder insisted that he must have reinforcements, if only a regiment. The urgency of the last request, presented against a din that told of a terrible fight in progress, prompted Ransom to send Magruder one of his regiments while dispatching his aide-de-camp to Huger for new orders. Huger consented to let Ransom go to the front, and the latter immediately put the remaining five regiments of his brigade in motion.

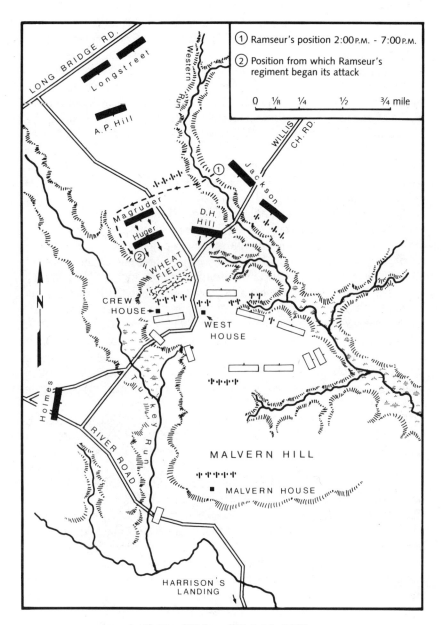

① Ramseur's position 2:00 P.M. - 7:00 P.M.

② Position from which Ramseur's regiment began its attack

Battle of Malvern Hill, 1 July 1862

Hastening toward the raging battle, Ransom's regiments crossed behind Wright and Mahone, forming on the extreme right of the Confederate line northwest of the Crew house. Scarcely had the men caught their breath when Magruder ordered the three leading regiments forward under "as fearful fire as the mind can conceive." Two of the three regimental commanders, one of them Ransom's brother Matt, went down with wounds immediately, and the regiments recoiled in the face of a withering fire. At this juncture, Ransom himself brought up the Forty-Ninth and Zebulon Vance's Twenty-Sixth North Carolina. He ordered his other regiments to join these two under cover of the bluff upon which the Crew house sat. Safe from the federal guns, the North Carolinians drew their line within 200 yards of the main Union position.

They started forward at twilight, undetected until, some hundred yards from the batteries, they raised a "tremendous shout." Hearing this cheer, the "enemy at once wheeled into line and opened upon us a perfect sheet of fire from musketry and the batteries." In the forefront of his regiment, Ramseur was hit in the right arm above the elbow, the ball mangling his upper arm and rendering it useless. Steadily advancing, the Forty-Ninth and Twenty-Sixth came within 20 yards of the guns before they "wavered and fell back before a fire the intensity of which is beyond description." In almost total darkness, Ransom's brigade retired to a point near that from which they had launched their attack.[58] Loath to leave his men, Ramseur at first declined to be carried from the battlefield. But the seriousness of his wound demanded that he be removed to a hospital. That night he made the long and bumpy journey to Richmond.[59]

The Seven Days were over. Five thousand Confederates had been sacrificed at Malvern Hill. Ransom's brigade lost 500 of 3,000 engaged; Ramseur's Forty-Ninth North Carolina over 100 of its 500.[60] In all, Lee's army sustained 20,000 casualties in the bloody week's work. McClellan's loss was less, about 16,000, but he was in full retreat toward his base at Harrison's Landing. From there he directed a stream of requests for reinforcements to Washington, claiming that Lee commanded a vastly superior army. After a month of this, Lincoln ordered him to move the Army of the Potomac from the Peninsula to the vicinity of Fredericksburg, Virginia, to aid in the defense of Washington. Though failing in his attempt to destroy McClellan, Lee had cleared the Peninsula of Federals and saved the Confederate capital. In doing so, he brought the horror of war closer to Richmond's residents. Ramseur was just one of thousands of casualties who choked the city. "The month of July of 1862 can never be forgotten in Richmond," one woman declared. "We lived in one immense hospital, and breathed the vapors of the charnel house." "The weather was excessively hot," she contin-

The battle of Malvern Hill—view from the wheat field below the Crew house.
(Battles and Leaders of the Civil War.)

ued, it "was midsummer, gangrene and erysipelas attacked the wounded, and those who might have been cured of their wounds were cut down by these diseases."[61]

Transported to the home of M. S. Valentine late on the night of the first, Ramseur was spared the filth and overcrowding of Richmond's military hospitals.[62] On 2 July he telegraphed his father: "Slightly wounded yesterday. Borne from field. [Regiment] suffered severely. Can give no particulars. Kindly taken care of in Richmond corner 9th & Capitol Street."[63] In truth, his wound was serious and painful. On 10 July special orders granted him sixty days' leave "for the benefit of his health." It would be a month before he could stand the trip to Lincolnton, there to continue his convalescence amid family and friends.[64]

While in Richmond, he had the pleasure of seeing his name mentioned prominently in Robert Ransom's account of his brigade's activities at Malvern Hill. After his tribute to the "resolute and gallant charge of the brigade" Ransom went on to mention "the conspicuous conduct of Colonels Rutledge, Ransom, and Ramseur, the two latter being severely wounded."[65] Late in July the Raleigh *Register*, sparring with its rival the *Standard* over whether the Twenty-Sixth or Forty-Ninth North Carolina had come closest to the Union guns on Malvern Hill, declared that the testimony of men who were there made clear that Ramseur's troops advanced farther and were the only ones to sleep on the field.[66]

Both before and after his return to Lincolnton, Ramseur experienced "most severe pains" in his arm, which was paralyzed. His family feared he would never regain use of the limb.[67] Still, relaxation at home must have been enjoyable. As always, his father's welfare had been on Dodson's mind. In May, after his father had acquired a new house, Dod had written David Schenck that "tears of gladness & gratitude" filled his eyes at the thought of his family's comfortable and happy situation. He wanted his father to devote all of his time to improving the property. Schenck should judge whether Jacob Ramseur, with financial assistance from Dodson, might resign his position at the mill. A month later Dodson wanted to know how improvements on the property were progressing. His father must "cultivate *fruit—good fruit*." He should also "draw his *wages* up to the 1st July—& lay in a good supply of bacon & flour & salt if it is to be had." Earlier Dodson had counseled David himself to put all available land into cultivation, "I tell you, food is going to be *gold*." Paper currency should be invested in hams, wheat, flour, and the like. Between what they could produce and the money he could send them, Ramseur expected his family to be comfortable.[68]

While Ramseur recuperated in Lincolnton, the Army of Northern Virginia campaigned almost continuously. In August a month of maneuvering culminated in the battle of Second Manassas, a decisive victory over General John Pope's Army of Virginia. Seeking to follow up this triumph, Lee invaded Maryland in September. On 17 September he and McClellan squared off once again in the sanguinary battle of Sharpsburg. In the course of that one day—the bloodiest of the entire war—Lee lost along Antietam Creek and in the adjoining woods and fields fully a third of his army. Besides the losses, Sharpsburg was a strategic defeat obliging Lee to withdraw to Virginia and relinquish the initiative.

The Sharpsburg casualties soon affected Ramseur's career. George B. Anderson, the North Carolinian whose success as a colonel and brigadier Ramseur had sought to emulate, was wounded in the battle and died 16 October. To command his brigade of four North Carolina regiments, Lee selected Ramseur. He did so on the basis of Ramseur's work at Malvern Hill and his superlative training of both his artillery and infantry units. Lee submitted Ramseur's name to the secretary of war and the adjutant general on 27 October.[69] Four and a half months previously, Dodson had closed a letter to David Schenck with "Hope I'll be with Old Stonewall soon."[70] The opportunity was now at hand, for the brigade he was to command belonged to Jackson's corps.

Ten days before his name went up for promotion Ramseur had left Lincolnton for Richmond, where he arrived on 25 October after stops in Raleigh and Milton. His purpose was to seek treatment for his arm. The paralysis remained, as did agonizing pain that required frequent use of morphine. Dr. Charles B. Gibson, "the most celebrated surgeon" in the capital, thought that the ball had carried clothing into the wound and that it would have to be removed surgically if the nerves were to heal properly. Ramseur's idea of rejoining his regiment, stated the physician, was insane.[71] Fortunately, Gibson did not recommend amputation, a very common treatment for wounds of this type.[72]

When Ramseur learned of his impending promotion he was troubled. Certainly he did not lack ambition. His pursuit of the colonelcy of the Forty-Ninth North Carolina was ample evidence of that. But he was only twenty-five years old, a tender age at which to assume such responsibility. He took his doubts to President Jefferson Davis, who discounted his misgivings and urged him to accept the command, but also advised him to return to Lincolnton until he was strong enough to rejoin the army. Davis's counsel echoed that of Dodson's friends and probably made easier his decision to take the commission.[73] On 1 November Secretary of War George W. Randolph signed the appointment that entitled Ramseur to wear the wreath and three stars of a general officer and sent it to the headquarters of the Forty-Ninth near Madison Court House, southwest of Culpeper. Five days later Special Orders No. 234 announced it to the army.[74]

Friends from his old regiment were quick to congratulate Ramseur. "I have your appointment of Brig. Gen. which I send you," Major Leroy M. McAfee wrote on November 11. "All are very much gratified and all regret you do not command this Brigade. You are assigned to Anderson's Brigade." McAfee asked Ramseur to try to have the Forty-Ninth transferred to his new command, as did regimental surgeon John K. Ruffin in a note left at Ramseur's hotel in Richmond. J. W. Wilson, the quartermaster, reported to his old chief on 10 November that the men hated to see him go but felt "much gratified at this appointment as it is an honor to us as well as yourself." A week later Wilson wrote again, inviting Ramseur to visit the Forty-Ninth before "you go home, or to your new command. . . . Your regiment is desirous of presenting you with some token of their regard."[75] What that token was, and whether Ramseur received it in person, is not recorded. But Ramseur's notes for a farewell message of appreciation survive. "My desire had been to perform my whole duty as your commander feeling assured that in that way only I could fairly gain your esteem & maintain my self respect." The men must know how pleased he was to receive their "parting gift as a token of your approbation of my success." He hoped that the fortunes of war would again throw them together to battle side by side.[76]

Ramseur returned to North Carolina in mid-November. During his convalescence, he had visited his cousin Ellen Richmond at Woodside, her father's home in Milton, fallen in love with her, and received her acceptance to his proposal of marriage. Dodson considered Nellie his "long cherished ideal of womanly perfection" and marveled that she should return his affection.[77] However wondrous to Ramseur, a detached observer would find their mutual attraction natural. Two and a half years his junior, Nellie possessed a quick mind and gracious manners. Like Dodson she was small in stature, attractive, with brown hair and eyes. She shared his strong Presbyterian faith. In short, she seemed to embody the virtues of womanhood held sacred by men of Ramseur's time, place, and temperament.[78] On Christmas Day Dodson sent his love to "the source of all my joys, how infinitely much I owe to you, how inexpressably [sic] much I love you for all this newfound happiness." On New Year's Day, Dodson's mind was in Milton. "Every day I love you more fondly and more devotedly," he confessed to Nellie, the "sentiment fills every corner of my heart until it has become as essential to my happiness as the heart is to existence."[79]

By January, Ramseur felt strong enough to join his command in Virginia. The brigade had since the wounding of George Anderson at Sharpsburg been commanded by Colonel Bryan Grimes of the Fourth North Carolina.[80] The other regiments were the Second, the Fourteenth, and the Thirtieth, all from North Carolina. The brigade had fought well on the Peninsula, at Second Manassas, and at Sharpsburg. It was part of the division known as Harvey Hill's, but commanded, since Hill's recent transfer to the Department of North Carolina, by Brigadier General Robert Rodes. Thirty-three years old, Rodes had graduated from the Virginia Military Institute, taught there briefly, then pursued a career as a civil engineer. A tall man of great presence, he had distinguished himself on fields from First Manassas through Sharpsburg and had been badly wounded at Seven Pines. His star was ascending, as was Ramseur's; the two of them would share glorious days ahead.[81]

The men of his new brigade might have regarded Ramseur with considerable coolness because he succeeded a beloved officer of great ability, and because, having spent most of his Confederate career in the artillery, he was almost a total stranger to them. One of his colonels later remembered, however, that Ramseur "at once disarmed criticism by his high professional attainment and great amiability of character, inspiring his men, by his own enthusiastic nature, with those lofty martial qualities which distinguish the true Southern soldier."[82] Impressed by the men in his regiments, Ramseur nevertheless thought their long service without a brigadier had left them in a condition of partial disorganization. This shortcoming he confidently expected to correct, predicting that the brigade would, by hard work, be in

Ellen Richmond Ramseur. "Every day I love you more fondly and more devotedly,"
Ramseur wrote Nellie in January 1863. "The sentiment fills every corner of my heart
until it has become as essential to my happiness as the heart is to existence."
(Collier's Representative Women of the South.*)*

"fine fighting trim" by the time General Joseph Hooker, who commanded the Army of the Potomac, "has the temerity to advance upon us."[83]

From Fredericksburg the night of 29 January, Dodson wrote that his brigade was on picket duty along the Rappahannock River, in view of Federal soldiers on the opposite bank. The moon shone on a foot-high blanket of snow, and "nature in her purity" evoked thoughts of Nellie.[84] Through late winter and early spring Ramseur and his men labored on picket and in drill. Despite long days in the saddle, often exposed to bitter cold and miserable weather—on one day the brigade "marched 7 miles through blinding snow, waded two deep creeks, reached camp at 9 p.m."—Ramseur's recovery from his wound progressed well. His arm remained in a sling, but "severe spasmodic pains" occurred less often.[85] Nellie's letters, though frequently lost or delayed in the mails, cheered him, and his mind often drifted from military duties to her, "especially in the still hours at night." He held no illusions about a quick end to the war, but neither did he doubt that the Army of Northern Virginia would defeat Hooker. "The vandal hordes of the Northern Tyrant are struck down with terror arising from their past experience," he assured Nellie. "They have learned to their sorrow that this army is made up of veterans equal to those of the 'Old Guard' of Napoleon." A brief warm spell had dried the roads, yet the Federals did not advance. The reason was clear to Ramseur: Hooker's desire "to postpone the day of his defeat and humiliation."[86]

Within the ranks of Ramseur's brigade existed this same belief in the invincibility of Lee's army. While not contemptuous of their foe, Ramseur's soldiers "hailed the dawn of the campaign with beautiful confidence in the future." They resented "evil-disposed persons" in North Carolina who "raised hue and cry against the war and thundered through their newspapers at the rear of Richmond." Though army regulations forbade political meetings, members of the Fourteenth North Carolina passed a series of resolutions and contrived to get them printed in the Richmond newspapers. "From our distant bivouac on the frozen banks of the Rappahannock," began one of these resolutions, "we conjure our fellow-citizens to beware, lest this struggle, already consecrated by much of the best blood of the State, be turned to our shame and humiliation." Manifestly, Ramseur's men were as prepared as he to open a new campaign.[87]

Free most nights to attend to his correspondence, Dodson scratched out many letters to Nellie with his left hand. He speculated about their married life after the war in an eastern garrison or in the vast western wilderness, reminisced about their days together at Woodside, and pressed Nellie to agree to a summer wedding rather than wait for the end of the war.[88] Desperately smitten, Dodson struggled constantly against the urge to return to Nellie. "I must overcome these longings," he said; duty, "stern and high, must reign supreme." A long interval between letters from Nellie invariably resulted in a plea that she pay more attention to her writing. Hurt by one of Nellie's silences, Dodson retaliated with a description of a "tea at Mr. Dickenson's, who has quite a pretty daughter. It was a pleasing episode in this wearisome soldier life of ours." At one point thirteen days passed with no word from Nellie, afflicting Ramseur with "a severe attack of the 'Blues.'" He requested that she number her letters so that he would know when one went astray. The fifth of April marked an anniversary for him. "'Tis two years ago today since I resigned my commission in the U.S.A.," he reflected, "years full of great events and wonderfull [sic] changes."[89]

On a somber note, Ramseur described the ruin by the hostile armies of the beautiful countryside around Fredericksburg. Broad forests had disappeared before soldiers' axes; earthworks and rifle pits scarred untended fields; horses trampled once-lovely grounds of mansions. In the aftermath of the Emancipation Proclamation, the North had forgotten the lessons of "our first Revolution: they have recklessly, yea madly, invested a weak, ruinous creature, Abraham Lincoln with dictatorial power. His word is henceforth law to Yankeedom." Unless Lincoln were impeached or abdicated in favor of another, there was no chance that hostilities would come to a close. "We certainly have a Stupendous task before us!" Ramseur averred, "a task which will test our manhood, and if successfully accomplished, will entitle those of us, who unflinchingly perform the part allotted to us, to the full title of heroes."[90]

By the middle of April, Hooker's army showed signs of stirring. Union pickets across the Rappahannock disappeared. A rattle of musketry echoed from the Confederate left. The Union observation balloon was up. Dodson promised Nellie he would not needlessly expose himself to enemy fire, for he considered his life "dearer to me *now* than ever before." Major J. W. Wilson, the quartermaster who had come with Ramseur from the Forty-Ninth, would write to Nellie should either Dodson or Caleb, Nellie's younger brother serving on Ramseur's staff, be wounded.[91] Another short lull, then on 27 April the Army of the Potomac began to march up the Rappahannock. Two days later the bulk of Hooker's force had crossed Kelly's Ford and U.S. Ford and was beyond Lee's left flank. In a hasty note to David Schenck, Ramseur reported heavy artillery and musket fire about a mile away. His brigade awaited orders to move. "I send you letters from my Sweetheart which you must put away carefully," Dodson wrote his friend. "You shall hear further from me if nothing happens to prevent."[92]

CHAPTER 4

MY BRIGADE BEHAVED SPLENDIDLY

AS IT ALWAYS DOES

Wednesday morning, 29 April, opened with mist and a fog creeping out from the Rappahannock, muffling the sounds across the river where elements of the Union army lay.[1] Robert Rodes's division, encamped near Grace Church southeast of Fredericksburg, moved in the early light to Hamilton's Crossing, about five miles below the town on the Richmond, Fredericksburg, and Potomac Railroad. Ramseur's brigade, which had been on picket duty, deployed along the southern bank of Massaponax Creek under orders to guard a ford near the confluence with the Rappahannock. From a position on the right wing of the Confederate army, Ramseur and his men listened to musketry in the direction of Fredericksburg and suffered casualties from the fire of Union batteries east of the river.[2]

As Ramseur kept his vigil along the creek, Robert E. Lee reviewed Hooker's movements and weighed possible responses. The Federals had thrown pontoons across the Rappahannock the previous day and massed troops under cover of the high western bank of the river. In reaction to this crossing, Stonewall Jackson early that morning had pulled his divisions—Rodes's among them—nearer the town. Clearly, a Federal attack in this quarter was a possibility. But as the day wore on the enemy showed no inclination to advance. Moreover, reports of Union activity far to the west grew increasingly ominous. General J. E. B. Stuart telegraphed that on the preceding evening the enemy had crossed the Rappahannock at Kelly's Ford, some twenty-five miles upstream from Fredericksburg. Later in the day came news that heavy Federal columns were moving from Kelly's Ford toward Germanna and Ely's fords on the Rapidan River. The routes they followed converged near Chancellorsville, a crossroads twelve miles west of Fredericksburg, whence several roads led to the rear of Lee's army.[3] Jeb Stuart's troopers had captured prisoners from three Union corps, confirming Lee's suspicion that the enemy to the west was numerous.[4]

To counter this threat, the commanding general ordered Richard H. Anderson's division to proceed to Chancellorsville. Stuart's cavalry would harass the Federals at every opportunity, slowing their progress and screening Lee's movements. Lafayette McLaws was to prepare to support Anderson. Jackson's four divisions would remain in their lines along the Rappahannock at least until the next day.[5] These six divisions, perhaps 57,000 muskets, were all Lee had to employ against the seven corps of Hooker's army. James Longstreet and two divisions of his First Corps had been sent to the Suffolk area. At best, the ratio would be one to two.[6] Certainly Lee could not wait for Hooker's pincers to close on him. He would strike one of the Union wings.[7]

Mist and fog returned on the morning of 30 April, lingering until noon.[8] Lee and Jackson conferred early. The latter initially preferred to attack in front of Fredericksburg. Lee pointed out that powerful Federal artillery on Stafford Heights east of the Rappahannock would make it difficult to get at the enemy. But if Jackson thought it could be done, Lee would give the orders. Jackson asked Lee's permission to examine the ground, and, having received it, spent the afternoon at that task. He returned in the evening convinced that an attack would be inexpedient. By the time of this report, Lee had decided that the enemy's crossing below Fredericksburg was a feint. The principal blow would come from the west. He determined to leave Jubal Early's division and William Barksdale's brigade, just over 10,000 men, to defend Fredericksburg. McLaws and three divisions of Jackson's corps would march to Richard Anderson's position on the road to Chancellorsville. Lee wanted the troops in motion by dawn.[9]

At three o'clock Friday morning Ramseur roused his men and prepared to depart. His brigade would lead the Second Corps. The column left Hamilton's Crossing at first light, heading north on the military road to reach the Plank Road, which ran from Fredericksburg to Chancellorsville.[10] It was a beautiful May day, warm and alive with newly opened apple, peach, and cherry blossoms. Anemone, sanguinaria, and houstonia added strokes of color to a rich green background in the woods and on hillsides. Fresh grass and wheat half a foot high grew in fields along the route.[11] The men sensed a fight, and prebattle adrenaline put spring into their steps.[12] Ramseur's brigade moved smartly to the Plank Road, turned left, and proceeded toward Anderson's position at Tabernacle Church, midway between Fredericksburg and Chancellorsville on the eastern edge of a heavily wooded area known as the Wilderness.[13] This was a region of few roads and widely scattered farmsteads; dense underbrush and choking vines underlay thickets of blackjack and swamp trees and hickory. It was terrain that could defy the best efforts of officers to keep a strict formation. If Hooker could be

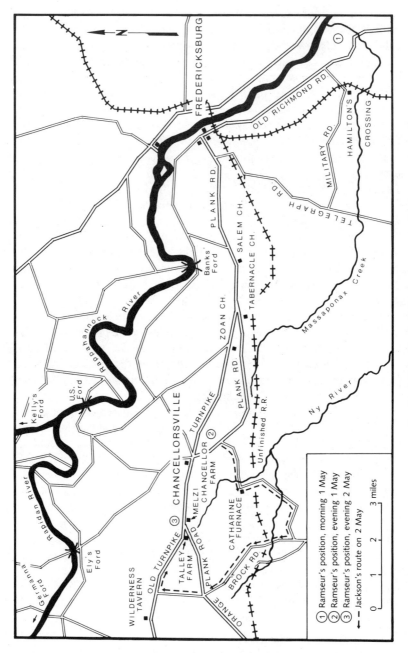

Battle of Chancellorsville, 1–2 May 1863

① Ramseur's position, morning 1 May
② Ramseur's position, evening 1 May
③ Ramseur's position, evening 2 May
--- Jackson's route on 2 May

0   1   2   3 miles

prevented from breaking out of the Wilderness, his advantage in men and artillery would be partially nullified.[14]

Anderson had reached Chancellorsville about midnight on 29 April, learned of the heavy Federal force approaching from the fords over the Rapidan, and fallen back to a position selected by Lee's chief engineer just west of Tabernacle Church and near Zoan Church. His men had entrenched on a small rise commanding the two roads—the Plank Road and the Old Turnpike—that diverged at Chancellorsville, came together again at Tabernacle Church, and led to Fredericksburg. Stonewall Jackson arrived at this crossroads about eight o'clock the morning of 1 May. McLaws's three brigades had preceded him by a few hours, and Ramseur's brigade, in the van of the Second Corps, was approaching. Jackson gave no thought to a stand at Tabernacle Church—his generals must prepare to seek out the enemy. William Mahone's brigade, which had come from Chancellorsville yesterday on the turnpike, should retrace its route with McLaws's division in support. Anderson's brigades under Carnot Posey and Ambrose Wright were to take the Plank Road. When the Second Corps arrived, it would fall in behind Anderson.[15]

The Confederates advanced at eleven o'clock and within fifteen minutes encountered a Federal column moving east on the turnpike. Ramseur on the Plank Road could hear the firing as he drew near Tabernacle Church. Wright and Posey, who led the advance on the Plank Road, had also discovered Federals in their front, and Jackson ordered Rodes to dispatch a brigade to their aid. Because Ramseur led Rodes's column, he received the command to join Wright and Posey.[16] Shortly after two-thirty, Ramseur's regiments came into Jackson's view, and he promptly put them in front, between Wright and Posey. Stonewall himself accompanied the North Carolinians and urged them on "with great vigor."[17]

Under the approving eye of his hero, Ramseur crisply deployed his brigade. He sent out skirmishers and sharpshooters, personally directing their movements with coolness and skill. Soon the hottest fighting of the day flared along the Plank Road. Where the terrain allowed, Ramseur maneuvered his men by regular brigade drill. Both A. P. Hill and Anderson witnessed this, admiring the efficiency of the regiments. Jackson more than once rode along behind Bryan Grimes's Fourth North Carolina, absorbed in the action. "Upon much resistance being shown by the enemy," Grimes wrote, Jackson "would say in suppressed tones, 'Press them, Colonel.' "[18]

Almost immediately the Federals, men of Henry W. Slocum's XII Corps, gave ground. For two miles the Confederates pressed westward, capturing prisoners, arms, and baggage. One of Ramseur's officers likened the pursuit to a fox hunt and remarked how beautifully the brigade responded to

The Wilderness of Spotsylvania, a second-growth woods with "an interminable mass of undergrowth." In 1863 and again in 1864 Lee's army fought in this forbidding, gloomy area. (Miller's Photographic History of the Civil War.)

its commander's direction.[19] As the line progressed through heavy woods, Ramseur utilized his skill as an artillerist to hound the retreating enemy. In every clearing he unlimbered artillery and assisted gunners in placing their rounds.[20] Hooker called off his advance by six o'clock and concentrated his army around Chancellorsville. In one final charge about six-thirty, Ramseur's brigade swept up the Plank Road to within less than a mile of Hooker's headquarters at the Chancellor house, a pillared mansion that gave the crossroads its name. Halted by artillery fire, Ramseur pulled back a short distance, set up a strong picket line, and settled in for the night.[21]

It had been a satisfying day for Ramseur. The Army of Northern Virginia had wrested the initiative from Hooker and pinned him in the oppressive tangle of the Wilderness. Now Ramseur's men found themselves under a bright moon that "filled the heavens with light" and cast eerie shadows in the surrounding forest.[22] They were so near the Union lines that orders were given in the lowest tones. For the first time the brigade employed the sign and countersign—"Liberty" was the challenge, "and Independence," the response. Up the road a few hundred yards the axes of Union pioneers rang as they labored to strengthen Hooker's position. A cold, damp night, punctuated by occasional Union shells, made sleep difficult.[23]

While the army tried to rest, Lee and Jackson met to plan the next day's course of action. Jackson thought Hooker would retreat across the Rappahannock that night. Lee disagreed. Hooker would not give up so easily. He must be attacked. But where? The Wilderness on the Confederate right was virtually impenetrable. In the center, Hooker's entrenchments would be strong and manned by overwhelming numbers. Jeb Stuart helped provide an answer by bringing word from one of his brigadiers, Fitzhugh Lee, nephew of the commanding general, that the Union right flank was "in the air." If Jackson could move undetected around Hooker's army to a point on the Federal right, there was a chance for a decisive blow. Jackson must try it. Lee sketched the approximate route of a flanking march but left the details to his lieutenant. When the two conferred again early the next morning, Jackson had learned that the route was practicable. He proposed to take three divisions—Rodes's, A. P. Hill's, and Colston's, which had been his own—leaving Lee with Anderson and McLaws. Some 28,000 men would make the flanking march; 14,000 would remain to occupy Hooker's five corps. It was dangerous, but the reward might be great. Lee agreed, and Jackson left to set the plan in motion.[24]

About eight o'clock on 2 May Jackson began his march. Rodes's division led, followed by Colston and A. P. Hill. Ramseur's brigade, which had been relieved of its duty on the Plank Road at daylight, took its place near the head of the column.[25] The march was purposeful, the men largely silent.

Blessed with another fair day, the troops had little discomfort until the sun
had climbed high and water proved difficult to find. The roads were moist,
remembered a South Carolinian, "just wet enough to be easy to the feet
and free from dust." The men rested and ate at noon, then resumed their
march through the warm, still afternoon.[26] They were disturbed only once,
early in the afternoon, when Federals struck the rear elements near Catharine Furnace.[27]

Shortly after two o'clock—for the second time in as many days—Fitzhugh Lee brought good news. He informed Jackson that a continuation of
the march past the Plank Road to the Old Turnpike would place the Confederates beyond the westernmost unit of the Army of the Potomac. Jackson
halted the column, climbed a hill with young Lee to observe the enemy's
lines, and saw a sight that must have thrilled even his dour heart. Stretched
out along the turnpike were the men of O. O. Howard's XI Corps, obviously
expecting no attack. Campfires were burning, arms stacked, the men at
ease. Hurrying back to Rodes, Jackson told him to continue past the Plank
Road to the turnpike.[28]

The pace picked up. Soon Rodes was on the turnpike. By four o'clock he
had deployed his division: Alfred Iverson and Edward O'Neal north of the
road; George Doles and Alfred Colquitt south of the road. Ramseur he
placed behind Colquitt as support. In another hour, Colston's division had
formed a second line, extending north from Ramseur's left, and A. P. Hill
part of a third. A mile down the turnpike lay the Talley farm and half a
mile east of it Melzi Chancellor's, two clearings in the forest that were to be
the immediate objectives of the attack. Talley's was on a slight hill that
commanded the Chancellor farm, where Howard had erected works facing
south. Rodes feared pressure from his right and directed Ramseur to watch
the flank so Colquitt could push ahead without worry from that quarter. At
five-fifteen, Jackson turned to Rodes and asked, "Are you ready, General
Rodes?" "Yes, sir!" said Rodes, eager to begin. "You can go forward then,"
replied Jackson.[29]

A nod from Rodes and buglers sent their calls to the waiting infantry.
Four hundred yards in front of the main line the skirmishers sprang forward, followed closely by the long ranks of Rodes's brigades. After feeble
resistance, the Federals fled in wild confusion, leaving the field strewn with
arms, accouterments, clothing, fieldpieces, and caissons. Past the Talley
farm swept the Confederates, raising the high whine of the rebel yell as they
went, and scattering thousands of terrified animals before them. Briefly
Howard's men rallied behind their works at Melzi Chancellor's; then, in the
early twilight of the forest, Rodes overwhelmed them and captured his
second objective. Colston's division caught up with Rodes in this clearing,

and the two divisions, now inextricably mixed together, made for Chancellorsville. Once past the open ground around Melzi Chancellor's, they entered the gloomy woods again and found themselves in near darkness. Lines became confused, communications deteriorated, and Rodes asked Jackson to bring A. P. Hill's division to the fore so that he could realign his winded troops. Jackson gave his assent, and Rodes withdrew his brigades.[30]

During the pursuit of his West Point religious instructor's panic-stricken corps, Ramseur found himself denied a satisfactory role. Ordered to protect Colquitt's right flank, he had covered but a few hundred yards when that officer halted his brigade and sent word that Federals were attempting to turn the Confederate right. Colquitt blocked Ramseur's path and that of Elisha F. Paxton's Stonewall Brigade on the Plank Road. Now 5,000 troops stood immobile while Ramseur hastened to the right. He found no firing there. Again the staff officer arrived from Colquitt to repeat the original message. Ramseur was beside himself. Colquitt's orders from Rodes had been specific: move ahead at all costs and let Ramseur watch the flank. Colquitt should resume the attack, insisted Ramseur. He would do his job of protecting the right. Finally Colquitt moved on, after which Ramseur "pressed on by the right flank to meet the enemy . . . reported . . . to be in that direction." For half a mile he continued the search, reporting disgustedly that "not a solitary Yankee was to be seen." His fruitless errand completed, Ramseur returned to his place in support of Colquitt, reaching Melzi Chancellor's on the turnpike about seven-fifteen. There, in entrenchments abandoned by Howard's troops, the brigade spent the night of 2 May.[31]

Although the day's fighting was over for Rodes's division, Stonewall Jackson wanted A. P. Hill to take up the attack. Hoping to renew his advance by moonlight, Jackson rode east to survey the terrain. In the confusion of darkness and forest, the Eighteenth North Carolina of James Lane's brigade mistook Jackson's group for Federal cavalry. A volley, then another crashed into the party, wounding Jackson in the arm and hand and disabling many others. A. P. Hill assumed command of the Second Corps until he, too, went down with wounds in both legs. Rodes, a brigadier general, briefly found himself a corps commander, while Ramseur took control of the division.

Soon after midnight, Jeb Stuart arrived to relieve Rodes. It was too late to do more before morning. The men could rest a few hours while their officers sorted out lines and prepared to renew the contest at daylight.[32] To the east on the Plank Road, the Army of the Potomac worked through the night with axe and spade. Their lines facing the Second Corps ran from Hazel Grove, southwest of Chancellorsville, north across the Plank Road and then on to the Rappahannock. East of Chancellorsville, from a point near Catharine Furnace to the turnpike, were the divisions of Anderson and McLaws. Under

*The battle of Chancellorsville—Confederate attack on the Federal XI Corps. (*Battles and Leaders of the Civil War.*)*

Lee's direction they had occupied Hooker while Jackson's corps made its march.[33]

Sunday morning, 3 May, a heavy dew covered the field at the beginning of what promised to be another beautiful day.[34] Stuart had A. P. Hill's division, now under Harry Heth, nearest the enemy, Colston in a second line, and Rodes, whose men had done the hardest fighting the day before, in a third line just east of Melzi Chancellor's. Part of Heth's men were in works erected the previous day by Slocum's XII Corps. All three divisions straddled the Plank Road. Ramseur, the middle brigade of Rodes's five, lay south of the road with his left touching it. Heth's men were almost exactly a mile west of Hooker's headquarters at the Chancellor house; Rodes was three-quarters of a mile west of Heth.[35]

About five-thirty, as Ramseur's hungry men were preparing breakfast, Stuart began his attack. The high ground on the right at Hazel Grove fell almost as soon as the advance got under way. Stuart grasped its importance as an artillery position and quickly batteries started on the way there. Between five-thirty and eight o'clock, the Confederate assault gained ground, especially to the north of the Plank Road. But Federal counterattacks pushed Heth and Colston back. South of the road a large body of disorganized men from both these Confederate divisions huddled behind Slocum's old works and refused to heed orders to face the enemy. The Stonewall Brigade forced its way through this static mass and restored the line temporarily; left unsupported, it too had to fall back.[36] A crisis was at hand for Stuart. Rodes was on his way up, but would need time to align his brigades. At this juncture the batteries ordered to Hazel Grove bought valuable time. Forty guns sent out the "most continuous and rapid [fire] ever delivered by the Confederate Artillery," pounding Union batteries at Fairview, an open area south of the Chancellor house, and Federal infantry along Stuart's front. Some of the guns fired three rounds a minute, as the artillerymen, Frank Huger among them, joyously worked their batteries.[37]

Ramseur's first great opportunity arose at this moment of danger. About eight-thirty, his brigade, together with the rest of Rodes's division, advanced against the enemy with orders to "engage him vigorously, moving over friend and foe alike, if in the way." For the next hour, remarks the most famous historian of the Army of Northern Virginia, "the battle was to be Ramseur's."[38] Dodson and Colonel Bryan Grimes of the Fourth North Carolina had just reached Slocum's old works when an officer of Jeb Stuart's staff rode up and ordered a brigade commander to charge. When that officer declined to do so without orders from his division, Ramseur broke in: "Give me the order and I will charge." Grimes suggested that the hard fighting of the previous two days dictated a supporting rather than a leading role for Ramseur's brigade, but Ramseur shrugged him off and repeated his offer. "Then you make the charge, General Ramseur," replied the staff officer. Hurry back, Ramseur told Grimes, and prepare the men to advance. James Lane, whose own brigade already had been wrecked that morning in attacks across the same ground, advised Ramseur not to go forward, but his counsel went unheeded.[39]

Detaching Parker's Thirtieth North Carolina to support the batteries at Hazel Grove, Ramseur brought his other regiments up to the breastworks behind which men from various units cowered three or four deep. Ramseur ordered these sullen troops forward. Not a man moved. Reporting this to Stuart, he received an order to assume command of the people behind the works and compel them to advance. Again the order to attack fell on deaf ears, whereupon Ramseur asked for permission to pass over the troops in his front, a request which Stuart "cheerfully granted."[40] Only a few moments passed before Ramseur, from a position near the left of the Second North Carolina, shouted "Forward at once!" The Fourth and seven companies of the Second, some of them literally "stooping like athletes" in anticipation of the order, raced toward the Yankees with a mighty yell.[41]

Across the backs of their own troops they went; Bryan Grimes, like his men disgusted with the "cowardly conduct" of these soldiers, put his foot on the back and head of an officer of high rank and "ground his face in the earth."[42] Plunging into an "interminable mass of undergrowth," the North

Carolinians braved a severe fire as they approached the log works of General Alpheus Williams. Pushing through junglelike foliage, now thick with smoke, they wrested the position from the Federals and found themselves on the edge of a marshy area adjacent to Union artillery at Fairview. Because no unit had supported their right, the Fourteenth under Colonel Bennett and three companies of the Second had stopped nearly 200 yards short of the works just captured. This created a bend in Ramseur's line that subjected the advance group to both direct and enfilading fire. They took a fearful pounding, but stood up "like a brazen wall in the face of the sheets of flame that were poured in upon them." Exploding shells turned branches into deadly missiles. Digging in on the reverse of Williams's trenches, the Confederates beat off repeated counterattacks.[43]

As Ramseur's men clung doggedly to their foothold near Fairview, pressure grew on the right. They could not hold much longer without support. Several times Ramseur sent word to John R. Jones's brigade back at Slocum's works that he needed help. Twice he returned in person to exhort these men to fill a gap of 600 yards between his right and the southern batteries at Hazel Grove. They would not budge. An exasperated Ramseur finally told Rodes that unless reinforced he would have to abandon the hard-won breastworks. Rodes himself, always a striking figure in battle, proved no more successful at dislodging the stubborn shirkers.[44] When Ramseur made his way to the front after his last appeal to Jones's soldiers, he found his men nearly out of ammunition. They held off their obstinate foe only by taking cartridges from the dead. Casualties had piled up, the woods were burning in places, and the ground itself was hot to stand on.[45]

At this point the Stonewall Brigade, now under Colonel J. H. S. Funk, appeared on Ramseur's right and moved into the gap. Jeb Stuart had spurred over to this famous unit, announced that the North Carolinians were hard pressed, and, in his usual ebullient manner, prevailed upon them to move. By lucky chance, Parker's Thirtieth North Carolina finished its work at Hazel Grove at the same time and headed toward the heavy fire on their left. Parker and Funk removed the threat on Ramseur's right, capturing several hundred prisoners in the process, and enabled the weary men of Grimes and Cox to retire in good order.[46] Bennett and the Fourteenth followed soon after, their ammunition, like that of their comrades at Williams's works, completely exhausted.[47]

Jeb Stuart ordered cheers for the North Carolinians as they emerged from the woods and declared that their commander deserved a major general's commission. "No, sir," replied Ramseur to the cavalryman's compliment, "I want to be Brigadier, and remain with my noble brigade." When the exhilaration of the moment passed and the numbed men grasped the extent of their

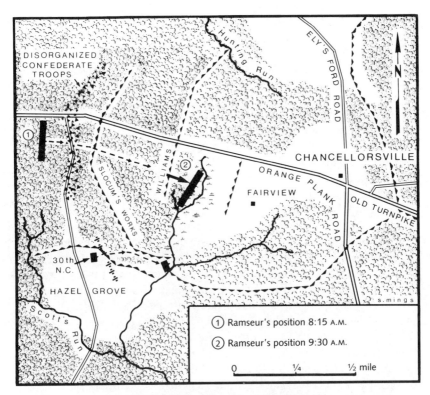

Battle of Chancellorsville, 3 May 1863

losses, many broke down. "On beholding the shattered remnants of the . . . brigade," reported an officer of the Second, Ramseur "wept like a child."[48] Seeing that his commander was overcome with emotion, Colonel R. T. Bennett of the Fourteenth stepped forward to praise the men, who responded with cheers and the rebel yell. Then, having replenished ammunition and dressed lines, Ramseur's regiments proceeded across the Plank Road to meet an expected Federal thrust.[49]

There they remained while Lee, who had worked his left to a point near Hazel Grove, linked up with the Second Corps for a final grand assault. Hooker was driven north from Fairview and Chancellorsville and took up a compact position from which he could protect his line of retreat across the Rappahannock. Deployed along the Plank Road on the afternoon of 3 May, Ramseur's brigade helped keep Hooker bottled up against the river while Lee took McLaws and Anderson to help Jubal Early deal with John Sedgwick, who had successfully stormed Marye's Heights that morning. On 3–4 May, Lee and Sedgwick fought a disjointed battle at Salem Church, four miles west of Fredericksburg on the Plank Road. That night Sedgwick crossed to the north side of the Rappahannock at Scott's Ford. "Fighting Joe" Hooker, who had been stunned by a shell on 3 May, ignored the advice of his corps commanders and ordered a withdrawal across the Rappahannock. By noon of 6 May, the Army of the Potomac was north of the river. That night Ramseur's brigade was on the march back to its old quarters at Grace Church. Eight days of hard campaigning had come to an end.[50]

Chancellorsville was Lee's masterpiece, a primer on the bold use of veteran troops in the face of a superior foe. But it cost the army 13,000 casualties, almost one in four of the men engaged. None of the brigades lost more heavily than Ramseur's. Of 1,509 men he carried into the battle, 788 fell. The Second North Carolina lost 75 percent of its number in fifteen minutes. Colonel Cox of that regiment suffered five wounds before leaving the field. The Second and the Fourth lost their flags when every member of their color guards was killed or wounded. Ramseur was hit in the lower leg by a shell fragment on the evening of 3 May. Reviewing his casualties several days after the battle, Dodson sadly informed David Schenck that his loss had "been *very* heavy."[51]

In return for this sacrifice, the brigade and its commander won plaudits from most of the army's highest leadership. Lee, Jackson, Stuart, A. P. Hill, Anderson, and Rodes—all had observed Ramseur's handling of the brigade at some point and been impressed. Jackson and A. P. Hill praised Ramseur for the precision of his maneuvering along the Plank Road on 1 May, and in his report Hill added that "Ramseur's brigade, under his gallant leadership, was conspicuous throughout the three days' fighting."[52] Jeb Stuart and Rodes complimented the brigade as it came out of the fighting on 3 May. Stuart's report spoke of Ramseur's "heroic conduct," and Rodes called attention to his "great gallantry and efficiency" and described as brilliant in style and unflinching in determination the attack on Williams's works. Rodes thought Ramseur made the "most glorious charge of that most glorious day." A month after the battle Robert E. Lee gave his judgment. In a letter to Governor Zebulon Vance of North Carolina, Lee asked that the depleted ranks of the brigade be filled. "I consider its brigade and regimental commanders as among the best of their respective grades in the army," wrote Lee. "In the battle of Chancellorsville, where the brigade was much distinguished and suffered severely, General Ramseur was among those whose conduct was especially commended to my notice by Lieutenant General Jackson."[53]

In his own report, Ramseur mentioned all his colonels by name and lauded the officers and men "for their gallantry, fortitude, and manly courage during this brief but arduous campaign." Their charge on 3 May had come at a critical moment when the enemy might have broken the Confederate line. They not only "checked his advance, but [also] threw him back in disorder, and pushed him with heavy loss from his last line of works." Proven equal to all they had been asked to do, the men richly deserved "the thanks of our beautiful and glorious Confederacy."[54]

Ramseur traveled after the battle to Richmond, where he received treatment for his wound at General Hospital No. 4.[55] The wound, a "severe" contusion of the shin, was painful, and rendered him "quite lame." Transferred on 8 May to Danville, he continued on to Milton and a reunion with his beloved Nellie. While there he undoubtedly felt deeply the loss of Stonewall Jackson, who died on 10 May of complications following the amputation of his wounded arm. A week flew by at Woodside, then Dodson returned to the army. On 17 May, Ramseur was in Richmond, where he waited three days for his cousin Caleb before rejoining his brigade on the Rappahannock River.[56]

Upon his return to the army Ramseur found a curt letter from Colonel J. H. S. Funk of the Stonewall Brigade. Funk understood that Ramseur claimed that Funk's brigade was among the troops who had refused to leave the shelter of Slocum's works, and that the North Carolinians had passed over them. Ramseur wrongly impugned the Virginians, asserted Funk. His command had assaulted the Federal lines early in the day and been forced to withdraw. After they reformed, Stuart came up and ordered them to "relieve (as I understood) your brigade who were out of amunition [*sic*]. I immediately advanced to the relief of the line in front who were gallantly holding their ground with thinned ranks and empty boxes." Funk remembered no troops passing over his men, whose casualties of more than one-third spoke for their actions. Funk hoped Ramseur would see that he was mistaken.[57]

Ramseur replied on 22 May that he was pleased to have Funk's letter. He had been troubled to think that the veterans once commanded by the immortal Jackson should ever falter in the discharge of their duty. He would explain "*why* I reported to Maj Genl Rodes that I had passed over Jones' [Brigade] and a *part* of Genl Paxton's." When he found the troops milling around behind the works and enquired as to their command, several answered, "I belong to the Stonewall Brig[ade]." Seventy-five or a hundred yards to the right, he received the same answer. "The crisis was on us," Ramseur continued. "Therefore I ordered my Brig[ade] forward over those of General Jones and over those who told me that they were of the Stonewall Brig[ade]." Naturally, Ramseur and his men thought they had run over at least part of Paxton's command. The men to whom he spoke could have been skulkers or members of other units who misrepresented themselves. Ramseur would be happy to correct his error by "having your letter published to my troops at Dress Parade."[58] This correspondence seemingly closed the matter; however, Ramseur's official report, dated one day later than his reply to Funk, said that "a small portion of Paxton's brigade" was behind the works and refused Ramseur's order to advance.[59]

Dodson offered his valedictory on Chancellorsville in two letters to David Schenck. In a short and glorious period of maneuvering, Lee's 53,000 men had forced Hooker's self-styled "finest army on the planet" across the Rappahannock. To those who wondered why Hooker escaped, Ramseur replied: "Is it not enough that we drove largely more than twice our numbers from the strongest field works I have yet seen?" The victory was decisive in that a Union triumph would have compelled the evacuation of Richmond. Had Hood and Pickett been with the army, a far heavier loss could have been inflicted upon the enemy.[60] Ramseur's own brigade had "covered itself with glory," but he doubted that the newspapers had given his unit its due. He had "no paid correspondent with my brig[ade], as many others have," and the Richmond papers always slighted troops not from Virginia. Had David seen anything in the North Carolina newspapers about "our *conduct* in the fight?" He must clip all notices. Dodson would send a copy of his official report to be read to "particular friends" and then filed away. Disingenuously he cautioned Schenck not to allow it to appear in print, such "publications being highly unmilitary." Whatever the newspapers might say, the official reports would, he was confident, be generous. As for the immediate future, Ramseur thought Lee planned an advance against Hooker. With Longstreet's detached divisions hurrying to the Rappahannock, the chance remained to deal a killing blow to the Army of the Potomac. Dodson had received thirty days' leave but would not take it with an offensive in prospect.[61]

Changes in the high command of the Army of Northern Virginia necessarily followed the death of Stonewall Jackson. Lee had for some time questioned whether the corps were not larger than one man could manage effectively in the wooded terrain over which the army operated. He therefore decided upon reorganization into three corps, the First Corps still under Longstreet, the Second under Richard S. Ewell, and the Third under A. P. Hill, whose division passed in somewhat altered form to Dorsey Pender. Ewell's Second Corps would consist of the divisions of Jubal Early, Edward "Allegheny" Johnson (successor to Colston), and Robert Rodes (now a major general). Ramseur's brigade remained in Rodes's division.[62]

Lee's army, thus reorganized, was ready for another campaign by the end of May 1863. There was much speculation about the nature of that campaign. Despite the loss of Jackson, the confidence of the army in its commanders was firm. Ramseur was certain that Lee and "his veteran army" would follow up Chancellorsville with another triumph.[63] Many newspapers across the South clamored for an invasion of the North. Officers and enlisted men in the army echoed this call. Dorsey Pender spoke for the former when he told his wife that "all feel that something is brewing and that Gen. Lee is not going to wait all the time for them to come to him." One of Ramseur's privates thought the army "equal to any undertaking and invasion would mean to us shoes, clothing, rations full and free, and all other supplies which the army so badly needed."[64] Indeed, provisions were much on Lee's mind. Virginia would be hard pressed to supply the army during another season of fighting. Pennsylvania and its riches beckoned. An invasion of the North might also fuel the peace movement in the United States; almost surely it would pull the Army of the Potomac away from Richmond. With luck, the European powers might be impressed. For all these reasons, Lee determined to invade Pennsylvania.[65]

At this time, Harvey Hill, commander of the Department of North Carolina, requested that Ramseur's brigade be sent to him in exchange for Alfred Colquitt's. Lee refused, saying that he considered "Ramseur necessary with the division to which he belongs." The secretary of war explained to Hill that he had presented to Lee "the inducement of the superior numbers of Colquitt's brigade." "You will see, however, that General Lee declines the exchange . . . preferring, no doubt, like yourself, despite its reduced numbers, Ramseur's veteran brigade."[66]

Before opening the campaign Lee reviewed the Second Corps. Whatever his intent, this was a brilliant device to inspirit the men for the hard work ahead. Ewell formed his divisions in three long lines across a plain near the Rappahannock. The soldiers watched with pride that warm afternoon as Lee cantered the length of each division. A gunner remembered that the thrilling spectacle enabled the men to "see that they were still formidable in number, and although Jackson was dead that the soul of the army had not passed away." In Ramseur's eyes the troops made a "splendid appearance," though he grieved to see the thinned ranks of his own brigade.[67]

Five days after the review Ramseur received orders to prepare for a march. "Where or why we go, none but Gen. Lee & his [Lieutenants] know," he wrote Nellie, but Hooker had moved toward Washington and the Army of Northern Virginia was probably "about to move in that direction." Uneasiness about greater separation from Nellie for a protracted period tempered Dodson's feelings about a possible invasion of the North. He wished they had married when he was nursing his wound at Woodside. For a time he had thought a lull might allow an early summer marriage. That no longer seemed possible. Walks about the grounds at Woodside, the roses in the garden there, the beautiful hills, Nellie's face in the moonlight—all these images reminded him how much he missed her and brought feelings of melancholy. A letter from her on 31 May, his twenty-sixth birthday, was most welcome, but news from Mississippi was depressing. He was "very anxious about Vicksburg." Should it fall, the war would drag on indefinitely. If Joseph E. Johnston and John C. Pemberton somehow managed to defeat the Federals in their theater, however, they could reinforce Braxton Bragg at Tullahoma and press William S. Rosecrans into Kentucky. With little conviction, Dodson told Nellie that all might yet be well in Mississippi. Whatever happened there, she should not feel uneasy about him during the coming campaign. As before Chancellorsville, he implored her not to "believe any disastrous news until fully confirmed."[68]

Rodes's division broke camp on 4 June, a fine, warm early summer day, and marched sixteen miles from Grace Church to Spotsylvania Court House. The following day the men covered twenty-one miles through clouds of dust raised by thousands of shuffling feet. After resting on 6 June, Ramseur's brigade waded the Rapidan at Somerville Ford, northeast of Orange Court House, on Sunday the seventh and camped four miles north of Culpeper. Showers on the sixth had settled the dust, making for a pleasant nineteen-mile hike. The division remained at Culpeper for two days. Excess baggage went to the rear, three-days' rations were cooked—sure signs of serious marching ahead.[69]

On 9 June Rodes sent Ramseur and other elements of the division to Brandy Station, on the Orange and Alexandria Railroad a few miles east of Culpeper, to assist Jeb Stuart's Cavalry Corps. Alfred Pleasonton's blue cavalry had surprised Stuart, whose troopers were tired from a strenuous two days of review, and engaged him in what proved to be the largest cavalry battle ever fought in North America. Ramseur's regiments came under fire but were not involved directly in the fighting. Hot marching to and from Brandy Station took up most of the day; by evening, the brigade was back at Culpeper readying for the next day's march.[70]

It was afternoon on 10 June before the column moved out. In two days the division crossed the Blue Ridge at Chester Gap, passed through Front Royal, waded both forks of the Shenandoah River, and arrived at Cedarville. There General Ewell directed Rodes to drive the Federals from Berryville, move on to Martinsburg, and enter Maryland via Williamsport. The other divisions of the Second Corps would attack Winchester and join Rodes in Maryland. On 13 June a small Union force evacuated Berryville in the face of Rodes's advance. The next day, after a march of nineteen miles, the

Confederates encountered on the outskirts of Martinsburg a Federal brigade under General Daniel Tyler. Rodes ordered Ramseur to attack at once. The other brigades would support him. "Notwithstanding their fatiguing march," Rodes later reported, "the troops exhibited great enthusiasm, and rapidly occupied the town and the enemy's position." In the lead, Ramseur's North Carolinians, spearheaded by the Fourteenth, chased the Federals for two miles over rough ground crisscrossed with stone fences. Five cannon with caissons and horses, 200 prisoners, thousands of bushels of grain, and some small arms and ammunition fell into Confederate hands.[71]

Rodes allowed his men to rest until ten o'clock on 15 June, then pushed on to Williamsport in a cruel march through intense heat. Ramseur's brigade was the first southern infantry to cross the Potomac; Alfred Iverson and George Doles were close behind, and Junius Daniel and Edward O'Neal followed the next day. At Williamsport, the officers first noticed "unmistakable signs of exhaustion" among the men. Heat, hard roads, and a shortage of shoes had left hundreds broken down and with bloody feet. A respite was imperative. For two days Rodes's five brigades rested in a meadow along the river while the commissary and quartermasters secured supplies in the neighboring countryside.[72]

A somewhat refreshed division departed from Williamsport on 19 June for Hagerstown, Maryland, where Rodes paused before crossing into Pennsylvania on 22 June. Proceeding through Greencastle and Chambersburg on the way to Carlisle, which they reached on 27 June, the soldiers envied the wealth of southern Pennsylvania.[73] "The war had not hurt them like it had us," J. A. Stikeleather of the Fourth North Carolina observed, "and the blighting effects of slavery were not seen there." Food was plentiful. Stikeleather mentioned especially the rich butter, light bread, and apple butter of the region. Lee's strict prohibition against taking private property from towns and farms was a hardship which W. A. Smith of the Fourteenth and countless others accepted only out of love for "Marse Robert." Plodding infantrymen resented the fact that many a cavalryman's horse was loaded down with plunder. Ramseur understood his men's frustration and told them it was improvident to pass up "so many ripe, luscious cherries on the roadside for those behind us to devour."[74]

The demands of the march prevented Dodson from writing to Nellie until his brigade entered Greencastle, Pennsylvania, on 23 June. The advance to that point had been "wonderfully rapid and . . . successful." His men were cheerful and full of fight, their conduct in every way satisfactory. But Dodson was "very sad and heartsick" at not hearing from Nellie. As the distance between them increased, so did his longing for her. Apart from these feelings, all was well: "We expect to make a bold and successful campaign."

Route of Ramseur's Brigade to Gettysburg, 4 June to 1 July 1863

Five days later the brigade was in Carlisle, occupying the old U.S. Barracks "which in the days of yore were inhabited by the gay and happy young officers of Dragoons & cavalry." The Yankees had left Carlisle so precipitately that they abandoned all "household ornaments & luxuries & left food to be consumed." Dodson had breakfasted one morning on iced salmon.[75]

Carlisle proved a welcome haven for three days. Afternoon showers kept the heat at bay, and lovely surroundings made rest easy. The Reverend B. Tucker Lacy, whom Jackson had appointed unofficial chaplain for the Second Corps, delivered an address on his old chief, and the Confederates ceremoniously raised their flag over the barracks. Ramseur enjoyed himself and exuded confidence at Carlisle. The absence of Federal opposition thus far astonished him. Bloody work no doubt lay ahead, but if God chose to reward the southern effort with victory, the present campaign could "result in a glorious and honorable peace."[76]

Orders to move toward the rest of the army ended this interlude on 30 June. Setting out for Cashtown, the brigades of Rodes's division covered twenty-two miles and bivouacked at Heidlersburg. Resuming the march on 1 July, they reached Middletown, where Rodes received word that A. P. Hill's corps was moving toward Gettysburg. The rendezvous was now to be there. Shifting the division's course to the south, Rodes started for Gettysburg with Iverson in the van and Ramseur the rear. Four miles from Gettysburg the men heard the unmistakable sounds of a heated engagement.[77] A battle was in progress between Heth and Pender of A. P. Hill's corps and John F. Reynolds's I Corps of the Army of the Potomac. The fight had opened early that morning when Heth approached Gettysburg from the northwest on the Cashtown Pike in search of shoes and found instead John Buford's tough Federal cavalry. A seesaw struggle ensued, as each side committed fresh units. By the time Rodes reached the field about three o'clock, Hill's corps had gained the upper hand.

Moving south along Oak Ridge, Rodes perceived that he could, under cover of woods, work his way to a position on the right flank of the Union force then opposing Heth and Pender. He deployed his division with Iverson, O'Neal, and Doles in the front row from right to left, and Daniel and Ramseur in reserve. Thus aligned, Rodes progressed a mile south down the ridge until he reached Oak Hill. From that eminence he could see the Federals in front of Hill and, off to his left, another body of Union troops fanning out north of town. As he watched, the Federals to his right changed position to meet him, anchoring their right behind a stone wall that stretched southwest from the Mummasburg Road. Placing Doles to counter any threat from the Federals north of Gettysburg, Rodes sent Iverson and O'Neal against the enemy in front. O'Neal's brigade quickly bogged down, then retreated.[78]

The battle of Gettysburg—view of the town from Oak Hill.
(Battles and Leaders of the Civil War.)

Iverson moved on, his left now uncovered, as the Union troops crouched behind their stone barricade. He had neglected to deploy skirmishers, and when the Confederates were nearly to the wall, the Federals rose up and poured a devastating fire into them. Much of Iverson's brigade fell in a few minutes. The remainder hugged the ground, surrendered, or stumbled back in disorder.[79]

With two of his five brigades smashed in but a few minutes, Rodes called on Ramseur to continue the attack. Ramseur rode up to find three of Iverson's regiments "almost annihilated." Conspicuous on a large gray mare— "the only officer in the field who had a horse under him"—Ramseur ordered the Second and Fourth North Carolina to support O'Neal; the Fourteenth and Thirtieth he prepared to carry the stone wall. Unexpected help came from Cullen A. Battle's Third Alabama, the only regiment of O'Neal's brigade still in condition to fight. When asked by some of Battle's soldiers if they could advance with his brigade, Ramseur answered, "Yes, N[orth] C[arolina] will stay with you." Masked by woods on the slope of Oak Hill, Ramseur formed these three regiments. Two lieutenants who had witnessed Iverson's debacle explained how the Federals had come in on his flank. Ramseur determined to turn the tables on them.[80]

Colonel Francis M. Parker of the Thirtieth, who thought Ramseur handled troops under fire with more ease than any other officer he knew, vividly recalled how Ramseur drew "his line . . . at a right angle to the wall . . . wheeled the line to the left, and then sent us forward at the double quick, or, rather, run." Ramseur's men and the Third Alabama moved with "irresistible force" into a galling fire. Parker went down with a wound in the face; Ramseur's horse was shot from under him within a few yards of the stone wall. The Second and Fourth, together with the Twelfth North Carolina of Iverson, added their weight to the attack, driving the Yankees back

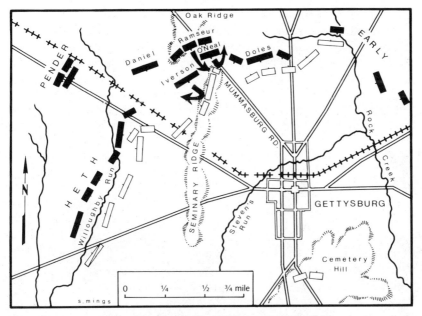

Battle of Gettysburg, Early Afternoon, 1 July 1863

in confusion and capturing 800–900 prisoners.[81] One brigade, witnessing Ramseur's coolness in the forefront of his regiments, interrupted their pursuit of the fleeing Union troops to give him three cheers.[82]

While Ramseur's men broke the enemy line in Rodes's center, the soldiers of Junius Daniel and George Doles were advancing on their right and left. Joined by Jubal Early's division, recently arrived on Doles's left directly north of town, Rodes's brigades inaugurated a general advance that continued into and through Gettysburg. Once again their opponents were the luckless men of O. O. Howard's XI Corps. As at Chancellorsville, the Yankees were put to rout, yielding 2,500 prisoners. Doles and Ramseur led the chase and were the first to enter Gettysburg.[83] While winded men caught their breath in the streets of the town, their commanders looked south to hills where Union officers frantically worked to construct a line. Ramseur, who had a second horse killed by a Federal straggler in Gettysburg, wanted to press forward and clear the enemy from that position, a sentiment shared by many of his men.[84] But General Ewell, who rode into the town soon after it fell, declined to attack the high ground—called Cemetery Hill by the locals—because he could not get fresh troops and artillery into position quickly enough.[85]

Eager to fight, Ramseur nevertheless contributed to the Confederate failure to seize the heights. Just after entering Gettysburg, he rode west to Seminary Ridge and asked General William Nelson Pendleton, Lee's chief of artillery, not to open on the Union position on Cemetery Hill, because to do so "would draw a concentrated fire upon his men, much exposed." David G. McIntosh, one of the more capable artillerists in the Army of Northern Virginia, remembered with bitterness this meeting between Ramseur and Pendleton: "The suggestion was as untimely and ill-judged as its acceptance was weak and unfortunate."[86] In Ramseur's defense, it must be said that he expected a renewal of the attack and wanted only to be able to deploy his regiments without taking artillery fire. But the order to take the hill did not come. Rodes placed his brigades in a defensive posture within the city, where they spent the night of 1 July.[87]

The halt on 1 July proved decisive. That night General George Gordon Meade, who had replaced Hooker as commander of the Army of the Potomac, concentrated his men in the famous "fishhook" south and southeast of Gettysburg. From Power's Hill and Culp's Hill southeast of town, his line stretched west along Cemetery Hill, then south down Cemetery Ridge. In addition to the advantage of high ground, Meade possessed interior lines. Union artillery crowned the heights and looked down on magnificent fields of fire. Posted on the western edge of Gettysburg, with their right at the foot of Seminary Ridge, Ramseur's men sat in line of battle for most of 2 July, troubled only by occasional artillery shells and light skirmishing. Off to the south, beginning about three-thirty, Longstreet attacked Meade's left. Bitter fighting continued for several hours. By the narrowest of margins, the Federals held Little Round Top, which anchored their southern flank, and Longstreet withdrew. Ewell later struck the Union right on Culp's Hill and East Cemetery Hill, reaching the crest of the former only to have darkness and a lack of support force his men back.

At dusk, Ramseur received orders to attack the northwest face of Cemetery Hill. Rodes's other brigades were to conform to his movements. Such an order would have been welcome twenty-four hours earlier when the enemy was disorganized and outnumbered. Now there was no chance for success. Moving to within 200 yards of the Federal position, Ramseur discovered a double line of infantry behind breastworks and backed by powerful batteries. "The idea of charging strong fortifications in the night time was an awful thing," wrote an officer in the Thirtieth North Carolina. "But everyone was willing to follow our Brigadier General wherever he would lead us. We had undivided confidence in his military skill and patriotism." Ramseur and Doles agreed to halt and apprise Rodes of their findings. Persuaded that the lateness of the hour and the strength of the enemy promised a "useless sacrifice of life," Rodes recalled his order. Ramseur withdrew 300 yards to a deep farm road. From there he would be ready to attack at daylight.[88]

Early Friday morning, 3 July, Dodson scrawled a hurried note to Nellie: "We were overwhelmed yesterday by numbers. Today we will have a hard fight—I pen these few lines from my saddle, hope you will receive them."[89] The hard fight came on that day to Ramseur's right, where Lee, in an action reminiscent of Malvern Hill, sent the divisions of George E. Pickett, Johnston J. Pettigrew, and Isaac R. Trimble against a strong Union force on Cemetery Ridge. "The position we had enabled us to see the whole affair," wrote one of Ramseur's officers. "Oh, what an awful sight it is to see an army marching upon another!"[90] Pickett's Charge was high drama, but it was doomed from the start. Its failure obliged Lee to draw back to Seminary Ridge, where he invited an attack from Meade on 4 July. That night, in a drenching rain, Lee's army began the long retreat to Virginia.

The Army of Northern Virginia marched slowly toward the Potomac, offering battle to its opponent several times. Rodes's division formed the rear guard.[91] From Hagerstown on 8 July, Dodson assured Nellie that he was fine, though his horse had been killed under him and he had "many hair breadth escapes." Northern numbers and their "Gibraltar of a position" had compelled the Confederates to withdraw. "My brigade behaved splendidly," he said, "as it always does." The men were in high spirits and hoped Meade would attack.[92] The Union commander chose not to press Lee, however, and on 14 July Longstreet's and Hill's men crossed the Potomac on pontoons. Ewell's corps waded the river. That afternoon the Federals launched against the rear guard a feeble attack, which Ramseur's brigade and a part of the Richmond Howitzers easily repulsed. After dark, in a cold rain, Ramseur's men struggled across the Potomac in water so deep some of the shorter men had to be carried by taller comrades.[93]

A few days later, at Martinsburg, Dodson admitted that things looked dark but insisted that the troops had suffered no loss of morale. Another ten days, the "hardest marching I have ever experienced," brought Ramseur and his brigade to Madison Court House. Fatigue and reflection on the events of the month—including the fall of Vicksburg on 4 July—had diminished Ramseur's capacity for optimism. "What must I say . . . about our bleeding country?" he asked Nellie. The European powers, especially England, preferred two weak nations in North America and would not recognize the South until one or both sides faced exhaustion. Still, Nellie should not be discouraged. The Confederate cause was just, the enemy wicked and cruel, and God would favor the righteous.[94]

By the first week in August, Ramseur had settled into camp near Orange Court House, and had time to focus on the price of Gettysburg. His brigade,

numbering 1,130 at the outset of the campaign, had been relatively fortunate, suffering only 196 casualties. The army as a whole carried 75,000
men into Pennsylvania and lost one-third killed, wounded, or captured.
Some of Dodson's dearest friends were gone: "Poor Pender, so full of every
noble and manly spirit . . . Poor McCreery too, fell, while gallantly charging." McCreery lay buried in the "land of the strangers." Lost also at Gettysburg was the almost mystical faith in the invincibility of Lee and his army:
"Our great campaign, admirably planned & more admirably executed up to
the fatal days at Gettysburg, has failed. Which I was not prepared to antici-
pate." Though one defeat did not spell disaster, it did foreshadow the path
ahead. If the South were to win, it would have much suffering to bear. "I
look the thing square in the face," he affirmed, "and am prepared to undergo
dangers and hardships and trials to the end." With determined effort and
sacrifice, "a glorious and honorable peace will be our rich and lasting
reward."[95]

Ramseur's brigade camped at Orange Court House for six quiet weeks.
The remnant of Alfred Iverson's brigade, taken from him because of his
dismal performance on 1 July, had been transferred to Ramseur during the
retreat from Pennsylvania. Ramseur drilled these soldiers with his own
regiments until early September, when Robert D. Johnston, who hailed from
Lincolnton, arrived to take charge of them. It was a relaxed time of reviews and light duty. Despite 1,000 casualties suffered since 1 May, Ramseur's regiments maintained high morale, and many of the Chancellorsville
wounded were returning to duty.[96] The brigade remained a showpiece on
the parade ground. A correspondent of the Richmond *Enquirer* who attended a review in late August reported that the "perfection of Ramseur's
men in drill is truly astonishing, and reflects the highest credit upon the
proficiency and skill of that officer."[97]

In much of the Army of Northern Virginia, however, morale was not
high. Desertions rose sharply after Gettysburg and Vicksburg, and regiments from North Carolina were among the hardest hit. Ramseur and others
blamed W. W. Holden, whose Raleigh *Standard* first wanted Jefferson Davis
to open peace negotiations and eventually urged North Carolina to seek
peace on its own. Ramseur's brigade voted almost unanimously—no open
dissenters, perhaps thirty abstentions—to condemn Holden. David Schenck
thought the doctrine Holden "insidiously taught" had prompted deserters
and traitors to resist Confederate authority to the point of open insurrection
in western North Carolina. Ramseur's reply assured David that the "army, I
think, I know—is *sound* and will do honor to the State"; surely "true men"
would step forward in North Carolina to put Holden down. Ramseur for his
part would do all he could to fight absenteeism in the army. He had submit-

General Robert E. Lee. Reviewing Confederate prospects after the fall of Atlanta in September 1864, Ramseu: insisted that "it will be all right as long as Gen'l Lee (God bless our old Hero!) and his glorious Army continue to baffle the tremendous efforts made to capture Richmond and overrun Virginia." (Courtesy of the Library of Congress.)

Lieutenant General T. J. "Stonewall" Jackson. "Jackson is playing the mischief with
*the Yankees," wrote Ramseur of his idol in June 1862. "Hope I'll be with Old Stonewall
soon." (Courtesy of the National Archives.)*

Lieutenant General Richard S. Ewell. Ramseur noted with pride that the charge of his brigade at Spotsylvania was "universally spoken of in the highest terms by off[icers] of distinction. Genl Ewell called me the 'hero of the day.' " (Courtesy of the Library of Congress.)

Lieutenant General Jubal A. Early. "I see the Richmond papers are 'pitching into' Gen'l Early for not taking Washington," Ramseur observed in July 1864. "If he had attempted it he would have been repulsed with great loss, and then these same wiseacres would have condemned him for recklessness." (Courtesy of the Library of Congress.)

Major General John B. Gordon. Gordon remembered that as his soldiers marched to the battlefield at Winchester "the far-off reverberant artillery was already giving painful notice that Ramseur was fighting practically alone, while the increasingly violent concussions were passionate appeals to the other divisions for help." (Courtesy of the Library of Congress.)

Brigadier General Bryan Grimes. "His joy was full deep in his heart," Grimes wrote Ellen Ramseur of the night her husband learned of the birth of their child, "tears of sympathy for you filled his eyes when speaking of you." (Miller's Photographic History of the Civil War.)

Major General Robert E. Rodes. Shortly after the death of his close friend Rodes, Ramseur delivered an impromptu eulogy: "When General Ramseur alluded to General Rodes," a captain noted in his diary, "I could not refrain from tears, and there were many other wet eyes." (Garnett, "Diary," pp. 9–10.) (Miller's Photographic History of the Civil War.*)*

ted a "plan to [General] Lee . . . to stop deserters for which he complimented me highly." On 16 September a deserter from one of Ramseur's
regiments was executed by firing squad, after which the entire brigade
marched past the corpse. Ramseur no doubt agreed with an Alabamian who
recorded in his diary that it was "a sad sight, but . . . necessary as a
warning and lesson to his comrades."[98]

Most of Dodson's energy in late summer went into the happier task of
arranging to marry Nellie. Expecting a furlough in mid-September, he set 17
September as the wedding date. When a cousin suggested that Nellie could
not be ready by then, Dodson answered that he hoped he was not being
unreasonable in insisting on "the immediate consummation of our engagement." Otherwise an active campaign in October would set the date back at
least to January 1864 and perhaps until spring. Nellie proposed 30 September as a compromise, but he agreed to put it off only until the twenty-third,
observing that Nellie was not fully "impressed with the uncertainties of
military life."[99]

Those uncertainties intruded in the middle of September, when Lee fell
back from his line along the Rappahannock to one behind the Rapidan.
Longstreet and part of his corps had been sent to Georgia to reinforce
Braxton Bragg, leaving the Army of Northern Virginia too weak to cover the
Rappahannock.[100] A period of constant skirmishing ensued, during which
the possibility of a major battle loomed. Though Dodson had his leave in
hand, and preparations for a 23 September wedding ceremony were well
under way, he could hardly absent himself from the army under these circumstances.[101] "I am heartsick," he confessed from his new position on the
Rapidan, "disappointment has almost unmanned me." Two weeks dragged
by; Ramseur hoped for a battle to settle the issue and allow him to take
furlough. On 27 September he complained to Nellie that they should have
been married by then: "*How happy* would *we* have been! Ah' me! This cruel,
cruel war!"[102]

On 8 October he received orders to march to Orange Court House.[103] Four
days later Lee began a flanking movement that culminated in an embarrass-
ing failure at Bristoe Station, where A. P. Hill rashly attacked a portion of
the Army of the Potomac before the bulk of the Confederate army had
reached the field. Meade, however, retreated beyond Bull Run, allowing the
Army of Northern Virginia to return to the south bank of the Rappahannock
on 18–19 October. Satisfied that Meade entertained no aggressive thoughts,
Dodson once again applied for leave to be married. Granted his request, he
was in Milton as quickly as the railroad could get him there. On 28 October
he married Nellie in a ceremony at Woodside, his long and anxious romantic
trial over at last.[104]

Woodside, Milton, North Carolina. Birthplace of Ellen Richmond, scene of her marriage to Dodson Ramseur, and the place where he recovered from two of his wounds, Woodside figured prominently in Ramseur's life. (Drawing by E. M. Sutherland.)

CHAPTER 5

WE INTEND TO FIGHT THE

THING OUT

The newly married couple spent nearly a month in the mountains of western North Carolina and with their families in Lincolnton and Milton, after which Ramseur returned on 23 November 1863 to the Army of Northern Virginia, then arrayed behind the Rapidan River. In his absence, two of his regiments had been mauled on 7 November in a skirmish at Kelly's Ford. The Second had acquitted itself well, but the Thirtieth, in the words of Robert Rodes, "did not sustain its reputation." Nearly 300 members of the Thirtieth had taken shelter in a cluster of buildings, refused to abandon them when ordered to fall back across ground subject to enemy fire, and meekly surrendered to advancing Federals.

Although Ramseur had heard about the incident while in North Carolina, he was surprised to see the extent of its effect. Almost a quarter of his brigade had been lost at Kelly's Ford, "which affair," he concluded, "was rather badly managed by the [officers] in command." Apart from that debacle, Ramseur's troops had formed sloppy habits, and he estimated two or three weeks would be necessary to police the camps, perfect fortifications, and get the regiments back into acceptable shape. Encouragingly, the men seemed happy to have their general back. One of Ramseur's officers remarked that the commander's presence "seemed to reanimate the Brigade, so that it was again as of old—joyous and gay, daring and brave."[1]

On 26 November, just three days after he rejoined his brigade, Ramseur wrote from near Morton's Ford that Federals had been crossing in force all day about twelve miles down the Rapidan. He regretted this turn of events because it compelled the Confederates to give up their "entrenchments & meet [their foe] in the open field." The ghastly casualties at Chancellorsville and Gettysburg had made Ramseur, stout fighter that he was, reluctant to throw his men into standup combat or assaults if there were a chance to fight from behind entrenchments. Gone was the disdain, so prevalent early in the war, for troops that preferred the protection of breastworks.[2]

To counter this latest Federal threat, Robert E. Lee decided to employ the Second Corps, temporarily under Jubal Early because Richard Ewell was ill. Early was to move three divisions toward Locust Grove, a hamlet just outside the forbidding forest where Joseph Hooker had come to grief seven months earlier. About midnight on 26 November, Robert Rodes received orders to march from his position near Morton's Ford to Zoar Church southwest of Locust Grove. The other two divisions, taking different routes, would unite with him near there.[3]

Promptly at three o'clock, under a "lunar halo" and in bitter cold, Ramseur started his brigade on the frozen road to Zoar Church, where Rodes placed him in line with the other brigades of the division. Pushing on after several hours toward Locust Grove, Rodes discovered that Union troops already held that ground and had opened fire on the division under Harry Hays which was advancing to Rodes's right on the Old Turnpike.[4] Rodes deployed his division, placing Ramseur on the right, and felt his way north until heavy skirmishing broke out along much of the line. Ramseur extended his right to link up with Hays's left and exchanged increasingly brisk fire with the enemy. Edward Johnson's division, the last to reach the field, occupied the Confederate left and in the hardest fighting of the day turned back a Federal effort to get in the Confederate rear. Shortly after sundown, Rodes shifted Ramseur from right to left to fill a gap between his and Johnson's divisions. About midnight, with Ramseur acting as rear guard, the Confederates fell back across Mine Run. There they entrenched in anticipation of a Union attack the next day.[5]

Driving rain chilled the Confederates on 28 November as they fortified on the west bank of Mine Run. When the rain stopped, the temperature dropped and doubled the soldiers' misery.[6] The Federals moved their entire force to the lines along Mine Run but made no attack. A Union cannonade the next morning promised action; however, once again Meade declined to force the issue. This timidity baffled the Confederates. Surely Meade had planned an offensive campaign when he crossed the Rapidan, yet now his troops were entrenching on the east side of Mine Run.

Throughout the last three days of November the southern generals and their men awaited the onslaught of the Army of the Potomac.[7] Constant expectation of a Federal assault racked nerves. One of Ramseur's men complained of having to "keep all our things on all the time and one-half of the men up all night, in case of an attack."[8] When Meade hesitated again on 1 December, Lee decided to take the initiative. That night he placed units in positions from which they could attack Meade's left the next morning. These preparations proved unnecessary. "With the rising sun we moved forward—the Yankee fires were burning—" Dodson wrote David Schenck,

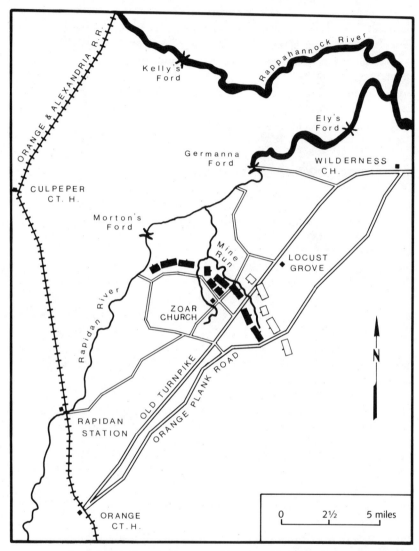

Area of Mine Run Campaign, 26 November to 2 December 1863

"but the rascals had cowardly sneaked off during the night." Though pursuit netted a few hundred prisoners, the Army of the Potomac made good its escape through the Wilderness to the fords over the Rapidan.[9]

A member of the Fourteenth North Carolina aptly characterized the Mine Run campaign as "one of hard marching day after day and preparations for battles that did not materialize." Another North Carolinian, in the Second, groused that the soldiers' "hard work and loss of sleep" had produced no favorable result.[10] Ramseur labeled it a short but severe campaign during which the Yankees "came over to whip us" then "ingloriously retreated without carrying out their purpose." Meade had wasted an opportunity to bring more than 60,000 men to bear upon 30,000 Confederates. Such conduct, thought Ramseur, would surely damage morale in the Army of the Potomac.[11] Southern soldiers pursuing the Federals found ransacked houses, smoldering ruins of outbuildings, remnants of crops put to the torch, dead stock, and stunned civilians all along the route. Such "wanton barbarity," Early reported, "could have been perpetrated only by a cowardly foe, stung with mortification at the ridiculous termination of so pretentious an expedition."[12]

Meade's cautious performance at Mine Run bolstered the spirits of Ramseur and others in the Army of Northern Virginia, but details of the Union victory at Chattanooga, which occurred the day before the Federals crossed the Rapidan, tempered enthusiasm. On 26 November unconfirmed reports indicated that Braxton Bragg's Army of Tennessee had been driven from the hills around Chattanooga; soon it became clear that the Confederates had offered little resistance. This upset Ramseur and strengthened his conviction that the Army of Tennessee was inferior to the Army of Northern Virginia and could not be trusted to carry its weight in the struggle for independence. "Bragg's army seems to have been disgracefully routed without anything approaching a stubborn fight," Dodson observed on 8 December. "I fear it will be hard to restore confidence to his shattered & demoralized masses." Ramseur believed P. G. T. Beauregard was the man to return the western army to fighting trim but doubted that he would be given a chance. "The [President] is still blindly holding on to Bragg," he complained, Davis's *"stubborness [sic] may yet prove our greatest disaster."*[13]

After Mine Run, the Army of Northern Virginia returned to its lines along the Rapidan to begin work on winter quarters. No sooner had Ramseur's brigade settled into the routine of shifting between picket and camp when it became clear that food was a serious problem. For the next four and a half months rations were so short and of such poor quality that officers and men alike suffered greatly. An inadequate transportation system, fraud on the part of carriers, and the reluctance of the Confederate government to seize the railroads were among the reasons for the extreme shortage.[14] In January Lee warned Secretary of War Seddon that without more food the army "cannot be kept effective." On 12 April 1864, with the winter behind them, the men still lacked food, and Lee bluntly told Jefferson Davis, "I cannot see how we can operate with our present supplies."[15] Ramseur's soldiers subsisted for part of December and most of January on a daily ration of ⅛–¼ pound of meat and 1⅛ pounds of flour. The amount of meat—salt pork or bacon, as beef was scarce—increased to ¼–½ pound a day late in January, which, together with a pint of cornmeal, kept men alive but left them vulnerable to scurvy and other diseases. Horses fared no better; in early January, Dodson sold one of his animals for want of forage.[16]

Ramseur saw to the feeding of his men as best he could. "Gen. Ramseur is very attentive to his men in that respect," Walter Lee of the Fourth North Carolina had written to his mother in the fall of 1863. He encouraged them to dig wild onions, recommended by the doctors to combat scurvy, and secured kettles in which each company could prepare them. It was beyond his power to increase rations, however, and the burden of supplementing the food issued to the soldiers fell on relatives in North Carolina. One private prefaced a plea for a box of food with the simple statement that the men "eat up everything they give us and feel hungry all the time." Another wrote matter-of-factly that the winter was "cold and our rations short, and our soup very thin."[17]

Though Ramseur received several shipments of food from Lincolnton, he constantly asked for vegetables, dried fruit, meat, chowchow, and liquor, the last of which he termed "almost indispensable to camp life." The shortage of food angered him because he considered it unnecessary. He insisted that the "army must be fed even if people at home must go without it." This sacrifice should extend to blacks as well as whites. Dodson instructed David Schenck to have his sister limit the Ramseur servants to ⅛–¼ pound of meat per day if they had sufficient vegetables to balance their diet: "Our whole people should do this & send the surplus to the army." Dodson's ration of "*fat* strong bacon & coarse corn meal" was leaving him weak. He assured David that he would give fifty dollars for one of "our old time dinners."[18]

As Lee's soldiers grimly fought off the hunger stalking their camps on the Rapidan, a new wave of desertions plagued the Army of Northern Virginia. At times a third of the army was absent without leave. As in the period following the retreat from Gettysburg, a significant number of the deserters was from North Carolina.[19] "I don't know why it is that so many is leaving," wrote one soldier in April 1864, "unless it is Short Rations." Indeed, North Carolinians in the army most often mentioned the shortage of food as a cause of desertion. But in North Carolina, whose western regions harbored so many deserters by 1864 that they moved about openly without fear, many citizens placed much of the blame on W. W. Holden, the editor-gadfly-politician who for months had been calling for a negotiated end to the war.[20] Ramseur had lashed out at Holden the previous summer and now did so again, calling him a traitor who tarnished the fame of North Carolina. When he learned that Holden would oppose Zebulon Vance in the 1864 North Carolina gubernatorial race, he was aghast. "Surely, Surely, North Carolina is not so *low*, so *disloyal*, as to bow to Holden as Gov—" he wrote, if so, "then Good bye to the Old State." A private from North Carolina was more direct: because Holden's newspapers led many to desert, "the N C Soldiers passing through Raleigh on Furlough ought to stop and hang the old son of a bitch."[21]

Ramseur's brigade was not immune to the contagion of desertion, but its losses were modest. Colonel Bennett of the Fourteenth remembered that his regiment escaped the problem to such a degree that it was ordered to the rear of the army to check defection from other units.[22] When a man did desert from one of his regiments, Ramseur meted out harsh punishment. Several poor wretches were shot. In February a member of the Fourth North Carolina cried out seconds before the firing squad cut him down that Holden's paper had brought him to this end. Ramseur took the view that many of the simple privates who left the army would not have done so without provocation from men such as Holden, but he refused to accept this as an excuse for their actions. The need for firm discipline caused him much anguish. "A most disagreeable duty awaits me," he wrote Nellie in late April 1864. "I have to march my Brigade out to witness the execution of three miserable deserters. Oh! Why will these poor miserable men commit this crime and folly."[23]

Ramseur and commanders of other North Carolina troops received unexpected help in their efforts to stem desertion from Governor Zebulon B. Vance. Hoping to "rekindle the fires of patriotism in the hearts of the North Carolina troops," and mindful no doubt of their votes, Vance arrived at Ramseur's camps on 26 March to begin a tour of the North Carolina regiments.[24] Assembled at Ramseur's headquarters to hear Vance were Lee, Jeb Stuart, Jubal Early, A. P. Hill, Richard Ewell, Robert Rodes, and others— "All the Generals of note in this army," wrote a much-impressed private in the Fourth North Carolina. Vance treated the generals and Ramseur's brigade to a rousing two-hour speech.[25] That evening the governor dined with the Fourteenth North Carolina, which had been his original regiment when he was with the army.[26]

Two days later, after reviewing all of the North Carolina regiments in the

Second Corps, Vance, a gifted stump speaker, took the stage for an address, had the men "in an uproar less than two minutes after he arose," and wound up four hours later "amidst deafening 'Rebel Yells.'" Stuart, Early, and Rodes spoke as well, making for a very long session.[27] During his ten days on the Rapidan the governor repeatedly emphasized that the people back home supported their soldiers and repudiated Holden and his peace party. Lee, as a gesture of thanks for Vance's remarkable service to morale, invited him to review the Army of Northern Virginia, an honor accorded no other civilian. Vance's address to the army following the review was a grand success.[28]

One reason Ramseur's men had not suffered a serious decline in morale during the winter months was that he left them little time to dwell on their problems. The idleness and filth that characterized the winter camps of too many regiments were unknown in Ramseur's brigade. Ramseur knew that if he were to bring a fit command to the battlefield he must be vigilant during slack times. He had been shocked in November to find that during his honeymoon discipline had fallen off markedly. Too loose a rein had caused, at least in part, the fiasco at Kelly's Ford. He could tolerate no sloth on the part of officer or enlisted man. Some had grown "careless & inattentive to the strict performance of duty," he observed. "I will have to proceed against some of my officers in the most rigorous manner unless they very speedily and decidedly mend their ways." He had no intention of losing the "high and enviable reputation my Brigade has so gloriously won."[29]

To this end, he insisted that the camps be kept clean and the men busy. He drilled the soldiers hard, often twice a day. Conscripts faced thrice-daily sessions. The Thirtieth, guilty of losing many prisoners at Kelly's Ford, received special attention, as on a late April day when it was drilled for two hours by Ramseur himself before an evening brigade drill that lasted two and one-half hours.[30] This drill, together with picket duty, corduroying roads, and other tasks, kept Ramseur's men occupied for the winter. Some were resentful, but the veterans knew that vigorous activity, including regular policing of camps, was preferable to an indolent existence that invited malingering and disease. As a member of the Fourteenth said, repairing a stretch of the Orange Plank Road was "hard labor but good for us," better than "stagnating in camp." One soldier who balked at this work was "bucked and gagged" and placed "in the snow some fifteen feet from the fire." After thirty minutes he gladly lent a hand.[31]

The result of this regimen was well-trained units with excellent morale. Evidence of the latter came on 27 January when, with rations at their leanest and the weather cold, Ramseur's brigade unanimously passed a resolution declaring they were "*in for the war without* condition." Rodes's other brigades did likewise, prompting Dodson to report to David Schenck that "our glorious Division . . . has shown to the world that we intend to *fight* the *thing out*—that we *won't be whipped* as long as anybody is left to fight."[32] In General Orders No. 14, 3 February 1864, General Lee announced these reenlistments to the army and called on other brigades to follow suit. Three days later the Confederate Congress approved a joint resolution thanking the "gallant brigade of North Carolina troops commanded by Brig. Gen. S. D. Ramseur" for offering their valuable services to the Confederacy after already displaying their valor and patriotic zeal on many battlefields.[33] Such recognition was flattering, but more important to Dodson was a certainty that his regiments were prepared for the next campaign. "My Brigade will be in fine condition next Spring," he promised in February, "*Small* 'tis sadly true, but true as steel—with an esprit de corps of which I am truly proud as I am to a certain degree the framer of it."[34]

The thinned ranks of his command worried Dodson throughout the winter. In late January he could muster just over 1,000 men, 40 percent fewer than a year before. He still grieved for those lost at Chancellorsville. They had been among his bravest soldiers, volunteers who were irreplaceable. By mid-February the brigade was up to 1,200, but most of the replacements were conscripts of questionable caliber.[35] Still, with proper training even conscripts could be made into soldiers. Ramseur thought that Congress should (as it was about to do) end substitution and force into service every man who had employed a substitute.[36] The "weak kneed gentry" who avoided duty through exemption he viewed contemptuously as shirkers of the worst sort. But he suffered no illusions about the likelihood of their being pressed into service any time soon. The one source of manpower that remained a realistic possibility was exchange of prisoners. Should the Federals agree to send back captured Confederates, most of Ramseur's losses at Kelly's Ford would be compensated and his brigade restored to its pre-Gettysburg strength.[37]

Ramseur's eagerness to press exempted men into service did not extend to David Schenck, exempt as a receiver for the Confederate government. David thought it his duty to enlist, but Dodson argued that he was too frail for active campaigning. If David insisted, Dodson would find a place for him on his staff, "but what's the use of [your] exposing [your] life, when it is not absolutely necessary!" Ramseur did fret over David's health, but his repeated warnings about the strains associated with life in the military were tinged with condescension. He would risk all for the cause; David need not make such a commitment.[38]

The absence of Stonewall Jackson, as much as that of his own dead soldiers, still saddened Ramseur. Though he trusted Lee blindly, he thought

Jackson's death had deprived the army of a spark it would never rekindle. When Union troops crossed the Rapidan at Morton's Ford on 6 February, the Confederates pinned them down but allowed them to escape safely across the river that night. "Oh! for the spirit of Jackson," Ramseur moaned, the southerners "ought to have captured & killed the entire batch. I would have done so—had my plan been adopted by Lt. Genl. Ewell." What that plan was, Ramseur did not detail. Perhaps he was overreacting to a perceived slight. Whatever the reason for his criticism of Ewell, he manifestly lacked confidence in his corps chief. Such an outburst directed against Stonewall would have been unthinkable. What the army needed, Ramseur thought, was Jackson and 30,000 men. Without them, each soldier would have to do more than before and trust in God to bring success when the next enemy offensive came.[39]

For Dodson and his brigade, the winter of 1863–64 had not been entirely without reliefs from hunger, work, and worry. Soldiers not on duty might fish, hunt the little game remaining in the valley of the Rapidan, or play cards. At night they listened as bands on both sides of the river played "The Girl I Left Behind Me," "When This Cruel War Is Over," and other sentimental songs so popular in the rival camps.[40] Predictably—and Ramseur no doubt thought fittingly—many turned to God in the midst of hardship. Men from the Fourteenth erected a chapel in which their chaplain presided over a nightly prayer meeting. Members of several regiments gathered there, and soon a "strong sentiment of religious fervor . . . swept over the camp and prevailed among the officers and the rank and file." Ramseur often attended the sermons, which he considered useful in maintaining morale.[41]

Heavy snowfall permitted snowball fights, the grandest of which took place on 23 March 1864, between Ramseur's and Doles's brigades of Rodes's division and the Stonewall and Louisiana brigades of Edward "Allegheny" Johnson's division. For the better part of a day the mock battle raged. Attack and counterattack rolled across open fields; prisoners and colors were captured; rebel yell answered rebel yell, until finally, with both sides exhausted, a flag of truce and exchange of prisoners ended a contest "marked by so much that was thrilling and followed by so little that was hurtful." Richmond newspapers devoted columns to it.[42]

An extended visit from Nellie, arranged in the face of numerous obstacles, was the high point of the winter for Dodson. He had wanted to bring her to the army almost as soon as he returned from their honeymoon, but Mine Run, active picket duty, scarcity of lodgings, and possible Federal movement frustrated his efforts. Images of his moments with Nellie crowded in upon him—his recuperation at Woodside after Malvern Hill and Chancellorsville, the trip to western North Carolina after their marriage—as

Snowball fight in a Confederate camp. (Battles and Leaders of the Civil War.)

he recalled "every scene & incident." A plan to share a house with Robert Rodes and his wife came to nothing.[43] On 12 December, as a steady rain fell outside his tent, Dodson brooded over the fact that Colonel Bryan Grimes of the Fourth North Carolina had located quarters for his wife while he had found none for Nellie. He missed her "all through the weary days & the long dreary nights" and admitted a fear that he would be killed before they could again be together. Christmas passed with Nellie in Milton and Dodson on the Rapidan still dependent upon the "horrid, tantalizing mails" for word from her. He felt "*a little blue*." A cold, wet spell in late December finally ended speculation about any immediate Federal activity and enabled Nellie to join him on 30 December. Three days later Ramseur received orders to return to picket on the Rapidan. Freed from that duty after a week, he arranged for lodging two miles from his camps, and the Ramseurs at last set up housekeeping.[44]

Nellie remained with her husband for three months, a period of great happiness for Dodson. "Can you imagine *how* much I enjoy her society?" Dodson asked David Schenck. How good it was to have "such a Wife!!!" They read together, rode horses along the Rapidan, and on some days Nellie accompanied him to the brigade camps. On a typical day he left the boarding house at nine o'clock in the morning, worked at his duties until four o'clock, then returned to dine. "Nellie and I have all the evening to ourselves," Dodson wrote David. "You *know* we have a cozy, comfortable, *spooney* time."

He said his happiest moments were when he left camp each evening to return to Nellie. Their weeks together were an idyllic respite from the hardships of active service, a time to delight in each other's company and plan for the future. Peace and a plantation, a happy home and a quiet, useful life—these were the goals toward which Dodson looked. Fervently he wished for a decisive campaign in the coming spring and summer.[45] He often detailed to David Schenck the joys of life with Nellie and reiterated his hope that the war would end quickly. David must not infer, however, that he was "growing careless or indifferent in the performance of my duty." "Far from it," he assured his friend, "I am still active and energetic."[46]

Nellie departed in the first week of April. Spring was parading its glories along the Rapidan, and good weather meant that the armies would soon resume their deadly relationship. Nellie would go first to Milton for a stay with her family, then travel to Lincolnton, with its more salubrious climate, for the summer. Would David look after her while she was in Lincolnton? Much as Dodson would like to visit them occasionally during the summer, "that can only be by being wounded—which I won't be anxious for."

A week after Nellie left, her brother Caleb brought Dodson a letter from her. The months of loneliness stretched far ahead and left him blue. He longed to "press my Darling to my heart." Picketing had helped keep his mind off Nellie. More rigorous drilling also filled part of the void, and Dodson expected that "some of the lazy fellows will be sorry you left me so soon." On the morning he answered her letter, the sun cast a warm glow over a landscape alive with the singing of birds and the color of blossoming trees. He drifted into a reverie about their life ahead, living on a beautiful mountain after peace had come. The tranquillity of his surroundings and thoughts of his wife evoked new optimism: "I feel so hopeful about the coming campaign. I have never felt so encouraged before. Surely Our Father will bless His faithful people."[47]

Indeed, the hardships of winter had not made Ramseur despair over prospects for Confederate victory. He predicted that when James Longstreet returned from Tennessee with his First Corps, Lee would crush Meade and cross the Potomac to collect supplies and cattle in Pennsylvania. Once these were brought back to Virginia, the army would await the onset of a new Yankee army composed of the remnant of the Army of the Potomac and reinforcements from the West. Joseph Johnston and the Army of Tennessee would have to mount a diversionary offensive into Kentucky. Meanwhile, the northern debt would pile up, gold would become scarce, and "Yanks will consider 'the job' bigger than they expected in which all concerned are apt to be hurt—Old Abe will be defeated . . . [and] the people will be ready & anxious to sustain the peace policy of the new [President]." Left out of this equation was potential French recognition. Louis Napoleon might intercede, but Ramseur distrusted all selfish European powers. Even without French help, he said, "I confidently expect that we will be enabled to whip the Yanks out single handed, by the assistance of the Lord of Hosts!"[48]

Several factors fired Ramseur's optimism. His own brigade was in excellent condition, finely tuned, and eager to begin the spring campaign. "I wish you could witness my Brigade drills," he wrote Nellie, "I know you would be edified." Visits to other units left him certain that morale throughout the army was high. The liberation of Plymouth, North Carolina, on 20 April, by Dodson's close friend Robert Hoke of Lincolnton gave promise of more good news from the Atlantic coast. Ramseur believed New Bern could be retaken, freeing another of Carolina's ports. Moreover, rumors placed the strength of the Army of the Potomac only slightly higher than that of the Confederate army. For once, the two might battle on even terms. Officers and enlisted men seemed to think the next campaign would be the last. One more victory might convince the Federals to allow the South to depart in peace: "I do pray that we may be established as an independent people, a people known and recognized as God's Peculiar People!"[49] If the South were to lose, did that make the North the chosen people? On this he did not speculate.

CHAPTER 6

THERE IS A RUMOR THAT I HAVE

BEEN MADE MAJOR GENERAL

Ramseur's brigade left its camps near Orange Court House on 2 May 1864 to resume picket duty on the Rapidan. A last look at the room he and Nellie had shared at the boarding house, and then Dodson was off to the outpost. There were reports of a Federal advance. Though Meade still commanded the Army of the Potomac, Ulysses S. Grant, new general in chief of the Union armies, would accompany it. Ramseur had guessed as early as 12 December that Grant would come east, just as John Pope had in the summer of 1862. If he thought Grant's presence significant, he did not say so in a letter home. He did note that the countryside along the Rapidan was beautiful, dotted with fields of wild violets. Nellie would like that.[1]

"Today I have carefully examined our front," he wrote on 3 May, "watched the Yankees dashing about on the other side to discover if possible their future movements." The next day dust floated over the trees on the Federal side of the Rapidan, and white wagon tops and burnished musket barrels were visible moving downstream toward Ely's and Germanna fords. Union deserters confirmed what the Confederates already suspected: Grant was attempting to turn Lee's right. He would cross the Rapidan and try to place himself between Lee and Richmond.[2] Once again the two armies would grapple in the Wilderness. The odds were not as favorable as Ramseur believed. The effective strength of the Army of the Potomac approached 120,000; Lee's army, counting Longstreet's corps ten miles southwest of Orange Court House near Gordonsville, mustered 65,000 men of all arms.[3]

While Grant moved his army across the Rapidan on 4 May, Lee put his three corps in motion eastward to intercept him. Ewell's Second Corps, encamped northeast of Orange Court House, marched about noon toward Locust Grove via the Old Turnpike; A. P. Hill's Third Corps, located closer to Orange Court House, took the Orange Plank Road; Longstreet left Gordons- ville about four o'clock for Brock's Bridge, whence he would fall in behind

Hill on the Plank Road. Ewell left Ramseur on the river with his brigade and regiments from Johnson's and Early's divisions under orders to remain until he was satisfied that there was no enemy at Culpeper or until instructed to rejoin the corps. Ramseur spent the night of 4 May on the Rapidan. Ewell and Hill bivouacked that night west of the Wilderness on the turnpike and Plank Road.[4] The bulk of Grant's army had already crossed the Rapidan—though its vast trains would take another thirty hours—and lay in the dense forest surrounding the Chancellorsville battlefield. At this point, as Jubal Early later observed, Grant was closer to Richmond than was his opponent.[5]

Ramseur crossed the Rapidan at Raccoon Ford early the next morning, moving north through a dense fog toward Culpeper Court House. All was quiet between the river and the town, and he reported that the Federal army had disappeared from that side of the river. His mission completed, Ramseur spent the rest of the day in a difficult march to overtake the Second Corps.[6] That morning Ewell had reached the edge of the Wilderness. Ahead, to the east, the Federals were moving through the forest. Proceeding southward on the Brock and Germanna Ford roads, they made contact first with Ewell and then with Hill. Grant immediately halted and struck Ewell on the turnpike and Hill on the Plank Road. Porter Alexander, Longstreet's chief of artillery and veteran of most of the big battles in the east, termed the day's fighting as desperate as any he had seen. The armies fought blindly in the woods until eight o'clock at night. The First Corps had not yet come up, and Lee threw every unit at hand into the fray. He planned to renew the struggle the next day, when Longstreet would be present.[7]

At six o'clock in the evening of 5 May, the commanding general ordered Ewell to have Ramseur's brigade in position early the next morning. Arriving that night, Ramseur rested his troops and then moved to a position in rear of Ewell's right. He would be the Second Corps reserve, available to support either "Allegheny" Johnson, in Ewell's center, or Robert Rodes, who anchored the right of the corps.[8] A gap of more than a mile yawned between Rodes and the left of Hill's corps, to the south on the Plank Road. Three clearings broke the forest in this gap: nearest Rodes was the Higgerson farm; next came the cropland of the Jones farm; finally, atop a plateau several hundred yards north of the Plank Road, lay the Chewning farm. The last of these clearings offered high ground from which the enemy might play havoc with Confederates to the north or south.[9]

A red eastern sky signaled the dawn of what would become an intensely hot sixth of May.[10] At five o'clock, after repulsing a brief Confederate demonstration by Early's division on Ewell's left, the Federals advanced along the length of the line. Two Union corps, John Sedgwick's VI and G. K.

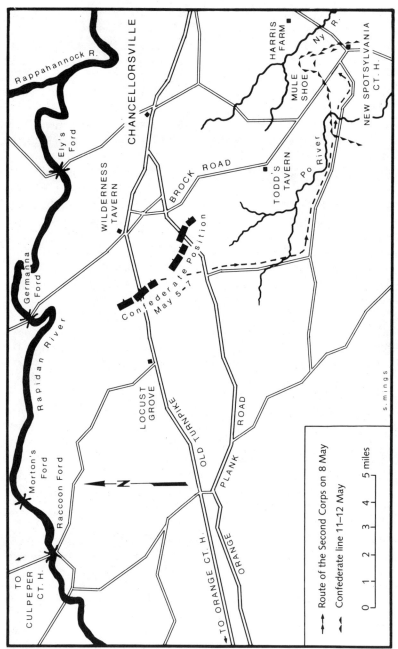

Area of Operations of the Army of Northern Virginia, 3–21 May 1864

The battle of the Wilderness—Confederate line awaiting orders.
*(*Battles and Leaders of the Civil War.*)*

Warren's V, hit Ewell; Winfield Scott Hancock's II Corps drove west on the Plank Road toward A. P. Hill. Ambrose E. Burnside's IX Corps was to have added its weight to the attack, crossing the gap in the southern line and coming in on Hill's left flank, but Burnside was not in position at the appointed time. Hancock achieved an early breakthrough, routing two of Hill's divisions. Only the timely arrival of Longstreet's First Corps prevented a collapse of Lee's right. Swift disposition and hard fighting enabled Longstreet to stem the Federal advance and launch a counterattack that by six-thirty was forcing Hancock to retreat east along the Plank Road.[11]

About the time Longstreet collided with Hancock, a serious threat materialized on Rodes's right. Ewell's corps had beaten back the attacks of Sedgwick and Warren,[12] but Burnside had finally found his way to the battlefield and was emerging from the woods at the northeast corner of the Jones farm, heading for the Chewning plateau,[13] and threatening to cut off the Second Corps from the rest of the army. Once abreast of the Confederate line, Burnside's column might envelop Rodes's right or Hill's left. Robert Rodes perceived this immediately and called on Ramseur to move into the gap to stop Burnside.

Moving at double-quick across Jones's field, Ramseur crashed into the leading elements of the IX Corps. He extended his skirmishers in force a

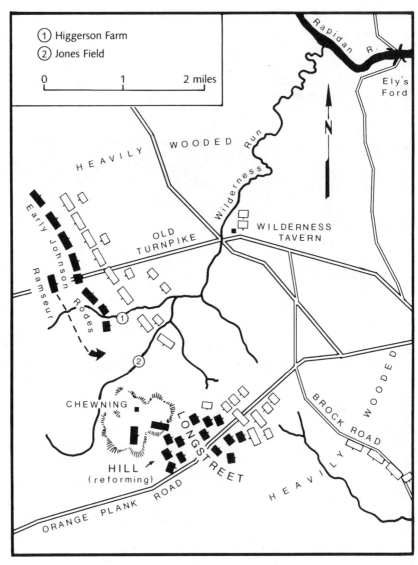

Battle of the Wilderness, Morning, 6 May 1864

half-mile to the south, "turned the enemy's line, and by a dashing charge with my skirmishers . . . drove not only the enemy's skirmishers, but [also] his line of battle, back fully half a mile." Prisoners and the equipage of an entire regiment fell into Confederate hands.[14] Among the trophies were copies of the Bible in the Ojibwa language dropped by members of a unit of Indian sharpshooters. Rarely had the North Carolinians met so exotic a foe. Whether from preconception or observation, one of the Confederates noted that the Indians fought "bravely in the wood" but when "driven into the open they did not again fire on us, but ran like deer."[15] Ramseur had accomplished much at little cost. His action had permitted Ewell's right "to connect with Lieutenant-General Hill's left" and thereby denied Burnside an opportunity to deliver a decisive blow. In the words of a careful student of the battle of the Wilderness, "Ramseur appeared at the vital point in the very nick of time."[16]

Ramseur's brigade remained in place the rest of the day, unmolested, while Lee sought to turn Grant's left and then, near sundown, his right.[17] Both efforts met with some success, but the Federals ultimately held their ground. With nightfall, an unnatural quiet settled over the field. Though the armies lay within a few dozen yards of each other, the only sounds in the dense woods were the muffled cries of the wounded. To Ramseur's right, where Hill and Longstreet had borne the brunt of the fight on 6 May, the sky was aglow with light from burning woods. Fire spread rapidly before a brisk wind, "terrifying the disabled wounded and scorching the bodies of the slain."[18]

In two days Lee had lost upwards of 8,000 men and inflicted nearly 18,000 casualties on the enemy. Six southern generals lay dead or severely wounded, including James Longstreet, shot down by his own men under circumstances eerily reminiscent of those that claimed the life of Stonewall Jackson a year earlier in the same deadly Wilderness.[19] The Federals had shown an uncharacteristic aggressiveness. They had attacked on the fifth and again on the sixth. Would Grant continue this pattern on the seventh, or would he emulate Hooker and withdraw across the Rappahannock to regroup? This question occupied the minds of officers and soldiers of both armies.

Before much of a dusty, warm Saturday, the seventh of May, had passed, it became clear to Robert E. Lee that Grant would not renew the contest on the same ground.[20] Jubal Early advanced at first light and discovered the Union position opposite his line empty. The Federals had abandoned their dead and large quantities of materiel.[21] Ewell so informed Lee, who thought Grant might move east toward Fredericksburg or south to Spotsylvania Court House, the latter on a direct line to Richmond. Cavalry reports from the area of Todd's Tavern, five miles northwest of Spotsylvania,[22] and a sighting of Union guns moving toward Spotsylvania[23] convinced Lee that Grant intended to march by his left toward Richmond. Accordingly, he ordered Longstreet's successor, Richard H. Anderson, to have the First Corps on the way to Spotsylvania Court House by three o'clock the next morning. The rest of the army would follow.[24]

The race to Spotsylvania would be difficult for the Confederates to win. Grant controlled the Brock Road, the most direct route. Anderson would have to march along a military road cut just that day by engineers, a rough path cluttered with stumps and felled trees. Because of the narrowness of this road, and because fires in the woods denied him a good place to rest his troops before beginning his march, Anderson decided to depart on the night of 8 May. He had his men in motion by eleven o'clock.[25] It was "cloudy, and exceeding dark" as they shuffled onto the road.[26] Someone raised the rebel yell. From unit to unit it spread to the left, through Ramseur's brigade, until it reached the last Confederates to the North. Two more times this process repeated itself. "The effect was beyond expression" for one southern soldier, whose comrades "seemed fairly convulsed with the fierce enthusiasm."[27]

While Anderson prepared his divisions for their march, Ramseur slipped to the right with his regiments and early on Sunday, 8 May, put them in motion with the rest of the Second Corps toward Spotsylvania. Rodes's division led the way, past carnage wrought by fighting on 5 and 6 May. The day was terribly hot and dusty. Partially buried corpses and dead horses littered the woods. Smoke from burning trees and undergrowth mingled with "the gases steaming up through the thin covering of the graves" to create a suffocating stench in the "hot, close air of the forest."[28] Ramseur's soldiers had better than fifteen miles to cover, and the heat took a high toll. Dozens of men fainted. Heatstroke claimed its victims. With a third of the distance still ahead, Ramseur received a message from Richard Anderson asking for help. Anderson and Jeb Stuart's cavalry had beaten Grant to Spotsylvania by the narrowest of margins and were doggedly holding their own in the face of a greatly superior force. Ramseur galloped down his line of march, dispatch in hand, and asked if the men would redouble their efforts. A hoarse shout answered in the affirmative, though some of the men "were so tired and worn out they could hardly halloo." Hurrying on, the leading regiments reached Spotsylvania Court House about five o'clock. The sounds of battle had been audible for some time.[29]

Their "distressing march" behind them, Rodes's brigades deployed and moved forward. They exchanged fire with Federals for twenty minutes, then launched a vigorous charge that erased the threat to Anderson's flank.[30] "We drove the enemy back half a mile to his entrenchments," Ramseur reported; he hoped to do more. Cullen Battle, another of Rodes's brigadiers, had led his Alabamians to the Union works, briefly taken a portion of them, and fallen back a short distance. Believing the Federals to be demoralized, Battle sought to prevail upon his men and those of two other brigades to carry the entrenchments. He seized a standard and called for an attack, but the men were too exhausted. When Ramseur joined Battle and exhorted the troops to make a final try, the results were scarcely better than before. Convinced that flesh had reached its limit that day, Ramseur and Battle abandoned their project. Rodes's division as a whole entrenched opposite the Federal lines. Edward Johnson's division formed on Rodes's right, while John Gordon, temporarily in command of Early's division, stood in reserve.[31]

As the unrelenting heat returned on 9 May, skirmishing erupted in several places along the line.[32] Troops labored all day improving their trenches, which soon would be the most formidable thus far constructed by Lee's army. The Third Corps, under Early, arrived and went into line on Ewell's right, near Spotsylvania Court House, covering the road to Fredericksburg. Though their works were strong, the Confederates' line had a serious weakness. Anderson's First Corps—Charles Field's division on the left, Joseph B. Kershaw's the right—stretched from a point close to the Po River about two miles northwest of the village, eastward across the Brock Road. Ewell's Second Corps—Rodes on the left, Johnson on the right—joined Anderson just east of the Brock Road. Near the road the line veered sharply to the north, so that Rodes and Johnson formed a salient jutting northward almost a mile. Johnson's right curved southeast to meet the left of Cadmus Wilcox, who commanded one of Early's divisions. Harry Heth's division extended Early's front southward to Spotsylvania Court House.[33] The salient, dubbed the "Mule Shoe" or "Horse Shoe" by the soldiers, troubled Lee. A thick growth of woods crowded close to it, especially on the west, which could afford cover for Federals preparing an attack. Lee's engineers decided, however, that with proper placement of artillery the salient could be defended. As a precaution a secondary line was begun within the northwest portion of the salient. Gordon's division held this line.[34]

Ramseur's brigade occupied the lower part of the western face of the salient. To his right were Rodes's brigades under Junius Daniel and George Doles holding the middle and upper parts of the western face. Entrenchment continued on 10 May. Musketry crackled here and there as Grant probed the Confederate defenses. Then, as the sun dipped low on yet another unseasonably warm day, twelve carefully selected northern regiments raised a cheer and exploded out of the woods, piercing the northwest corner of the salient, and capturing some 300 prisoners. Swiftly the Confederates counterattacked, Ramseur's brigade among them, and drove the Federals

The battle of Spotsylvania—views of Confederate entrenchments.
(Battles and Leaders of the Civil War.)

from their foothold in the Mule Shoe. Union supporting troops had failed to advance, or the damage might have been more serious.[35] Still, the temporary Federal success underscored the vulnerability of the salient.

On the next day, while hard rain prevented fighting, scouts reported the enemy moving toward Fredericksburg, and Lee gave attention to the pursuit of Grant. He instructed Ewell to remove twenty two guns posted in the salient to a place from which they could be quickly sent away.[36] That night noises from the Federal lines suggested that Grant was massing troops for an attack, and George H. Steuart, one of Johnson's brigadiers, asked that the guns be recalled. Ewell subsequently ordered their return. By four o'clock in the morning, the guns were on the way back.[37]

Ramseur was awake before dawn on 12 May.[38] Thunderstorms had drenched the field during the night, chilling the soldiers and hindering sleep. By four-thirty in the morning, rain had given way to a fine mist. Thick fog limited visibility to a few rods.[39] Ramseur had his men under arms as the first hint of light penetrated the clouds and forest. About five o'clock, cheering and gunfire echoed from the right. In minutes the sound swelled and warned of a "terrible assault" coming from the northern end of the salient. Ramseur's ears told him that the enemy was gaining ground. He placed the Second North Carolina, his brigade reserve, in line facing north, perpendicular to his other regiments. With his flank thus protected, he awaited orders to join the fight.[40]

The clamor heard by Ramseur and his men came from the tip of the salient, where a massive Union assault had overrun the southern works and threatened to divide Lee's army. The Federals, striking just as the twenty-two absent cannon arrived back at their previous position, captured them at one stroke. With little artillery support, and bedeviled by damp gunpowder, Edward Johnson's division had managed only token resistance. Thousands of Confederates surrendered, among them Johnson, George Steuart, and most of the Stonewall Brigade.[41]

The victorious Federals had fought their way down the salient to the clearing around the McCoull house, where John B. Gordon's division had stopped them. Lee himself had ridden to the front, been restrained by Gordon, and watched as that officer directed a brilliant counterstroke that slowly turned the tide. With help from James Lane's brigade of Wilcox's division, which advanced along the eastern side of the salient, Gordon pressed forward toward the original line. But Gordon's division was too small to cover the entire width of the salient.[42] On his left, where the Federal attack was heaviest, the Confederates were still in danger. Robert Rodes, whose division held the lower left side of the Mule Shoe, grasped the nature of the crisis and reacted at once. He had Junius Daniel change his brigade front from west to north and ordered Ramseur to align on Daniel's right. When Ramseur pulled his men out of the trenches, Kershaw extended his right northward to fill the gap.[43]

Rodes's orders were specific: Ramseur was to "check the enemy's advance and . . . drive him back." Ramseur shifted his regiments into a single line. From right to left were Parker's Thirtieth North Carolina, Cox's Second, Grimes's Fourth, and Bennett's Fourteenth. Exposed to enemy fire while forming, many of Ramseur's men fell. Ramseur rode up to Colonel Parker, and, over the din of fighting to the north and east, told the colonel that they must take back the works now held by the enemy. In a voice loud enough for many of the regiment to hear, Parker proudly answered that his troops could do it. "This was a serious time with us," recalled one of Parker's soldiers, "and would have been more so, if we could really realize our position." From their new formation, Ramseur's men, who had had neither breakfast nor an opportunity to fill their canteens, could see Union flags fluttering above the captured works.[44] Moving down his line, Ramseur cautioned them to keep their alignment, not to fire, and to advance slowly until they heard the command "Charge!" Then they should move forward at a run and stop only when the Federals had been driven beyond the entrenchments relinquished by Johnson's division. As he prepared, mounted and confident, to lead his brigade against the enemy, Ramseur reminded an officer of the Fourth of "an angel of war."[45]

Tense minutes passed before the shouted order to charge rang out. The brigade rushed at double-quick toward Federals behind the reverse side of the secondary works halfway up the salient. A sergeant in Junius Daniel's brigade watched "the peerless Ramseur" and his regiments, who "always seemed to be in the right place at the right time," dash ahead. "For a moment it seemed . . . our brigade . . . held its breath," wrote this soldier, "as these men went forward, apparently into the very jaws of death."[46] Ramseur's horse went down almost immediately—the first of three he would lose this day. A ball ripped through his right arm below the elbow.[47] Struggling to keep up, he saw the Federals flee the first line of trenches. The Confederates paused to realign. The Fourth and the Fourteenth were jumbled together, their flags not five paces apart. Above the din of battle a soldier began to sing "The Bonnie Blue Flag," others following his lead until he fell dead, accidentally shot from behind by a fellow North Carolinian. The brigade stayed at these works but a few minutes. They fired a volley or two, and then, responding to an order from Bryan Grimes, who had seen Ramseur fall and taken it upon himself to get the men moving again, set out for the northern part of the salient.[48]

Ramseur, right arm hanging useless at his side, soon started after his

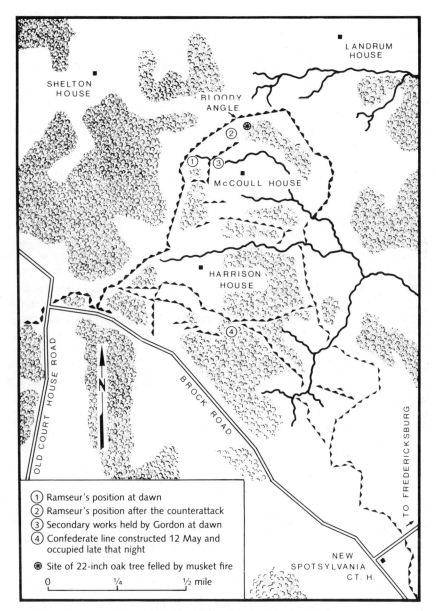

Legend:

1. Ramseur's position at dawn
2. Ramseur's position after the counterattack
3. Secondary works held by Gordon at dawn
4. Confederate line constructed 12 May and occupied late that night
⊛ Site of 22-inch oak tree felled by musket fire

0 ¼ ½ mile

The Mule Shoe at Spotsylvania, 12 May 1864

soldiers, by now in process of clawing their way up the western face of the salient.[49] From traverse to traverse they grimly moved on, clearing Federals from the woods east of the works. Closing in their rapidly thinning line, the men poured a "continuous storm of leaden hail into the enemy's ranks, as he slowly, but stubbornly retired, until he reached the line of works . . . from which he was driven almost at the very point of the bayonet." It was the only instance during the entire war in which any number of Ramseur's men used their bayonets. Arriving at a position in the northwest corner of the salient, and unable to go farther, the regiments pivoted to their left and reclaimed a segment of the original Confederate line. The soldiers pulled bodies out of the pits at the breastworks, waded into rain water "red with human gore," and prepared to hold on. This counterattack had been, stated Richard Ewell admiringly, "a charge of unsurpassed gallantry."[50]

Digging in behind the works, Ramseur's men delivered a telling fire into the enemy in their front. But Federals retained a portion of the Confederate line to the right, and were, as Ramseur reported, "enfilading my line with a destructive fire, at the same time heavily assaulting my right front." He advised Rodes that he could not hold without help. At about nine o'clock one of Rodes's staff officers guided Nat Harris's Mississippi brigade of William Mahone's division into position on Ramseur's flank. An hour later, Samuel McGowan's South Carolinians came up.[51] Federals continued to occupy a stretch of works in front of Harris, however, and to deliver a persistent enfilading fire that accounted, according to one of Ramseur's men, for two-thirds of the North Carolinians' casualties. "In this extremity," Ramseur later reported, "Colonel Bennett, Fourteenth North Carolina, offered to take his regiment from left to right under a severe fire, and drive back the growing masses of the enemy on my right." Midday approached as Ramseur accepted Bennett's "bold and hazardous offer . . . as a forlorn hope." In a very difficult maneuver, Bennett extricated his regiment from the line, moved across the rear of the rest of the brigade, and secured the right flank by giving the Federals "cold steel and other reforms."[52]

The battle had raged for seven hours. By any standard, the units in the salient had already put in a long day. Rain continued to pelt them. They had not eaten for almost twenty-four hours. The enemy did not let up, however, as Grant piled in more troops. If he could expand his toehold, he might yet break Lee's army. The Confederates were hard at work on a new line across the base of the salient. They must have time to make it strong before Ramseur and others could withdraw. But the Union troops evicted from the northern arc of the Mule Shoe had retreated no farther than the opposite side of the entrenchments. In some places they jammed into traverses and fired down the ranks of southern soldiers to both right and left.[53]

Hour after hour the fighting continued with incredible savagery.[54] Men stabbed each other through traverses, clubbed one another with their muskets. A torrent of bullets and shells flew all around, the "air away up hundreds of feet was groaning with all the hideous deviltry of war." The volume of musketry was such that it felled a 22-inch oak tree.[55] One of Ramseur's men discovered afterward, to his amazement, that he had fired 120 rounds in the course of the day. Colonel Bennett of the Fourteenth took a wound in the face. The adjutant of the Thirtieth was pulled by his hair over the works and made a prisoner. Four bullets passed through Ramseur's overcoat.[56] "A perfect rampart of dead" lay in the blood-stained water on either side of the breastworks. The wounded "bled and groaned, stretched or huddled in every attitude of pain." Exhausted beyond caring, men sat on the bodies of their slain comrades for rest.[57]

Nightfall brought no slackening of the slaughter, it only served to increase "the awful terror of the scene." Of all battles during the war Spotsylvania offered "unexampled muzzle-to-muzzle fire; the longest roll of incessant, unbroken musketry," thought John Gordon, "the most splendid exhibition of individual heroism and personal daring by large numbers, who, standing in the freshly spilt blood of their fellows, faced for so long a period and at so short a range the flaming rifles as they heralded the decrees of death."[58]

It was past midnight when the engineers completed a new line across the bottom of the Mule Shoe. For the Confederates at the top of the salient, it had been, as one South Carolinian put it, "a question of bravery and endurance." Ramseur's brigade, "black and muddy as hogs" and hollow-eyed as though recovering from a serious illness, reached the new line sometime after three o'clock the morning of 13 May.[59] Their nightmare had lasted more than twenty hours. Even the maelstrom at Chancellorsville paled in comparison. A captain in the Second North Carolina called the twelfth of May the "crowning glory of the career of Ramseur's Brigade." For Colonel Bennett, it was quite simply the most memorable day of the war. A private in the Fourth North Carolina found it hard "to realize what our brigade did actually accomplish that day." No survivor would forget the "hottest and hardest fought battle that has ever been on this continent."[60] This reaction was typical. Henceforth soldiers in Lee's army would call that awful salient not the Mule Shoe or the Horse Shoe but the "Bloody Angle."

Once again Ramseur and his brigade had met a crucial challenge in magnificent fashion. "To Colonels Parker, Grimes, Bennett, and Cox, to the gallant officers and patriotic men of my little brigade," as he said in his official report, "the country owes much for the successful charge, which I verily believe turned the fortune of the day at that point in our favor."

The battle of Spotsylvania—struggling for the works at the "Bloody Angle."
(Battles and Leaders of the Civil War.)

Richard Ewell and Robert Rodes thanked Ramseur on the field. Ewell told him he was the hero of the day. General Lee sent for Ramseur to thank him and his men for their service and conduct.[61] Rodes and Early spoke to the brigade, stating that it had saved Ewell's corps and deserved the gratitude of the nation. After the war Colonel Charles S. Venable of Lee's staff described the restoration of the Confederate line along the northern end of the salient as a "wonderful feat of arms, in which all the troops engaged deserve the greatest credit for endurance, constancy, and unflinching courage; but without unjust discrimination, we may say that Gordon, Rodes and Ramseur were the heroes of this bloody day." Venable's judgment was that of the army. Ramseur did not exaggerate when he wrote Nellie that the charge made by his men was "universally spoken of in the highest terms by off[icer]s of distinction." Eighty years after the battle Douglas Southall Freeman observed that seldom in the war "had one brigade accomplished so much in fast, close fighting." It was another display of Ramseur's "remarkable leadership in offensive combat."[62]

In a left-handed scrawl Dodson informed Nellie that his life had been mercifully preserved, though his brigade had lost heavily. He labeled the conduct of the troops that were overrun early on 12 May shameful; "matters looked scarey [*sic*] for awhile," but his men's splendid behavior had staved off defeat.[63] Neither his report nor his letters mentioned John Gordon's brigades or the other units that helped to roll back the Federals in the salient.

As after Chancellorsville, Ramseur professed, not very convincingly, an indifference to newspaper reports or the lack of them. When David Schenck expressed astonishment at the skimpy mention of Ramseur in the North Carolina press, Dodson answered that it came as no surprise: "I don't keep a newspaper correspondent with me, nor do I seek out the Special Correspondent of any of our city papers." He insisted to Nellie that praise from Ewell, Rodes, and Lee counted far more than "partial, prejudiced (and often incorrect) newspaper accounts." But he did send her a newspaper piece by a correspondent for the London *Herald* that credited his brigade with restoring the line on 12 May and ended with a gratuitous slap at the Stonewall Brigade: "Those brave North Carolinians had thus, in one of the hottest conflicts of the day, succeeded in driving the enemy from the works that had been occupied during the previous night by a brigade which, until the 12th of May, had never yielded to a foe—the Stonewall."[64]

The rains that soaked combatants in the Bloody Angle on 12 May continued for three more days. Thus did nature veto any plans for a large-scale resumption of fighting. Only light skirmishing and trudging soldiers violated the quiet of Spotsylvania's soggy forests. Grant transferred troops from his right to his left. Lee responded by moving Anderson's divisions to Early's right, leaving Ewell's corps on the left flank. On 17 May sunshine and a brisk wind dried clothing and brightened spirits.[65]

Grant took advantage of the improved weather next day to launch a major assault against Ewell at the base of the old salient. Poised behind formidable works, and supported by ample artillery, the Confederates "could not believe a serious attempt would be made to assail such a line." When the Federals advanced several brigades deep along Ewell's entire front, southerners welcomed the opportunity to "pay off old scores" by directing a fire against the attackers that quickly drove them back in confusion. Several times the blue infantry regrouped and came on, only to be rebuffed. Though large numbers of Union troops were involved, their repulse was so easy that Ramseur dismissed the attacks as feeble.[66]

Information received the next day, 19 May, suggested that Grant might be sidling around the Confederate right once again. Lee ordered Ewell to demonstrate against the Union right to determine whether the Federals still occupied that portion of their works. Ewell moved west through heavy forest, Ramseur's brigade in the lead.[67] A week of rain had left roads so muddy that Ewell took only his infantry—reduced to but 6,000 in the fighting since 5 May—without artillery support.[68] He crossed the Ny River at three o'clock in the afternoon. Thirty minutes later near the Harris farm Ramseur made contact with Federals in such strength that he thought awaiting their attack "would cause disaster." Accordingly, he sought permission to throw them off balance by moving forward. His regiments, advancing at double-quick across an open field through renewed rain, "drove the enemy rapidly and with severe loss" until superior northern numbers partially enveloped both Ramseur's flanks. Retiring some 200 yards, he reformed his command while Bryan Grimes's brigade came up on his left and Cullen Battle's on his right.[69]

Trouble promptly arose to Grimes's left, where John Gordon's division fell back in disorder before a Federal attack on the flank, endangering all of Ewell's small corps. Ramseur retreated to his original position, where, with timely aid from John Pegram's Virginia brigade, he checked the enemy.[70] In an intensifying downpour, Ramseur's and Pegram's men engaged the Federals in a standup fight with no cover, a throwback to earlier days of the war. Three hours and more elapsed until approaching nightfall stayed the contest. The two forces remained within shouting distance for some time, their battle blood still aroused. Federal cheers provoked wild rebel yells, and twice Ramseur hallooed into the gathering twilight, "Come on Yankees." But no attack came, though Confederates could hear Union officers urging their men to make a last assault.[71]

After dark, Ewell returned to his breastworks. He had located the Federal flank at the cost of a sixth of his corps. Ramseur's brigade, which probably did the hardest fighting, suffered many casualties but acquitted itself well. Ramseur believed that his brigade and Pegram's, together with Junius Daniel's, "saved the day & that glorious corps" by holding in the wake of Gordon's retreat. Ewell reported that the firmness of Pegram's and Ramseur's brigades enabled him to maintain position until nightfall and withdraw unmolested.[72]

The sharp action of 19 May marked the end of combat in the vicinity of Spotsylvania Court House. In twelve days, Grant had lost another 18,500 men; Lee's casualties, slightly more than half as many, included several general officers killed or badly wounded. "We are being conquered by the splendor of our own victories," wrote a member of Longstreet's staff to his wife.[73] The South could not sustain this ratio of casualties.

With the Army of Northern Virginia bleeding to death, Grant meant to allow it no respite. He moved by his left again on the night of 20–21 May, heading southeast toward Guiney's Station, whence he could turn directly south and make for Richmond. The next good defensive position available to the Confederates was some twenty miles south of Guiney's Station behind the North Anna River. Lee chose Hanover Junction, two miles south of the

North Anna and twenty-two miles north of Richmond, as his point of concentration.[74] Setting out on the pleasantly cool afternoon of 21 May, Ewell's Second Corps marched until eleven o'clock that night. An early start the following day brought it to Hanover Junction ahead of Grant.[75] Lee posted the Second Corps on his right, astride the Richmond, Fredericksburg, and Potomac Railroad. From 23 May through 26 May, Grant tested the Confederate lines behind the North Anna. Ramseur's brigade took part in skirmishing each of these days, especially on the afternoon of 26 May. The following morning showed that the Army of the Potomac had withdrawn across the river and was moving southeast.[76]

As Lee reacted to this latest attempt to get around his right, Ramseur stepped up in the hierarchy of the Second Corps. When Richard Ewell's health and capacity to command had given way, Jubal Early assumed temporary control of the Second Corps. To direct Early's division, Lee selected Ramseur, who heard of the change on 27 May as the army moved southward along the railroads that ran north from the capital. The next day Early's divisions were deployed south of Totopotomoy Creek on the old Seven Days battlefield, their right resting near Beaver Dam Creek.[77] Ramseur knew something of the environs of Richmond, but this difficult terrain had befuddled Confederate plans to crush George B. McClellan in 1862. On the afternoon of 29 May he met with Jedediah Hotchkiss, topographer of the Second Corps, who gave him a new map of the area northeast of the city.[78]

Ramseur's first trial as a divisional commander came the next day in a situation he had more or less foreseen. He expected that Grant would try another flanking movement, and that Lee would attack before the Federals could entrench, "altho our noble chief would rather that Grant attack him." This analysis proved correct. Lee undertook to arrest the Federal slide toward the Chickahominy by "striking at once at that part of their force which has crossed the Totopotomoy in General Early's front." He instructed Early to advance eastward to Bethesda Church. Richard Anderson's First Corps would act in support.[79]

On the warm afternoon of 30 May Early found the Federals at Bethesda Church.[80] Rodes's division pushed a Union brigade back to the east of the crossroads, while Ramseur brought up his division, John Pegram's brigade in the van. Ramseur and Early were at the head of the column when a single Union gun began an intermittent fire from woods on their left. Ramseur wanted to silence the pesky cannon. Early advised against it, but at length agreed to let Ramseur use Pegram, together with one of Rodes's brigades, to "feel the enemy, and ascertain his strength."[81] Ramseur started his men forward, whereupon the Union cannon retired to a line of works. Emerging from woods into a field, the Confederates saw massed artillery on the oppo-

In fighting near the Harris farm on 19 May 1864, Ramseur believed that his brigade and two others "saved the day." These two soldiers were among those of Ramseur's command who gave their lives that afternoon. (Courtesy of the Library of Congress.)

site side. When they reached the middle of the field Federal guns blazed into action. "Our line melted away as if by magic," remembered a soldier of the Forty-Ninth Virginia, "every brigade, staff and field officer was cut down." The Thirteenth Virginia took similar casualties. "No orders were given to fall back," noted a diarist of the Thirteenth, "and nearly the whole [of Pegram's] Brigade were killed or wounded."[82]

This was an inauspicious debut for Ramseur, and won him no favor with the veterans of Early's division. One bitter survivor said that Ramseur ordered the charge "without knowing anything about the ground or the force he was fighting." He was "to blame for the whole thing and ought to have been shot for the part he played in it."[83] The evidence confirms that Ramseur acted hastily, though his letters, which referred to Bethesda Church as a "hard fight" in which his good friend Colonel Edward Willis was killed, contained no hint that he considered his conduct rash. Jubal Early's report

of the action did not mention Ramseur. In connection with Pegram's heavy casualties, Early observed simply that the "enemy was not discovered until the brigade was very close to the line." The whole operation confirmed that Grant was still moving toward the Chickahominy, and Early pulled back to a position a mile west of Bethesda Church on the Mechanicsville Road, remaining there while Lee shifted the rest of his army to the Chickahominy.[84]

On 31 May Dodson informed Nellie of his temporary command of Early's division. His arm wound was healing nicely; full recovery was but a few days off. He thanked God for sparing him in the "terrible battles of the 12th 19th & 30th" and trusted in Him to "cause this cruel war to end & reunite us in peace & safety, happiness and independence." Though the rigors of the past month had precluded his writing frequently, he had thought of Nellie "so often & so tenderly during this arduous & bloody campaign—Oh! how I have sometimes longed to lay my head in your lap & rest." What the enemy would do he could not say, though Grant seemed to have given up plans of attack. The Army of Northern Virginia was in good spirits, fully capable, and confident of defeating Grant as it had all the other generals who had matched skills with Lee.[85]

Events soon proved Ramseur wrong in his prediction that Grant had lost his taste for the offensive. The Army of Northern Virginia held by the evening of 2 June a strong line that ran north from the Chickahominy to the Totopotomoy.[86] Grant's army lay opposite. Both sides had dug in, and the northern general had run out of room to maneuver. "No further flanking marches were possible," commented one of Grant's generals. "Richmond was dead in front."[87] Frustrated by his inability to get around Lee, Grant decided to run over him. At dawn on 3 June the Federals attacked along the entire line. In less than half an hour—one Union officer estimated eight minutes—7,000 of Grant's soldiers were killed or wounded. Sporadic fighting continued throughout the day, but the southern defense did not crack.[88]

Ramseur, whose division was in line across the road from Bethesda Church to Mechanicsville, visited his sharpshooters as the attack began. He ordered them to hold their ground, then rode off. Almost immediately he returned to tell them to seek safer ground. As he wheeled to go back to the breastworks, his horse tripped and fell, "throwing his brave rider who rolled over and over in the dust." "Horse and man seemed to rise together," recalled an officer of the Twenty-First North Carolina, "and went away amidst a storm of shot and bursting shell." This was not Ramseur's only close call on 3 June. Later in the day, he wrote Nellie, a bullet came so close to him that he jumped.[89]

The profligate waste of lives at Cold Harbor capped thirty days of unbroken campaigning during which the Army of the Potomac sustained casualties nearly equal to the initial strength of Lee's army. Confederate losses were at least 50 percent smaller, but far above the level Lee could afford. Moreover, of fifty-eight general officers with the Army of Northern Virginia in early May, twenty-two had been killed, seriously wounded, or captured. When the illnesses of A. P. Hill and Ewell were taken into account, the picture became even more grim. For the immediate future Jubal Early would retain control of the Second Corps and Ramseur would remain in divisional command.[90]

On 4 June Dodson sat on the ground in the rear of his breastworks and wrote Nellie a long letter describing the past month's events. Musketry and artillery boomed to his right, while skirmishers kept up a "continual popping at each other" from their respective pits in front. A light rain fell, smearing the ink on his paper. The Federals had been everywhere repulsed on 3 June, he reported, and if they persisted in such tactics their army surely would be destroyed. His brigade had covered itself with glory on 7,

12, and 19 May, and his military superiors had shown their appreciation by giving him Early's division while Ewell was sick. "There is a rumor that I have been made Maj. Genl," he continued; if so, "I will endeavor to do my whole duty—I will be the more rejoiced on your account." One bonus of higher rank was that his place in battle would be away from the front lines, with sharply diminished risk of being wounded.[91]

Though Ramseur apparently did not know it when he wrote Nellie, his commission as a major general for "assignment to the Command of Early's Division [Army of Northern Virginia]" had been signed by Secretary of War Seddon on 1 June to rank from that date.[92] He was then one day past his twenty-seventh birthday, the youngest West Pointer to achieve the rank of major general in the Confederate army. Special Orders No. 138, dated 4 June, announced Ramseur's good fortune to the army.[93]

This promotion closed a brilliant career as brigadier general during which Ramseur and his brigade had earned an enviable reputation in the Army of Northern Virginia. Exceptionally well-trained and responsive to Ramseur's direction, the brigade had added luster to its name on successive battlefields and was referred to by some as the "Ironsides of the army." Ramseur's bold and decisive behavior in combat, coupled with his firm control over his troops, made the brigade an offensive weapon capable of delivering powerful blows against heavy odds. His almost constant presence at points of danger, often in company with his pickets or sharpshooters, contributed to a strong bond between him and his soldiers.

Major James W. Wilson, brigade quartermaster, wrote in 1863 that "Genl R. . . . is admired by all and his brigade is *devoted* to him." W. A. Smith of the Fourteenth North Carolina said Ramseur "had the martial qualities that make a brave, capable officer and won the esteem of his men. We regretted to lose him, as under him we had won renown and commendation." The soldiers' faith in his ability enabled him to "lead them anywhere," according to E. H. Harding, a clergyman in the brigade. "If he was guiding them, they never distrusted, never hesitated, never quailed" and "had the most unbounded confidence in his daring, skill, and military resource." Ramseur infused his men with something of his own nature, concluded Harding, and they "seemed to feel the same kind of personal enthusiasm towards him that the corps felt toward General Jackson."[94]

A higher tribute than that, Ramseur could not expect. "In this war we must judge men by their action," he had written Nellie in April 1864. "Success is certainly, whether justly or not I will not determine, the test of merit."[95] He had passed this test as a brigadier. The question whether he could do so in a larger command would be answered on new and difficult fields.

CHAPTER 7

NATURAL OBSTACLES ALONE

PREVENTED OUR TAKING

WASHINGTON

A period of relative quiet followed the Federal assaults at Cold Harbor on 3 June, affording Ramseur an opportunity to rest after the relentless marching and fighting of the previous thirty days. To be sure, skirmishing did not cease, and until a truce went into effect on 7 June, dead and wounded remained between the armies in the broiling sun, but there was a sense of pause, a feeling that each side was fought out.

Ramseur was ill. Bread and meat of poor quality and muddy drinking water had left him weak and starved for vegetables and fruit. He had been getting far too little sleep. He managed a short note to Nellie on 7 June, expressing his love for her and desire to be with her, and his intention to take advantage of the lull to nap. Two days later he wrote again, having slept twenty hours and awakened quite refreshed: "I have just made Carter *bathe* me thoroughly and after a change of clothing I have taken a mint julep a friend sent me and am now waiting to eat some bacon & bread & as a rarity some onions and pickled cherries." He had no letter from Nellie—that would have added the crowning touch to one of his better days in some weeks. As he put it a short time later, he needed the "sweet influence" of her "gentle spirit after the storms of the past month."[1]

Freed for the moment from the strain of combat, Ramseur contemplated the future course of the war in Virginia. It seemed to him that Grant had grown tired recently and would not, unless heavily reinforced, again ask his troops to attack Lee's lines at Cold Harbor. His next move probably would be to cross the James River in an attempt to cut lines of supply and communications between Richmond and the South. If a siege resulted the Confederate army and people would have to be patient. As uneventful days slipped by, Ramseur believed Grant to be building toward another grand effort. God had allowed Lee to thwart "immense hosts" thus far, and Dodson asked that

He might again "enable us to baffle all the designs of our evil enemy." Whatever Grant's plans, many dangers and hardships lay ahead. "Perseverance must be our motto"; liberty was worth any sacrifice.[2]

The days after Cold Harbor allowed time for Ramseur to become acquainted with his new command. He had brought Nellie's brother, Caleb Richmond, with him as an aide; otherwise, he retained members of Jubal Early's staff who did not accompany Old Jube to Second Corps headquarters.[3] Ramseur's and the other brigades of Robert Rodes's division had fought beside Jubal Early's division on many fields. Through his long association with the Second Corps, Ramseur undoubtedly had become known among Early's soldiers. A good many of them probably recognized him on sight. Thus, although Ramseur did not come from within the division—the usual method of replacing a divisional chief was to select one of his deserving brigadiers—he was no stranger. Two of his three brigades were made up of North Carolina regiments. Robert D. Johnston, born ten weeks before Ramseur in Lincolnton, led one, which had been Alfred Iverson's and was temporarily under T. F. Toon of the Twentieth North Carolina until Johnston should recover from a Spotsylvania wound. W. Gaston Lewis was in charge of the second, which had been Robert Hoke's and would be A. C. Godwin's when he returned from a northern prison. The third brigade, composed of Virginians, was John Pegram's, though Pegram, too, was out with a wound, and Robert D. Lilley commanded.[4] The division numbered about 2,000 effectives,[5] little more than the paper strength of two regiments when the war began.

On 12 June, after Early had summoned his major generals to headquarters, orders went out to cook rations and be ready to move. Aroused about midnight, soldiers formed and were on the march by three o'clock the morning of 13 June. Leaving their camp near Gaines's Mill behind them, they started toward Richmond, thinking their route would take them south across the Chickahominy to head off Grant. But they went west and then turned north. A cool morning gave way to heat and dust, as the three divisions plus two battalions of artillery marched away from the capital. The soldiers were mystified as to their destination. Some suspected that Stonewall Jackson's old corps might be bound for the Great Valley of Virginia, scene of so many triumphs in the spring of 1862.[6]

Those who imagined they were going to the Shenandoah Valley were correct. Federals under Major General David Hunter were marching up the Valley toward Lynchburg, a key center of supply and transportation for the Confederate army in Virginia. Lee directed Early to take the Second Corps to Lynchburg via Louisa Court House and Charlottesville, repel Hunter's army, and strike a decisive blow if possible. Should Hunter retreat down the

Valley into Maryland, Early was to follow him, thereby freeing the Valley of Union troops, threatening Baltimore and Washington, and perhaps compelling Grant to reinforce the national capital at the expense of the Army of the Potomac, which might then be driven from Richmond. General John C. Breckinridge, who had been vice-president of the United States under James Buchanan and a Democratic candidate for the presidency in 1860, was falling back before Hunter with a small force; he would cooperate with Early.[7]

The march to Charlottesville went smoothly. Liberated from the muddy trenches outside Richmond, soldiers were in fine spirits and marched efficiently. The third day out they passed Trevilian Station, where Wade Hampton had defeated Philip Sheridan's Federal cavalry a few days earlier. Dead horses still lay on the field, and freshly dug graves were numerous. By afternoon of the sixteenth, the Second Corps reached the Rivanna River outside Charlottesville, having covered more than eighty miles in four days.[8] Early immediately set about rounding up railroad cars, and by dawn on the seventeenth had enough to transport half of his corps to Lynchburg, some sixty miles distant. Ramseur's and part of Gordon's division boarded and soon were on their way. Rodes and the rest of Gordon's division would follow as rolling stock became available. Early accompanied Ramseur on the first train.[9]

What should have been a three-hour ride from Charlottesville to Lynchburg took the entire morning and more on the deteriorating road of the Orange and Alexandria Railroad. The lead train chugged into Lynchburg about one o'clock, and Early and Ramseur stepped off to find the city palpably excited. Hunter was less than five miles southwest of town, advancing slowly against a ragtag cavalry force under John Imboden. John Breckinridge lay in bed sick. Ramseur's old friend Harvey Hill, who happened to be in town, had put together a line just west of Lynchburg manned by Breckinridge's small brigades, some reserves and invalids, and the cadets from the Virginia Military Institute.[10] These defenders, anxiously awaiting Early's arrival, had nearly lost hope, when train whistles signaled their rescue. One of them watched happily as the initial train, "plastered over sides and tops with men," came to a halt and "out swarmed men like blackbirds, piling their knapsacks into huge piles." Ramseur hurried his troops through Lynchburg, past the motley force Hill had assembled, to a position selected by Early about two miles beyond the town on the Salem Turnpike. Backed by two pieces of artillery, Ramseur's brigades checked Hunter's progress. Skirmishing and artillery fire continued until dark, when Hunter's army bivouacked in Ramseur's front.[11]

Early's timely arrival cheered the townspeople, but Hunter and his

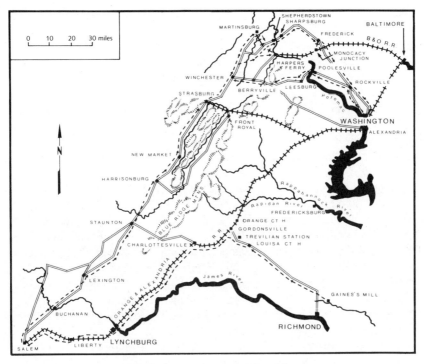

Early's Route, 13 June to 17 July 1864

18,000 men remained a serious threat. Even with his entire corps and the small army of Breckinridge, Early would be badly outnumbered. He was up by two o'clock the morning of 18 June checking his lines. Ramseur's division ran north and west of the Salem Turnpike; Breckinridge was on his right, Gordon's division his left. The Confederates thought Hunter would attack, but the morning passed quietly. Through the afternoon, artillery exchanged fire and Hunter probed the Confederate line at several points. Ramseur "handsomely repulsed" the heaviest attack of the day with considerable loss to the Federals.[12] The afternoon was nearly gone before Rodes's division arrived in Lynchburg. At a loss to explain Hunter's caution, Early decided to strike the enemy the next day. But in early morning darkness, prior to the designated hour of attack, the southerners discovered that, incredibly, Hunter was retreating. Lynchburg was safe. Jubal Early prepared to carry out the second part of Lee's instructions by pressing Hunter's army as it retired to the west.[13]

Ramseur spearheaded the Confederate pursuit that covered twenty-five miles on 19 June. Outmarching their Union counterparts, Ramseur's brigades caught up with Hunter at Liberty, driving a weary Federal rear guard through the city as night fell.[14] The chase continued on 20 and 21 June, through Buford's Gap in the Blue Ridge to Salem, where the Confederates, who had sped beyond their supplies, reluctantly halted. Hunter fell back to Lewisburg, thereby taking himself out of the Valley—and out of the war— for several weeks. Having covered sixty miles at a speed befitting Stonewall Jackson's "foot cavalry," the Second Corps rested and cooked rations on 22 June at Botetourt Springs, northeast of Salem. Weary and footsore infantrymen took their ease at the springs while Early's artillery and wagons caught up.[15]

At dawn the next day, Ramseur's division led the way north, toward Lexington and Staunton in the Valley.[16] Lee had left to Early's discretion a possible movement down the Valley and into Maryland, and Old Jube had decided to take the war across the Potomac.[17] Ramseur crossed the James River at Buchanan, his men clambering single file on boards laid over a burned bridge. He made a short detour on 24 June so his soldiers could see Natural Bridge; one of his bands played under the rock arch while their comrades marched by the landmark Thomas Jefferson had found so lovely.[18]

The twenty-fifth brought the Second Corps to Lexington, where each of the divisions marched by the grave of Stonewall Jackson. Field officers dismounted, men uncovered and reversed arms, flags dipped, eyes moistened, and a "hush as deep as midnight" fell over the column as it approached the hero's resting place.[19] On the other side of town the soldiers viewed the ruins of the Virginia Military Institute, burned to the ground by Hunter earlier in the month. Robert Rodes had taught there; many of the better officers in the Army of Northern Virginia had studied in its halls. The gaunt ruins of the Virginia Military Institute, together with those of many other homes and buildings along the route Hunter had taken, engendered deep bitterness against the foe. A staff officer riding with Ramseur's division had never seen such destruction, and for the first time in the war "felt that vengeance ought not be left entirely to the Lord."[20]

On 27 June, two weeks after they had left their lines at Cold Harbor, the divisions of the Second Corps reached Staunton. They had, reckoned one of the soldiers, marched 229 miles in ten days and 6 miles on the eleventh. Ramseur considered it some of the hardest marching of the war. And more was to come. Hunter had escaped, but Dodson thought Early's little army would yet strike a heavy blow. "We are going still farther," he wrote Nellie from Staunton, "& all our communications will be cut. We hope to relieve Richmond & make Yankeedom smart in a sore place."[21]

Indeed, there was a general feeling in the corps that Early was headed for the Potomac. An Alabamian noted in his diary that soldiers were "under the impression that we are going to invade Pennsylvania or Maryland. It will be a very daring movement, but all are ready and anxious for it." Daring was a mild word for what they were about to do. With scarcely 10,000 infantry, and cavalry known to be unreliable, Jubal Early was going to mount an offensive in the very shadow of the enemy's capital. Henry Kyd Douglas, who had been on Jackson's staff, thought it "safe to say no other General in either army would have attempted it against such odds."[22]

Provisions arrived from Waynesboro on 27 June, and the troops discarded everything but necessities in anticipation of a rapid march. The Second Corps left Staunton the next morning with five days' rations in the wagons and two in haversacks. Early's soldiers were enthusiastic. They were on familiar ground, over which they had maneuvered with great success on more than one occasion. Many lacked shoes, but they kept a fast pace.[23] The agricultural abundance of the Valley was manifest, with lush fields of wheat and grass stretching to the foothills. From New Market on 30 June, Early wrote Lee that he hoped to do "something for your relief and the success of our cause shortly." Ramseur, in a letter to Nellie, was more specific: "We intend to cut loose from our communications & *take Washington . . . or try.*"[24]

Reaching Winchester on 2 July, Early spread his army from Martinsburg to Harpers Ferry and cleared that part of the Potomac of enemy units. Ramseur proceeded through Leetown and Charlestown on 3 and 4 July, linking up with Rodes on the fourth to drive a Federal force from Halltown to Harpers Ferry. Then they captured Bolivar Heights and bottled up the Federals in Harpers Ferry, which the Union commander evacuated that night.[25]

Rodes's division and most of Ramseur's, after staying in front of Harpers Ferry on 5 July, moved the next day up the Potomac to Shepherdstown, where they crossed into Maryland. John Gordon had crossed the previous day. Lewis's brigade of Ramseur's division remained behind to occupy Harpers Ferry, which yielded considerable stores, with skirmishers. Ramseur's other two brigades bivouacked the night of 6 July near Sharpsburg, Maryland.[26]

Unlike many of his men, Ramseur was making only his second visit to Maryland. He had missed the Sharpsburg campaign while recuperating from his wound at Malvern Hill. Kyd Douglas, a native of Shepherdstown, pointed out landmarks on the battlefield. It was at Sharpsburg that George B. Anderson had received the mortal wound that resulted in Ramseur's promotion to brigade command. Thoughts of Anderson, whom he had admired greatly, must have been on Ramseur's mind as he and Douglas rode along. Scars of the battle almost two years earlier were still everywhere apparent; houses, fences, and trees showed countless marks made by minié balls and artillery shells. While Ramseur was camped at the battlefield, his brother David, a surgeon with the army, stopped by for a visit. David looked well, and his stay cheered Dodson.[27]

Early had wanted to maneuver the Federals out of Maryland Heights before continuing on to Washington, but their position proved too strong. He now determined to swing north, through the gaps in South Mountain, and descend on the capital from the northwest. Ramseur, in charge of the trains, marched on 8 July to Boonsboro, and then through Turner's Gap to Catoctin Mountain, some five miles from Frederick, Maryland, before stopping for the night. Lewis, after burning trestlework and what stores he could not carry off, had left Harpers Ferry the previous night and rejoined the division on the road to Frederick.[28] Before eight-thirty on 9 July, a day so fine the soldiers remarked on its beauty, Ramseur entered Frederick, scattering enemy skirmishers before him.[29] As Ramseur's soldiers proceeded through the clean and prosperous-looking city, they heard citizens taunt them with warnings of Federal regulars ahead. Once clear of Frederick, Ramseur moved toward Monocacy Junction, a short distance south on the Baltimore and Ohio (B & O) Railroad. Early's other divisions followed close behind.[30]

Near the Junction, Ramseur found a strong Union force under General Lew Wallace. Blockhouses guarded the Georgetown Road bridge and, a quarter-mile upstream, the B & O Railroad bridge over the Monocacy River. Federals occupied earthworks on either side of the Georgetown Road east of the Monocacy. Two miles above the railroad bridge, where the road to Baltimore crossed the river, Wallace had deployed troops west of the Monocacy. Every route to the southeast was thus blocked. Ramseur's division moved down the Georgetown Road, nudged Wallace's skirmishers to the east side of the river, and went into position opposite the rifle pits. Early placed artillery along Ramseur's line, and a brisk duel broke out between southern and northern guns. When Rodes's division came up, Early ordered it to Ramseur's left, covering the road to Baltimore.[31]

While Early made these dispositions, Ramseur tried with little success to clear the wooden bridge on the Georgetown Road. He informed his commander that any attempt to force the bridge under direct fire would be too costly. Was there no other way across the river? Shortly before noon, with intermittent musketry and cannonading in progress along Ramseur's front, Early decided to ride down the Monocacy to see if the enemy's left could be turned. Wallace concluded at roughly the same time that the wooden bridge was vulnerable to Confederate attack, and he ordered it burned. Soon flames and black smoke billowed skyward. About twelve-thirty, the charred main timbers tumbled into the Monocacy.[32]

While Early examined the ground on his right, he noticed that John Mc-Causland, a young general of cavalry, had forded the river slightly more than a mile below the Georgetown Road bridge. Once east of the river, Mc-Causland struck Wallace's left, throwing it into confusion. Limited numbers prevented McCausland from accomplishing much, but Early ordered John Gordon's division to cross at the same place and attack the enemy flank while Ramseur demonstrated in Wallace's front as a distraction. Gordon promptly crossed and came to grips with the enemy. When firing became audible from below, Ramseur sent Johnston's brigade against the blockhouse beyond the B & O Railroad. Driven back at first, Johnston's men reformed, and, as Gordon's assault gained momentum, Ramseur prepared for a general advance.[33]

About four-thirty, under pressure from Gordon, the Federals retreated from their position opposite Ramseur, enabling him to push his division across the B & O Railroad bridge. Rodes attacked on the left, and, while Gordon's tired men watched, Ramseur and his old division chief harassed the withdrawing foe.[34] Early halted the advance before sunset. Wallace was in full flight, and more Federal prisoners would only hinder Confederate movement. At a cost of 700 casualties, Early had brushed aside the one major Union force between his army and Washington. Wallace's losses totaled about 1,300. The victorious Confederates learned from captured Federals that a division detached from the Army of the Potomac had been on the field.[35]

Having swept Federals from the Valley and obligated Grant to weaken his army, Jubal Early set his sights on the most tantalizing prize of all—the enemy capital, some forty miles distant. Next morning he put his troops in motion toward Rockville, Maryland, with Breckinridge in the lead.[36] Ramseur remained behind with orders to destroy the iron railroad bridge over the Monocacy. It was a very hot morning. Dust hung over the departing infantry, as Ramseur's soldiers tackled the bridge. Powder on hand proved insufficient to blow it up, no part of it would burn, and a battery failed to "knock it to pieces with solid shot." Time was passing, and Federal cavalry were prowling the area. Ramseur admitted defeat and headed his brigades southeast on a march that would continue past midnight. More than once Union cavalry applied so much pressure on his rear guard that Ramseur stopped to deploy. After a miserably long, brutal day, Ramseur's weary troops bivouacked with the rest of the army a few miles south of Rockville. They had come thirty miles.[37]

The eleventh of July was, if anything, even hotter. In column at an early hour, the men marched under a blistering sun on a "dusty road that was almost suffocating." Hardened though they were, many soldiers could not stand the heat and dust, and officers slowed the pace.[38] By noon, Early had

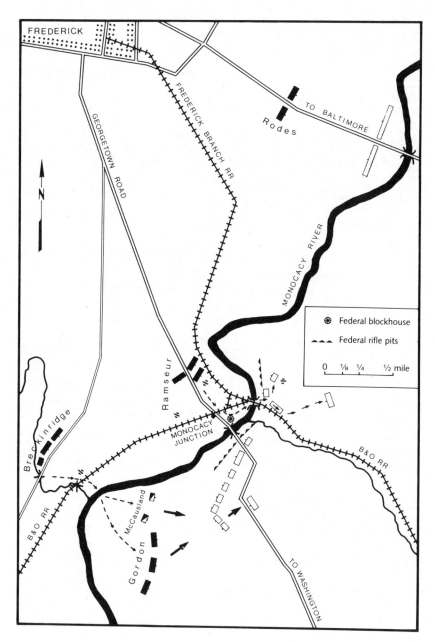

Battle of the Monocacy, 9 July 1864

ridden ahead and was in sight of Fort Stevens, part of the Washington fortifications about four miles north of the White House. Jubal Early could congratulate himself on being closer to Washington than any other Confederate general had been during the war. A smile possibly crossed his lips as he now "discovered that the works were but feebly manned." The men, tired and suffering, must hurry on. Rodes was in the lead. If he could get there soon enough, Early might be able to punch his way into the city.[39]

This possibility proved fleeting. Before Rodes was in position, clouds of dust drifted up from behind the Federal entrenchments and Early could see Union troops filing into them. Clearly, an easy breakthrough was not to be. Rodes's skirmishers, having pushed Union skirmishers to their trenches, could do no more. Although prisoners had talked of a ragged group of "counter jumpers, clerks in the War Office, hospital rats and stragglers" holding the fortifications at Washington, Early had known since yesterday that troops from Grant's army had reached the city. The dust he had seen might mean more veterans coming up. He must await the arrival of his whole army, reconnoiter, and weigh the chances for a successful assault.[40]

While Early inspected the enemy's lines and pondered options, the spent soldiers of Ramseur and Gordon added their numbers to the investing army. To the south, the dome of the U.S. Capitol rose majestically. Off to the right of the Capitol, west of the Potomac, another building stood out—Arlington House, prewar home of Robert E. Lee. Fitful skirmishing took place in Ramseur's front, on the Confederate left, and on down the southern line to Gordon on the right. Late in the afternoon Early put aside his field glasses, convinced that the Federal defenses were "very strong and constructed very scientifically." This belief, together with an awareness of his men's exhaustion, prompted Early to give up thoughts of an attack on 11 July.[41] Much later, with the sun gone, the last of his troops stumbled into position.[42]

That evening, Ramseur received a summons to join Early at Silver Spring, the handsome estate of Francis Preston Blair just north of Washington. In this comfortable setting Ramseur, Rodes, Gordon, and Breckinridge met with their commander to discuss strategy. It had been a difficult day, but for the moment that was forgotten. Over wine requisitioned from Blair's well-stocked cellar, the generals teased Breckinridge. Capture of the city, they said, would permit him to reclaim his seat as president of the Senate.[43] Turning to the question at hand, Early reviewed the perils of their position. It was now certain that the entire VI Corps was in Washington. David Hunter was en route to Harpers Ferry, whence he could menace the Confederate rear. Whatever action they decided upon must be prompt, for the passes through South Mountain and the fords of the upper Potomac would soon be closed. All present agreed that they had come too far to turn back without a fight. Barring unforeseen problems, Early "determined to make an assault on the enemy's works at daylight next morning" and instructed his divisional leaders to see to necessary preparations.[44]

The sun had yet to appear when Early understood that a second corps from the Army of the Potomac had arrived in Washington. He postponed the attack pending another examination of the fortifications. First daylight shone on parapets thick with Union soldiers, leaving the invaders no choice but "to give up all hopes of capturing Washington." Even a successful assault on the fortifications would entail ruinously high casualties; an unsuccessful assault would result in "the loss of the whole force." The latter would prove "very serious, if not fatal" to the Confederate cause. Therefore, with great reluctance, Early decided to return to Virginia.[45]

After a day in front of Washington on 12 July, the army began its march to the Potomac that night. Passing through Rockville and Poolesville, it reached White's Ford, above Leesburg, Virginia, about midnight of 13 July. Across the river by evening of 14 July, Early rested his divisions near Leesburg, then moved toward Snicker's Gap in the Blue Ridge. On 16 July Ramseur and Rodes repulsed a Federal column that had come down from Harpers Ferry to harry the retreat, crossed the Shenandoah at Castleman's Ferry, and encamped at Berryville on the seventeenth.[46]

The return to the Valley ended the fifth week of constant campaigning, during which Ramseur's division had covered hundreds of miles and taken part in one battle and extensive skirmishing. Ramseur had gained much experience in a short time and was well pleased with his own progress and the achievements of the Army of the Valley. "I may be pardoned for saying that I am making a reputation as Maj. Gen'l," he wrote Nellie. He went on to say that the "greatest hardship I have to endure is my separation from you." Early's army had whipped the Yankees at the Monocacy and come within five miles of the Federal Capitol. "Natural obstacles alone prevented our taking Washington," Dodson observed. Extreme heat and dust on 11 July had rendered the soldiers unable to attack, and time "was thus given the enemy to get a sufficient force into his works to prevent our capturing them." By morning of the twelfth, the enemy had "more men behind the strongest built works I ever saw than we had in front of them."[47] Dodson also wrote that he was concerned about his brother David. About 400 badly wounded soldiers had been left behind in Frederick, Maryland, and David, as an army physician, was detailed to look after them. Had he but known of David's assignment, which meant certain capture by the Federals, Ramseur thought that he could and would have prevented it.[48]

On 23 July Ramseur reiterated to Nellie his belief that the "trip into [Maryland] was a success. I see the Richmond papers are 'pitching into'

Gen'l Early for not taking Washington. If he had attempted it he would have been repulsed with great loss, and then these same wiseacres would have condemned him for recklessness."[49] General Lee agreed with Ramseur and Early that the expedition had been fruitful. Lynchburg had been saved, Grant compelled to release a portion of his army to defend Washington, and many military stores and other supplies captured. Jubal Early himself best caught the spirit of his army's recent campaign. Speaking to Kyd Douglas as the withdrawal to Virginia got under way, he said, "Major, we haven't taken Washington, but we've scared Abe Lincoln like hell!"[50]

On 19 July Early ordered Ramseur to take his division and the cavalry of J. C. Vaughn to Winchester, seventeen miles west of Berryville. His mission was to drive back a force said to be advancing from Martinsburg, and to remove all sick and wounded and stores from Winchester. Daylight of 20 July found him two miles north of Winchester, whence he sent Vaughn north to feel out the enemy. Vaughn reported that the Federals were not numerous. About noon Vaughn requested a battery and asked how far he should drive the enemy. Ramseur sent him four guns and instructions to press the foe to Bunker Hill, twelve miles north of Winchester. Two hours later a staff officer came from Vaughn to ask that Ramseur prepare an ambush into which Vaughn would draw the enemy. Because his men were tired, woods large enough to conceal his division were not near, and the supplies, sick, and wounded were ready to depart, Ramseur declined to attempt an ambush.

Another two hours passed on this hot afternoon, and then, about four o'clock, Ramseur heard musketry to the north. Quickly he put his division on the road. Advancing toward the firing, he met Vaughn and his cavalry coming back. Why was Vaughn retreating, he asked? Was the enemy present in force? No, Vaughn replied, the Federals had but one regiment each of infantry and cavalry and a battery of four guns. Ramseur saw a chance to overwhelm a weaker adversary. Placing Johnston's brigade on the right and Lewis's on the left, with Pegram's brigade under Robert Lilley in reserve, he threw skirmishers fifty yards forward to entice the enemy into attacking. With luck, there might be opportunity for a decisive counterattack.

Broken woods obscured part of the field, but in minutes Ramseur glimpsed what looked to be at least three large regiments on Lewis's right, moving rapidly against the Confederates. Shifting Johnston to meet this threat, Ramseur discovered just as firing swelled that the Federals overlapped Lewis's left by 200 yards. He ordered Lilley to extend the line in that direction. But Lilley moved so sluggishly that before he got in position two of Lewis's regiments "broke & ran like sheep." Ramseur was about to order Johnston's brigade to charge on the right when he saw his left collapsing.

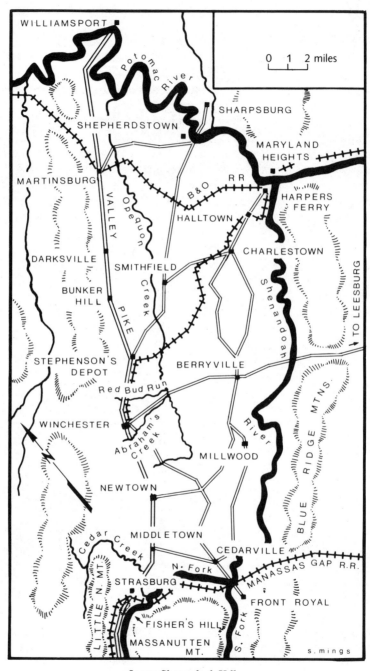

Lower Shenandoah Valley

He galloped toward Lewis and "by every means endeavored to check the flying panic stricken men"; however, all efforts were unavailing. Ramseur's soldiers swirled around him "in the most perfect rout I ever saw," each regiment from left to right sprinting for the rear in a "perfect & unaccountable panic." Four guns and more than 250 men, including General Lilley, fell into Union hands. Fifteen minutes after the collapse, the Federals withdrew toward the north.[51]

This reverse at Stephenson's Depot, as it came to be called, devastated Ramseur. Though he found out that he had in fact been outnumbered by a wide margin, he was convinced that Johnston could have turned the enemy's left and won a victory had Lewis held for even five minutes more. "I censured my command severely for running," he wrote David Schenck. "I called it unnecessary & cowardly. For this reason I've no doubt there will be a good deal of correspondence about it." At least his division would know what he expected and should be ready to fight the next time.[52]

To Nellie, Dod expressed profound anger: "My men behaved shamefully. They ran from the Enemy. And for the first time in my life I am deeply mortified at the conduct of troops under my command." Had these men "behaved like my old Brigade would have done under similar circumstances —a disgraceful retreat would have been a brilliant victory." He had done all a mortal man could do, yet he knew "newspaper editors & stay at home croakers will sit back in safe places and condemn me."[53] In Ramseur's view, Vaughn, who had been in contact with the enemy all day, had given him false information; Lilley had been slow to advance; and Lewis had failed to make his regiments fight. All three bore responsibility for the poor behavior of their commands, and Ramseur "unhesitatingly said so." His superiors would vindicate him, of that he was certain.[54]

As he had expected, Ramseur received sharp criticism for his handling of the affair at Stephenson's Depot. The Richmond *Enquirer*, asserting that Ramseur had been completely surprised, demanded an investigation. It mentioned darkly that rumors damaging to him had gained circulation. From Brigadier General Lewis, who was in Staunton recovering from a wound, the *Enquirer* understood that Ramseur was under arrest. Having printed all this hearsay, the *Enquirer* went on to remark that the "reputation of such an officer as Ramseur, who has won his way to distinction upon many more important fields than this, should not be victimized by rumor."[55] The Richmond *Sentinel* also carried a harsh account, which Ramseur labeled entirely inaccurate.[56] A Virginian in Pegram's brigade, one of those who had thought that Ramseur's promotion was unjust to officers in Early's division, recorded a version of the affair very unfavorable to Ramseur. According to this man, Ramseur had moved toward the enemy without checking the

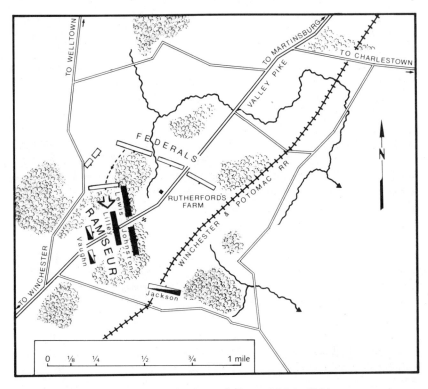

Engagement near Stephenson's Depot, 20 July 1864

ground, repeating his mistake at Bethesda Church. "While I was making good time to the rear I met Ramseur and he was crying." Later on, Jubal Early rode by and enquired why Pegram's brigade had broken: "We said 'Gen. Ramseur was to blame for it.' " Early then rebuked Ramseur and told him not to bring on any more actions.[57]

Early's own writings do not bear this out. In his 1867 memoir, he stated that Ramseur relied too heavily on Vaughn's information and "did not take the proper precautions in advancing." The error committed on this occasion by "this most gallant officer," Early continued, was most "nobly retrieved in the subsequent part of the campaign." Lee, quoting a report from Early three days after the battle, observed only that Ramseur attacked, encountered a much superior force, and was compelled to fall back on fortifications at Winchester.[58] Early, Rodes, and Gordon all gave Ramseur assurances of their sympathy in person, acknowledging that even veterans were susceptible to such routs.[59] Robert Rodes, who was a loyal friend, felt duty-bound to do more. In a letter of 12 September to Richard Ewell, he stated that "by a natural desire to shirk their responsibility for this disaster, and the less laudable one inspired by their dislike of Ramseur, to throw the blame upon Ramseur, the men and main officers concerned have succeeded in winning public opinion to their side, and . . . very nearly ruined Ramseur." His friend acted "most heroically, as usual exposed himself recklessly, but could do nothing with the men; they were under the influence of panic." Rodes offered his opinion that the principal cause of the debacle was the "conduct of the men" and hoped Ewell would find an opportunity to place Ramseur's case fairly before his brother officers in Richmond.[60]

Nellie put the setback in proper perspective. It was unfortunate, she wrote, that he had been unfairly criticized. But neither his friends "nor indeed *anyone* in this part of the country seems inclined to censure *you* in the least, but simply express regret that the affair should have happened." Then, gently, she chided him for worrying so much about what the newspapers might say. He could not live through "this war & rise to fame without passing through some shadows for a moment, no man ever did yet." Christian fortitude should come into play; "let us not succumb to the first trial of faith, but act with that firm confidence which your name . . . [and] character well justify."[61]

For some time Ramseur feared that Stephenson's Depot had jeopardized his elevation to divisional leadership. "I am [appointed to] Maj Genl temporarily," he explained to Schenck, "that is while I have command of Early's [Division], which I suppose will be as long as he is Lt. Genl (which *he* is temporarily), or if his [appointment] is made permanent I think mine will be—tho' I understand the friends of a certain Virginian are making use of the Winchester disaster to cry me down in Richmond." When other officers made known their support of him, Ramseur's apprehension diminished. In mid-September he assured Schenck that he had "lost nothing in the Army— the whole fault of the disaster . . . is put where it belongs—on the [Cavalry] & part of Lewis' men who ran most shamefully without fighting five minutes."[62] As for the soldiers in his division, "I think I am getting up a good spirit among them." They seemed embarrassed about their conduct and had done well in subsequent skirmishing. Still, there lingered in Ramseur a burning desire to atone on the battlefield for the reverse at Stephenson's Depot.[63]

Through the period from late July to mid-September, Ramseur paid close attention to political developments in the North. He well understood that the presidential election of 1864 might prove critically important to southern hopes for independence, and that Lincoln faced a difficult challenge if his armies had not captured Richmond or Atlanta by November. In late July

Dodson worried over reports from Georgia but hoped that John Bell Hood
would be able to drive Sherman back. August passed with Grant and Sherman stymied before Richmond and Atlanta, and Ramseur began to believe
the peace party might unseat Lincoln. He did not doubt that Lee would
defend the Confederate capital successfully. It was to Atlanta—"there is the
vital point"—that he looked with some trepidation.[64]

By the end of August, nearly all of Ramseur's comrades talked of peace
as imminent. Robert Rodes predicted an armistice before the year was out.
A Confederate prisoner who had escaped in New York and walked back to
Virginia told Ramseur that northerners were tired of Lincoln and the war
and would elect a peace candidate. Others who had been among the Yankees spoke similarly. "War clouds seem now to be passing away," wrote
Ramseur on 31 August, and the "sweet voice of peace is beginning to be
heard." He had been reading many northern newspapers, of which only
abolitionist sheets refused to consider peace without a restored Union. All
others, even Republican papers, called for peace with union if possible, but
peace "at any cost—on any condition." If moderate counsel prevailed at the
Democratic convention then in session in Chicago, "wise and good men will
unite to stop the great carnival of blood which Lincoln has inaugurated."[65]

The news Dodson had dreaded most came from Georgia in early September—Atlanta had fallen. On a cold and rainy sixth of September, he relayed
what he had read to Nellie: "My Darling this is certainly a time to try our
souls. We see in Yankee papers that Sherman has defeated Hood and captured Atlanta! We do not wish to believe this—but . . . are compelled to be
apprehensive and anxious." If Hood's army were still intact and Lee—"God
bless our old Hero!"—held fast in front of Richmond, all might still be well.
When he learned a few days later that Hood had escaped with the Army of
Tennessee, Ramseur felt encouraged. Perhaps the western cavalry could
disrupt Sherman's supply lines. Better yet, if Hood could be reinforced from
the south or the trans-Mississippi, he would have the strength to mount an
offensive.[66]

Developments on the political front were nearly as disappointing as the
news from Atlanta. The platform adopted by Democrats in Chicago did
nothing to cheer Ramseur, who described it as "ingeniously contrived to
mean War or Peace so as to catch all the opponents of the Lincoln Administration."[67] Their selection of George B. McClellan as presidential candidate
seemed propitious at first. But McClellan's letter of acceptance proved more
warlike than expected,[68] leaving Dodson disheartened about the chances
for peace: "However neither platforms nor letters will avail anything—
Everything depends upon the issue of this fall [military] campaign." A Confederate victory in Georgia or Virginia would create a loud demand for peace

in the North. Even a stalemate might suffice. "If on the other hand we suffer defeat and disaster at any important point," he cautioned Nellie, "the war will be renewed and the Rebellion on its last legs will be trumpeted through Yankeeland." Whatever transpired in the election, *"duty is very plain.* We must fight this fight out—there must be no turning back now—too much precious blood has been shed for the maintainance [*sic*] of our rights—to great a gulph [*sic*] has been opened up between us & our foes to allow even the idea of reunion to be entertained."[69]

During these weeks of Ramseur's keen attention to northern politics and western military developments, Early's army maneuvered in the lower Valley, constantly on the move, venturing back into Maryland on more than one occasion, and skirmishing with Federal cavalry and infantry.[70] A Confederate victory over General George Crook on 24 July at Kernstown, in the course of which the southerners taken prisoner at Stephenson's Depot were liberated, followed by a Confederate cavalry raid into Pennsylvania that resulted in the burning of Chambersburg, proved more than the Lincoln administration could tolerate. In early August Grant sent Philip Sheridan to Harpers Ferry to gather a large force with which to wrest control of the Shenandoah from the Confederates once and for all. If successful, Sheridan would deny the agricultural bounty of the Valley to Lee's army and prohibit the use of the area as an invasion route.[71]

Ramseur himself did not fear a critical military failure in the Shenandoah Valley. Although Early's cavalry was no match for Sheridan's, the Army of the Valley was more than holding its own. The Confederates repeatedly offered battle, but their foe merely skirmished with them and then withdrew to Harpers Ferry or another entrenched position. Ramseur was confident that in a showdown the southern infantry could defeat the northern despite Sheridan's numbers. Meanwhile, Early's strategy of constant movement had "forced old Abe to send a heavy force to check our peregrinations. We have at least 45,000 or 50,000 men opposed to us." In addition, the Army of the Valley was feeding itself and sending wheat and cattle to Lee's army at Petersburg. We have been "very successful, God grant that we may continue to strike telling blows for our bleeding country."[72]

The Federals could not be prevented from destroying many of the fine farms of the lower Valley. "Plantations are ruined & blackened remains of once splendid mansions are to be seen on all sides," Ramseur wrote in September. It seemed to him sacrilegious to "despoil such an Eden-like spot by the cruel ravages of war." He was thankful that Lincolnton and Milton had been spared the presence of "mean cowardly foes . . . who respect neither helpless age nor tender woman." Surely God would visit upon such a nation and such an army the "just indignation of His terrible wrath!"[73]

Despite outrages by Sheridan's soldiers, the Shenandoah retained its basic attractiveness, and Ramseur wished Nellie could see its magnificence "at this beautiful season of the year." Autumn foliage in the forests, lush meadows, and broad, undulating fields of grain beckoning the harvester confirmed that "nature is still triumphant" in the face of the pillaging Union army.[74] Arduous as the incessant marching was under Early, Ramseur thought it much preferable to the vexations and trials of endurance and patience confronting Lee's men at Petersburg. He hoped he would not have to join them for the winter. "Altogether we consider ourselves very fortunate," he admitted somewhat sheepishly, for while the Army of Northern Virginia was stuck in the hellish earthworks south of Richmond, Early's soldiers had enjoyed abundant food, delightful weather, and a "great variety of scenes . . . in the most beautiful part of the Valley of Virginia."[75]

Ramseur's health was excellent, though he was losing his hair, which always had been thin, quite rapidly. "You would be astonished to see me now," he wrote Nellie. "I weigh about one hundred and fifty and *look as handsome* as you ever saw me *with my hat on*. You must be prepared to see me nearly if not quite bald."[76] His headquarters consisted of two small tents, rather the worse for wear, several wagons drawn by thin mules, and—the most interesting and attractive feature to Dodson's mind—a flock of chickens and ducks that lived under the wagons. Spartan these accommodations were, but adequate, and the company of Caleb Richmond, Kyd Douglas, and other members of Ramseur's staff brightened life in camp. Dodson's brother David, captured by the Federals when he was left with Confederate wounded near Washington while Early fell back to Virginia in July, was paroled in August and visited Ramseur. To Dodson's great relief, David had emerged unscathed from his ordeal in a Yankee prison.[77]

As the army moved about the Valley and across the Potomac, Ramseur spent what free time he had in various ways. His arm, wounded at Spotsylvania, had healed sufficiently to allow him to hunt.[78] Trips to Maryland permitted Dodson to buy items of clothing for Nellie that were difficult to find in North Carolina and Virginia. When he could persuade Marylanders to accept Confederate money, the usual exchange rate was six C.S. notes to one U.S. note, though on one occasion he managed three to two.[79] Perhaps the most pleasant diversions were dinners and teas with residents of the Valley. He developed a great fondness for the family of Kyd Douglas's fiancée, who lived near Winchester. These generous people insisted that Nellie stay with them if the Army of the Valley made winter quarters nearby.[80]

Early autumn made Dodson acutely aware of his separation from Nellie, for it was the season when he had spent many of his most delightful moments with her. One bright, warm September day near Winchester his gaze took in the wooded slopes of the mountains, conjuring memories of strolls with Nellie in the hills around Woodside in September 1862. He often relived the "days of our early love, courtship, & marriage," though the contrast between those relatively carefree times and now was painful. He took comfort from anticipating his pride at being able to tell their children that he had fought and helped win some of the great battles of this second war for independence.[81]

What solace Dodson derived from such musings was shadowed by the profound influence the war exerted on his and Nellie's lives. He was frustrated that he was unable to support her as he thought he should. As early as January 1864, Dodson estimated that his monthly pay equaled but $3.50 in gold, yet the Confederate Congress balked at legislation to correct for inflation. "Everything is so high," he complained that winter, "I can hardly live in the plainest way on my pay."[82] He received no money at all from the government for the period 1 March to 7 July, and when his back pay finally came he had no safe way to transfer it to Nellie. In the meantime, she was reduced to asking for money from friends. More than once Dod committed large sums to the mails because Nellie was without funds. Each time he nervously asked in followup letters whether she had gotten the money.[83] An added burden was Jacob Ramseur, who suffered continuing financial instability. Dodson always shared his income with family in Lincolnton, and he entered into an arrangement whereby he and his father traded in yarn produced at a mill in Lincoln County.[84]

Dodson's enforced absence from home was all the more oppressive through summer and early fall 1864 because Nellie was pregnant. More than ever he had reason to look to the future, to lay out the course their lives would take. But the maddening war mocked attempts to do so. From Bunker Hill on 30 August he asked how she felt. What was she thinking? He had not heard from her in days because of a senseless quarrel between the postmaster general and a railroad president.[85] In the second week of September he finally received several of her letters and was relieved to discover that her pregnancy was proceeding normally. "Every letter I get from you gives me hope that all will be well with you," he wrote back, and if Early decided to move up the Valley, away from Sheridan, Dodson would request a furlough so he could be in Milton when the child arrived. Late in the month, after campaigning had resumed in earnest, he knew their baby would be born with its father far away: "As *the day* approaches I grow more and more anxious to be with you—But these recent battles & defeats will render it almost impossible for me to leave this army." A tender experience marking the culmination of their love for each other was to be denied them, and Dodson lamented it. "How much I do regret to lose all this lovely, precious time of our young life," he told Nellie, and "to be separated from you is to lose it all."[86]

On 17 September Ramseur's division was encamped a mile east of Winchester on the road to Berryville.[87] The chill of fall was in the air. Farmers sowed their winter wheat, and luxuriant grass, nourished by recent rains, grew thickly in the countryside.[88] Federal cavalry tested Ramseur's pickets in the morning, but were quickly driven back toward Berryville. Ramseur expected Sheridan to advance in earnest before long, a view not shared by Jubal Early, who had developed over the past weeks an open disdain for Sheridan's abilities.[89] With the Federals showing so little aggressiveness, Early believed he could divide his small army with impunity. Leaving Ramseur outside Winchester on the seventeenth, he took Rodes and Gordon north to Bunker Hill, and the next day went on to Martinsburg, twenty-two miles from Winchester.[90]

Officers at Ramseur's headquarters reacted to Early's departure with alarm. They suspected Sheridan's army numbered at least 40,000, nearly four times the strength of their own. "Genl Early, in these bold movements," Henry Kyd Douglas recorded in his diary, "seems to rely too much upon the caution and timidity of Sheridan." To Douglas, the "air seemed to have a sulphurous smell" promising trouble.[91] The next day Early marched Rodes and Gordon back to Stephenson's Depot, where they were within six miles of Winchester. Ramseur posted Robert Johnston's brigade about two miles east of the rest of the division, just north of the Berryville Pike. Johnston's pickets were scattered along the edge of some woods that skirted Opequon Creek. These men were within a mile of the stream, just beyond which, they knew, the enemy lurked in considerable numbers. Thus did the eighteenth come and go, another calm, beautiful autumn day. "I shall be glad," a still uneasy Kyd Douglas noted that evening, "if tomorrow passes away as quietly."[92]

At first light on 19 September, a courier dashed up to Ramseur's headquarters and announced that Federals had crossed Opequon Creek and were moving toward Winchester. If this were the serious offensive for which he had looked, the hour was at hand to atone for Stephenson's Depot. Pegram's and Godwin's brigades soon were on their way to join Robert Johnston. When all were united, Ramseur still would muster no more than 2,000 muskets, and it quickly became apparent that there was weight behind the Union advance. Sheridan's troopers had swarmed up out of a wooded ravine so quickly at daybreak that Johnston's pickets fired but a single round before falling back. Johnston was now retiring westward very skillfully.[93]

Bradley T. Johnson, one of Early's cavalry leaders, witnessed the stubborn resistance of Johnston's brigade. He saw a mass of Federal cavalry,

500 yards in front of which was "a thin grey line moving off in retreat, solidly and in perfect coolness and self-possession." The enemy would deploy and their buglers sound "Charge!"—whereupon Johnston's brigade would halt, "face by the rear rank, wait until the horses got within 100 yards and then fire as deliberately and coolly as if firing volleys on brigade drill." The Union cavalry would break and withdraw, the Confederates would resume their retrograde movement, and the whole scene would be reenacted. In this way Johnston held off the enemy while Ramseur brought up the other brigades.[94]

When he reached Johnston on the Berryville Pike, Ramseur deployed his full division. The line straddled the pike about a mile and a half east of Winchester on an elevated plateau between Red Bud Run and Abraham's Creek, two tributaries of the Opequon. Looking to his immediate front and right, Ramseur saw open country; to his left, where the ground dropped off to Red Bud Run, patches of woods offered cover to the Federals. From the Opequon to Ramseur's position, much of the Berryville Pike ran through a ravine bordered by thick woods. Along this part of the road, the enemy might form in relative safety. Guarded on its flanks by small bodies of cavalry, and supported by the guns of William Nelson's battalion of artillery, Ramseur's division resisted growing Federal pressure. The better part of an entire Federal corps, aided by ample cavalry and artillery, pushed against the small southern brigades.[95]

About nine o'clock, a Union surge overpowered a portion of Ramseur's line. Confronted by "Yankees in overwhelming force," a few Confederates "did some tall running," evoking the awful memory of Stephenson's Depot. Ramseur rushed into the midst of his men, hoping by example to calm them. Failing in this, he grabbed a musket, rode over to the foremost of those who had fled, and knocked him down. Again and again he brought his weapon down on the heads of those who refused to halt, and "by this means and the exertions of my staff and some gallant [officers] of the [Brigades]" got his division back in line. A brief counterattack actually jolted the Union mass eastward a short distance, but the Federals quickly regrouped and came on again. Unable to remain where he was, Ramseur ordered his division back a few hundred yards. There it steadfastly held Sheridan's army at bay.[96] Kyd Douglas had observed these soldiers on battlefields going back to 1862; in his opinion, never "did that division or any other do better work."[97]

Jubal Early had joined Ramseur before the heaviest Union attacks began, and he also admired the conduct of his old division. During the night he had learned of a meeting between Grant and Sheridan on 18 September, and the enemy's advance across the Opequon near dawn of 19 September persuaded him that Grant had ordered Sheridan to strike a heavy blow. By Early's

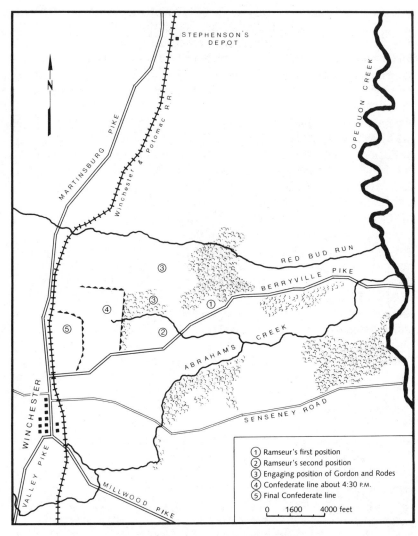

Battle of Winchester, 19 September 1864

order the divisions of Rodes and Gordon were speeding toward Winchester to reinforce Ramseur.[98] Neither then nor later did Old Jube admit that the separation of his army on 17 September had been unwise, but he must have considered himself lucky that Ramseur's soldiers were buying enough time for the Army of the Valley to reconcentrate.

A few minutes past ten o'clock, John Gordon's division came into line on Ramseur's extreme left, leaving a gap into which Robert Rodes, hard behind Gordon, promptly guided his brigades. As these troops had marched to the field, Gordon remembered, "the far-off reverberant artillery was already giving painful notice that Ramseur was fighting practically alone, while the increasingly violent concussions were passionate appeals to the other divisions for help."[99] Early's line now ran from Ramseur on the right, holding the Berryville Pike, north to Red Bud Run, where Gordon anchored the left. It had just taken shape when Sheridan sent the VI and XIX Corps against Ramseur, occupying him in front while attempting to turn his right. The crisis had not passed for Ramseur's "bleeding brigades." They must hold their own while Gordon and Rodes prepared to assault Sheridan's right in an attempt to reverse the tide of battle. Early termed it a moment of "imminent and thrilling danger, as it was impossible for Ramseur's division, which numbered only about 1,700 muskets, to withstand the immense force advancing against it."[100]

Fighting furiously, Ramseur's soldiers absorbed the shock of Sheridan's attack, recoiled slightly, then, as Rodes and Gordon hit the Union flank, inched their way forward. As the two southern divisions plowed into their right, the Federals hesitated, then wavered, and fled in disorder and with considerable loss. It was about noon. Firing died away. Some of Early's soldiers lay down to rest, convinced they had won a victory. At two o'clock, John Breckinridge added his brigades to Early's force, placing one on the left and two on Ramseur's right.[101]

Breckinridge's brigades hardly had settled into their positions when a commotion began on the left. Two divisions of Federal cavalry and George Crook's VIII Corps had broken through a small Confederate force watching that flank, and the cavalry was sweeping down the Martinsburg Road toward Winchester. Breckinridge and some artillery halted the blue horsemen, but not before they had gotten into Early's left rear. The infantry of Gordon and Rodes, hearing musketry behind them to the northwest, fell back in disarray. Seeing this opening, Crook advanced and bent the Confederate left further to the south. Resolute fighting by Ramseur on the right and some of Breckinridge's troops on the left permitted Early to rally most of the soldiers who had broken behind some old works just outside Winchester. The Confederate line now approximated an L, with the apex facing northeast.[102]

*The battle of Winchester—advance of the Federals on the morning of 19 September 1864. (*Battles and Leaders of the Civil War.*)*

Shortly after five o'clock, as Early surveyed his new line, a messenger brought word of an enemy flanking party on the right. With masses of Federals still hovering on his fragile left flank, the specter of an envelopment of his right persuaded the commanding general that his position was untenable. Grimly he gave the order to withdraw. Almost at once he realized that the supposed Federal force was in fact Ramseur's division, "which had merely moved back to keep in line with the other troops." But it was too late to rescind the order to retreat. Minds now focused on escape and would not return to fighting. Sheridan's cavalry again got on Early's left, confusing the men of Rodes and Gordon and dictating the abandonment of Winchester. Ramseur's division, as it had all day, "maintained its organization" and covered the retreat. While the army marched to Newtown, Ramseur repulsed pursuing Federals at Kernstown. On 20 September Early continued southward to Fisher's Hill, some twenty-odd miles from Winchester, where he intended to make a stand.[103]

The battle had been very costly. Early's Army of the Valley carried about 12,000 men into the fight, of whom over 2,000 were killed or wounded. Another 2,200 were captured in the chaotic final phase of action, bringing total casualties to better than one-third. Sheridan's army of 40,000 lost nearly 5,000 killed and wounded.[104] Bad as the northern figures were, however, they did not cripple Sheridan. Early, on the other hand, would be hard put to find any replacements. A heavy toll in officers added to the sad reckoning. Heading the list was Robert Rodes, mortally wounded by a shell fragment just as his division began its attack on the Union right. Ramseur grieved for his old friend and longtime divisional chief. They had fought very well together ever since the glorious victory at Chancellorsville. In his own division, Ramseur lost Brigadier General A. C. Godwin, who had been released in a prisoner exchange in August and made brigadier to head Hoke's old brigade.[105]

For a good part of the day, the Confederates had battled stubbornly. Early asserted in his memoirs that they "deserved the victory, and would have had it, but for the enemy's immense superiority in cavalry." As it was, taking into consideration the disparity in numbers and equipment, "the enemy had very little to boast of." Sheridan had failed to crush the Army of the Valley when he had ample tools with which to do so, a circumstance Early attributed to the "incapacity of my opponent."[106] Ramseur agreed that the southern infantry was more than a match for Sheridan's and that the battle was under control until Union cavalry shook loose late in the day: "we whipped their infantry but their cavalry 7000 or 8000 strong broke our cavalry on the left [and] got in behind us followed by a strong column of infantry."[107]

Indeed, the soldiers of Ramseur's brigades needed to make no apologies for their part in the battle. "Ramseur's division, the first on the field, was the last to leave it," Kyd Douglas later wrote. "It had held its own during the long day, and when the army was defeated it was thrown across the rear and, that night, covered the retreat."[108] This was the feeling of the men themselves. T. F. Toon of the Twentieth North Carolina, Johnston's brigade, stated that "although Early was defeated, Ramseur's division was not." Another of Johnston's soldiers wrote that his regiment had "stood firmly, fighting manfully among Ramseur's 1,700 heroes." A major in Godwin's brigade praised his men who, "amid great confusion . . . fought with a desperation rarely equaled, and . . . contributed largely in preventing a disastrous rout." These three spoke for comrades who, smarting from the panic at Stephenson's Depot and Ramseur's resultant tongue-lashing of them, had turned in a gritty performance against "overwhelming numbers of blue-coated soldiers."[109]

Ramseur's conduct was equally praiseworthy, "as brilliant as anything in his career and . . . full atonement for any charge of negligence in the affair at Stephenson's Depot." Kyd Douglas pronounced him "unquestionably the hero of the day."[110] Ramseur had kept his brigades well in hand under constant pressure. His prompt and vigorous response to the signs of an impending stampede early in the morning quieted the soldiers and stabilized his line. "This much I can say," Dod wrote David Schenck in reference to that moment of danger, "I *made* Early's old [Division] do splendid fighting at Winchester." Once that fleeting moment of crisis passed, Ramseur's troops never again showed any signs of breaking and were the bulwark of Early's defense through the afternoon. After Rodes and Gordon caved in, Ramseur's brigades, which had been in action several hours longer, retained their composure: "I brought up the rear—my [Division] organization unbroken—I was rear guard & repulsed several attacks and saved our wagons and artillery."[111]

Ramseur unquestionably felt he and his men had demonstrated that Stephenson's Depot was an aberration. Yet, except on a personal level, Winchester was a "sad blow, coming as it does, on the heels of the affair at Atlanta." Whether Sheridan's victory would rescue Abraham Lincoln's faltering candidacy remained to be seen. "But let us not be discouraged," he exhorted Nellie, "& all will be well."[112]

CHAPTER 8

HE DIED AS BECAME A

CONFEDERATE SOLDIER AND A

FIRM BELIEVER

After the defeat at Winchester on 19 September, Jubal Early's battered army fell back to Fisher's Hill, above Strasburg on the Valley Pike. Early considered this the only position from which he could reasonably contest a Federal advance up the Valley. Retreat beyond Fisher's Hill would oblige him to give ground to the gaps in the Blue Ridge above Staunton, a circumstance he wished to avoid.[1] Sheridan followed closely but did not force an engagement on the twentieth or twenty-first. While awaiting the enemy's next move, Early juggled his divisional commanders. He gave the brigades of Robert Rodes to Ramseur, who thus took over the division in which he had made his reputation. John Pegram, senior brigadier in Early's old division, replaced Ramseur. To John Gordon, Early assigned the small division of Gabriel C. Wharton, formerly under John C. Breckinridge, who on 21 September received orders to return to his Department of Southwest Virginia.[2]

After making these adjustments, Early did his best to fashion a defensible line. Unfortunately, terrain dictated that he cover all the area between the North Fork of the Shenandoah on his right and Little North Mountain on his left, a distance of well over three miles. From right to left, roughly a quarter-mile south of a tributary of the North Fork of the Shenandoah called Tumbling Run, Early placed Wharton, Gordon, Pegram, and Ramseur. Ramseur's left rested a mile short of Little North Mountain. Early extended his line westward to that eminence by dismounting and stationing behind slight works the greater part of Lunsford L. Lomax's cavalry. So few were the defenders that at some points they might be mistaken for skirmishers. Moreover, Early had concentrated most of his strength on the right, where the ground lent itself to defense, while virtually ignoring his left, which he himself later admitted "could be flanked." Knowing his army to be too weak to resist a determined assault, Early hoped Sheridan would lapse back into his pre-Winchester lethargy.[3]

Federal skirmishers ventured forward early on the warm autumn morning of 22 September, their challenging fire crackling along the lengthy line. Behind them were infantry in considerable numbers, standing in formation but seemingly in no hurry to advance. Officers and enlisted men in Early's army were all too aware of their own vulnerability. An artilleryman on Ramseur's left remembered that soldiers looked around "to examine with a critical eye our means, or rather our want of means, of defence."[4]

Ramseur worried about the dismounted cavalry between him and Little North Mountain. Their previous record in the Valley was undistinguished, yet they occupied a position susceptible to a flanking movement. Ramseur and Lomax agreed that the enemy might strike near Little North Mountain, in which case neither thought the cavalrymen would offer more than token resistance.[5] A shortage of ammunition added to Ramseur's concern, and at an early hour he asked Colonel William Allan, Second Corps chief of ordnance, when his men could expect to receive additional cartridges. Federal skirmishers grew more insistent as the morning slipped by, but Ramseur, who anticipated a major enemy assault, felt constrained to limit his response lest his troops empty their cartridge boxes. At midday Colonel Allan learned that a fresh supply of ammunition was close at hand, whereupon he informed Ramseur that "he might safely use up all he had."[6]

Shortly after receipt of this good news, about one o'clock, a sizable body of Federals made its way toward Ramseur's skirmishers posted on a hill half a mile north of the main southern line. Protected by piles of fence rails, the badly outnumbered Confederates stubbornly held their ground. Their comrades, who thought their skirmishers would be "swept away without any trouble," looked on with surprise and admiration as the attackers halted, wavered, and then retired in some disorder. Spurred on by the "cheers of the whole line of battle half a mile behind them," the southerners on the hill redoubled their fire. They fought with the spirit of Spartans, thought one private, but all who witnessed this action knew what would be the outcome. Union artillery found the range and ripped holes in the rail breastworks; another heavy column of infantry advanced, and the skirmishers gave up the unequal contest and sprinted back to the rest of their division. Inexplicably, the Federals stopped, content for the moment with having dislodged Ramseur's skirmishers.[7]

During this activity in front of the division, soldiers on the left had spied Federals on the slopes of Little North Mountain. When first urged to study that part of the field, Ramseur looked and thought he saw nothing more than a fence row. But a glance through his field glasses revealed a double

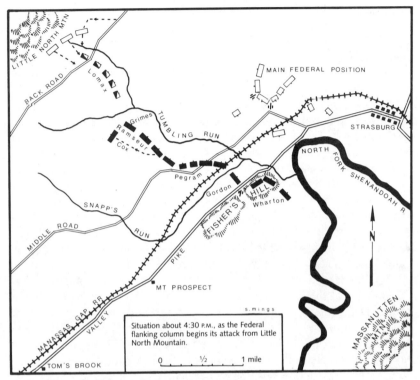

Battle of Fisher's Hill, 22 September 1864

column of Union infantry. Bryan Grimes, whose brigade was farthest west, reported at three o'clock that enemy cavalry also was approaching from that direction. He implored Ramseur to reinforce Lomax's troopers with a brigade or two of infantry. Ramseur declined to do so without first communicating with Early. About four-thirty, the Federals drove in John Gordon's skirmishers on the right and opened with their artillery. Several volleys of musketry to the left signaled the beginning of a concomitant flanking movement.[8]

At the sound of firing from Little North Mountain, Ramseur belatedly ordered William R. Cox's brigade, which had been his own, to pull out of line and proceed toward Lomax's position. Within minutes, however, Lomax's troopers abandoned their works and the Federals roared down upon the Confederate flank, hitting Grimes's brigade simultaneously in left, front, and rear. The men of Grimes and Cox fought briefly, as Ramseur attempted to bring his other brigades into line to the left.[9] Early ordered other units to

Ramseur's aid and had Pegram shift his brigades to meet the onrushing enemy. These movements, undertaken in the midst of a vigorous Union assault, led to confusion in Ramseur's and Pegram's divisions which the enemy exploited with a general attack along the entire line. Confederate resistance quickly collapsed, and soldiers, wagons, cannons, limbers, and caissons clogged the Valley Pike as Early's army fled to the south.[10]

Though hampered by increasing darkness, John Gordon, John Pegram, and several staff officers managed to rally a few men near Mount Prospect, a mile and a half south of the original Confederate line. As at Winchester, Ramseur had charge of the rear guard, which in this instance consisted of two regiments of Battle's brigade and parts of each of his other brigades. Supported superbly by their artillery, Ramseur, Gordon, and Pegram put together enough of a defense to allow the bulk of the army to continue its retreat in more orderly fashion. After dark Ramseur set an ambush. Pulling his soldiers off the turnpike, he allowed the Federals to draw abreast, then directed a telling fire into their flank which sent them scurrying back up the road. Sheridan ceased pursuit at Tom's Brook, while Early's troops marched all night, arriving at Mount Jackson on the morning of 23 September.[11]

The Army of the Valley regrouped at Mount Jackson, driving off Federal cavalry in the afternoon. Toward evening of a cool, damp day, the divisions moved south to Rude's Hill. On the morning of 24 September, Early formed his divisions in line of battle at Rude's Hill. From this elevation, enemy cavalry was visible to the right, infantry to the left, each attempting to get around the Confederate position.[12] Lee had telegraphed Early the night before that Joseph B. Kershaw's division of the First Corps had been dispatched to reinforce the troops in the Valley, and Ramseur relayed this information to his brigades as they waited under arms at Rude's Hill.[13] He also spoke warmly of Robert Rodes, whom the soldiers of the division had idolized. The news about Kershaw naturally lifted spirits, and Ramseur's praise of Rodes moved many to tears.[14] Shortly after Ramseur spoke, with Federal flanking columns fully under way, Early ordered a withdrawal in line of battle. Under constant pressure from the enemy, the army made its way to a point several miles south of New Market. The next morning, 25 September, the divisions began a four-day march that took them through Port Republic, outside of which Kershaw's brigades joined them, to Waynesboro, in the shadow of the Blue Ridge west of Rockfish Gap.[15]

Following this seventy-five-mile retreat from the battlefield at Fisher's Hill, a period of more than two weeks ensued during which the Federals evinced no interest in forcing a showdown. There was opportunity to evaluate the performance at Fisher's Hill, an exercise that gave no member of the army satisfaction. Early reported to Lee that his loss included twelve guns and about 1,300 men. Fewer than 300 of the casualties were killed or wounded; the remaining 1,000 had either been captured or had taken to the mountains when the line collapsed. "I very much regret the reverses that have occurred to the army in the Valley," Lee replied, "but trust they can be remedied."[16]

Ramseur was less magnanimous. "Too busy and too much mortified" to give a full account of the recent campaigning in the days immediately after Fisher's Hill, he now offered his views to Nellie and to David Schenck. He thought Early's line had been poorly drawn. At the weakest point, the extreme left, the Federals faced only Lomax's cavalry. Concentrating on that inviting target, the enemy had crushed Lomax and then "poured in our flank & rear." The men were "very much stampeded & did not keep cool or fight as well as they have heretofore done." For the present he would maintain official silence on Early's disposition of forces, but at the proper time would state his opinion plainly.[17]

The reverses in the Valley, when added to the fall of Atlanta, convinced Ramseur that the war party would triumph in the northern elections that fall. Adding to his gloom was a rumored Union movement toward Orange Court House that made him anxious about Lee's ability to hold his own. "They learn to stick to McClellan's plan of approaching Richmond from three directions," he wrote, making necessary a supreme Confederate effort. Unless Lee was reinforced, Ramseur predicted the loss of Richmond. From what quarter might help be drawn? The Yankees reportedly were rebuilding Manassas Gap Railroad, a sign that Sheridan wanted a dependable supply line to enable his force to stay in the Valley through the winter. Were this true, the Second Corps probably would remain as well, unless Lee became so hard pressed he recalled Early. Hood's army might stand a better chance of helping the Army of Northern Virginia. If Hood struck Sherman a telling blow soon—"time is an important element"—he could reinforce the army at Petersburg, and with added strength "our great Gen'l Lee" might win a victory that would bring peace in 1865. There was little in this thinking to inspire confidence, and when Sheridan's cavalry drubbed Early's Confederate horsemen on 9 October at Tom's Brook, Ramseur poured out his frustrations: "I declare I am sick at heart from these repeated disasters—but I hope this is the last."[18]

Though Sheridan did not seek a decisive victory over Early in the weeks after Fisher's Hill, he kept his men busy in a way that created bitterness among his southern opponents. The Federal commander, John Gordon later wrote, had "decided upon a season of burning, instead of battling; of assaults with matches and torches upon barns and haystacks, instead of upon armed men who were lined up in front of him."[19] Surveying the countryside around New Market on a crisp October day, Ramseur sorrowfully recorded that the "beautiful and fertile Valley has been totally destroyed. Sheridan has had *some* houses, *all* the mills & barns, every straw & wheat stalk burned. This Valley is one great desert." Supplies for the Confederate army had to come from the upper reaches of the Shenandoah. Life was wretched for those who lived in areas visited by Sheridan's troops. Ramseur did not know how they would survive amid such desolation. Hoping for a chance to punish the enemy, he expressed his willingness to "take a musket and fight to the bitter end, rather than submit to these miserable Yankees. I think they have placed themselves outside of the pale of civilization by the course they have pursued in this campaign."[20]

Ramseur's resolution to continue the struggle against a foe greatly superior in numbers and resources had remained firm through successive setbacks. His letters betrayed no willingness to accept less than independence for the Confederacy. Holding to his belief in the superiority of southern infantry, he argued that with enough cavalry to hold the blue horsemen in check Early could defeat Sheridan. He hoped Nellie had not grown discouraged by the stream of bad news from the Shenandoah. The Confederates were recruiting in the upper Valley and, with Kershaw's division and cavalry and artillery replacements on hand, they should "go after the Yankees and drive them down the Valley." "Tho' peace may be a long way off," he conceded, "I feel sure that Justice & right will finally triumph. . . . Surely all true Southrons would prefer *anything* to *submission*."[21] When David Schenck admitted that reports of recent weeks had left him depressed, Ramseur insisted that he must not indulge such thoughts. Undoubtedly it was a time of trial, but southerners must "show that we are made of the true metal. Let us then be brave cheerful and trustful." He implored David not to give up, as "we are bound to succeed. The God of Justice will order all things for our good."[22]

Ramseur's return to his old division after the death of Robert Rodes strengthened his faith in the army's ability to best the enemy. This assignment was "very pleasing" to him, for he trusted these brigades implicitly.[23] They had broken with the rest of Early's force at Fisher's Hill, but Ramseur considered that unfortunate rout to have been preordained by the faulty deployment of the Confederate troops. Though proud of the way Early's division had fought under him at Winchester, he never felt those men measured up to the soldiers with whom he had campaigned as a brigadier. And he must have known, as Rodes had pointed out to Richard Ewell in his letter defending Ramseur's conduct at Stephenson's Depot, that in the ranks and among the officers of Early's division were men who disliked him and disapproved of his appointment to lead them. Indeed, this sentiment may have influenced Early's decision to assign Ramseur to Rodes's division.

Ramseur's brigades now included the one formerly his own, under William Ruffin Cox; George Doles's Georgians, commanded by Philip Cook since Doles's death at Bethesda Church; Cullen Battle's Alabamians; and Junius Daniel's North Carolinians, commanded by Bryan Grimes since Daniel had been mortally wounded in the "Bloody Angle" at Spotsylvania. As of 30 September, the division numbered about 2,500.[24] Most of them were well acquainted with Ramseur. According to General Cox, the men of Ramseur's old brigade received with "great gratification" the news that he would lead their division. Members of Rodes's staff had asked Early to give the division to Ramseur, and the general feeling among officers and men of the other three brigades seems to have been that although Rodes's death was a serious blow to the Confederacy, Ramseur was the best choice to be his successor.[25]

Transfer to Rodes's division also meant that Ramseur no longer was standing in for someone who might resume command, as had been the case when he took over Early's division. In light of this, he felt his appointment as major general should be made permanent. "But you know I have from the first made it a principle not to ask for promotion," he wrote Schenck. "I have no friends *at Court.*" He would not object if a move were made in his behalf, however, particularly since he had heard that other generals were maneuvering to secure the position. Some influential North Carolina man should write outlining Ramseur's qualifications to Braxton Bragg, a fellow North Carolinian whose military ability Ramseur always had questioned but who served in Richmond as a kind of chief of the Confederate general staff. Ramseur had several months' experience as a major general and was the ranking officer in the division; two of his brigades were composed of North Carolina regiments; his past services, as brigadier and as major general at Winchester, were such that he was entitled to a division. Whoever communicated with Bragg, Ramseur added, should make reference to the opinions of Lee, Ewell, and Early.[26]

On the day he wrote to Schenck regarding promotion, 10 October, Ramseur also sent a letter to Nellie in which he discussed the impending birth of their child. This was the subject that had most occupied his mind since Fisher's Hill, a period for him of "the most intense anxiety and solicitude on your behalf." A furlough was out of the question: "Since our disasters over here in the Valley . . . I think my duty is plain. I ought not to leave *now* even if I could do so." But whenever duty permitted a moment of freedom, he had assured her a few days before, his mind turned instantly to Nellie "and always with reference to the great event of our lives." He longed for the time when they might rear their family in a mountain home, free from the threat of domination by a Yankee government.[27] "I would like to get a telegram from you daily until the crisis is past," he wrote from near Staunton. "Won't you send them to me?" He knew that Nellie's mother and grandmother would do all that was necessary, and two of his sisters might be in Milton to help with the delivery; still, it was the harshest trial of his life to be separated from her now. He would come as soon as poor weather curtailed campaigning.[28]

During the first week in October, Sheridan had marched slowly down the Valley, burning as he went, and Early had followed. Reaching New Market on 7 October, the Confederates encamped there for several days.[29] Lee had sent Kershaw, Thomas Rosser's cavalry, and additional artillery to Early after Fisher's Hill so that the Army of the Valley might resume the offensive. "I have given you all I can," read one of Lee's dispatches, "you must use the resources you have so as to gain success. The enemy must be defeated, and I rely upon you to do it."[30]

Such an expression of confidence after Early's ill fortune in September kindled in Old Jube a desire to hit the enemy at the first opportunity. When he heard that Sheridan had moved north from Fisher's Hill and might be preparing to send troops to Grant, Early decided to confront his opponent. The army left New Market at dawn on 12 October, Ramseur in lead, and arrived at Fisher's Hill the following morning. Taking part of his command through Strasburg to Hupp's Hill on a reconnaissance, Early discovered Federals in evident strength north of Cedar Creek, a stream that joined the North Fork of the Shenandoah River just east of Strasburg. "This was too strong a position to attack," Early later reported. "I therefore encamped my force at Fisher's Hill and waited to see whether the enemy would move."[31]

Early drew his line at Fisher's Hill on 14 October. General Gabriel Wharton's division, formerly under John C. Breckinridge, was on the right, east of Fisher's Hill; to Wharton's left, in order, were Kershaw, Gordon, Pegram, and Ramseur. Early wanted Sheridan to retreat, in which case there might be an opening for a southern thrust, or to attack, but on this pleasant fall day the Union commander did neither.[32] Much to Ramseur's disgust, the enemy remained inactive on the fifteenth. He could not explain why they declined battle on these two days, but he hoped for an engagement before long.[33] A third quiet day passed on Sunday, 16 October, with the armies in sight of each other. From high ground, topographer Jed Hotchkiss and others observed Federals at work fortifying their position. Early sent Gordon and one of his brigades to Hupp's Hill at daylight on the seventeenth to ascertain the strength of Sheridan's lines. Gordon found no potential for a frontal assault.

Early thus faced a difficult choice. His army had few provisions left, and none could be procured from that devastated part of the Valley. He could retire, but in doing so he would have taken troops from Lee and accomplished nothing. Choosing not to retreat and knowing he was too weak to hit Sheridan head-on, Early selected a third alternative: "I then determined to try and get around one of the enemy's flanks and surprise him in camp."[34]

Having made this decision, Early sent John Gordon and Jed Hotchkiss to the northern end of Massanutten Mountain, whence they could examine Sheridan's position. These officers saw that the Federals were well prepared to meet a threat to their right but had neglected to cover their left. No doubt, thought Gordon, Sheridan believed a turning column could not negotiate the rugged slope of Massanutten to descend on his eastern flank. A pathway wide enough for men to pass single file led around the end of the mountain, however, and if the Confederates started a march at dark they could cover the distance in time to strike at dawn. Hotchkiss showed Early the proposed route on a map he had sketched while on the mountain. Early agreed to the plan, pending confirmation of the adequacy of the path.[35]

Ramseur's thoughts were not on military questions that Monday, 17 October. Late the previous evening he had received a message from the signal corps. Wigwagged from station to station down the Valley from Staunton, it read simply, "The crisis is over and all is well." Nellie had given birth to their child.[36] Immediately he had sent for Bryan Grimes to share the news. "His joy was full deep in his heart," Grimes later wrote Nellie, "tears of sympathy for you filled his eyes when speaking of you." Ramseur told Grimes that he thought his child was a boy. By coincidence, Grimes learned after he left Ramseur's headquarters that he, too, had become a father, whereupon he returned to tell Ramseur. Seated around the gnarled roots of an old oak, the two spoke of their wives and babies and the future.[37]

Now Dodson asked Nellie to give him all the details. Had he a son or a daughter? Was Nellie truly well? He could not put into words his feelings when he thought of how she had suffered for him. He had thought he could not love her more but now he did, "more devotedly, more tenderly than ever before." Thanking God for bringing her through the labor safely, he marveled at the mercy He had shown *"both of us."* Reluctantly, he closed his letter: "Oh me! I want to see you *so bad*. God bless my Darling & may He soon reunite us in happiness & peace a joyful family."[38]

The next day, feeling his new responsibility, Ramseur made out a will, after which, about two o'clock, he rode to Early's headquarters for a meeting.[39] Along with the other divisional commanders he listened as Early outlined his plan of attack. John Gordon, senior major general in the Second Corps, was to take the three divisions of the corps—Ramseur's, Pegram's, and his own, under Clement Evans—across the North Fork of the Shenandoah at Fisher's Hill, around the end of Massanutten Mountain, over the river again at Bowman's Ford near the mouth of Cedar Creek, and north to a position near the J. Cooley house. Commencing the attack from that point, Gordon's divisions were to make for Belle Grove, a large house west of the Valley Pike known to be Sheridan's headquarters. Kershaw's division was to march through Strasburg, across Cedar Creek at Bowman's Mill, and advance against the Union flank as Gordon made contact. Wharton was to move his division down the Valley Pike and add the weight of those brigades to the attack. Thomas Rosser's cavalry was to guard Early's left, while W. H. F. Payne's troopers were to accompany Gordon with the objective of capturing Sheridan. Gordon was to open the attack at five o'clock in the morning; Kershaw and Wharton would advance when they heard Gordon's fire.[40]

It was an audacious plan. With fewer than 10,000 infantry, Early meant to challenge an army more than double that number which had soundly thrashed him twice in the past month.[41] But if surprise were complete and all went well, he might have his revenge on Sheridan before the sun set on 19 October.

After the meeting adjourned, Ramseur, Gordon, and Hotchkiss rode along the route the Second Corps would take. Finding nothing to occasion a change in strategy, they returned to their camps late in the afternoon. Hotchkiss then took Ramseur's pioneers back to build bridges and clear the trail of trees.[42] In preparation for the march, soldiers laid aside canteens and removed all other articles that might, in the stillness of the night, make a noise audible to Federal pickets along the river.[43] About dark, Ramseur moved his division to the Valley Pike, where the men rested an hour while Early and his generals conferred and set their watches. At eight o'clock, the Second Corps—Gordon in front, then Ramseur and Pegram—began its flanking march.[44] In its ranks were many veterans who had followed Stonewall Jackson around Joseph Hooker's right at Chancellorsville.

Quickly the divisions were across the North Fork of the Shenandoah and moving single file on what a captain in one of Pegram's brigades called "a pig's path" strewn with logs, stones, and other obstacles. Under orders not to talk, the men silently made their way through the cool night air. A gentle breeze rustled leaves, while to the left could be heard the steady flow of the river. Massanutten Mountain loomed to the right.[45] Ramseur and Gordon, friends as well as fellow soldiers, sat on a bluff and watched as "the long gray line like a great serpent glided noiselessly" along the trail above the Shenandoah. Ramseur talked "most tenderly and beautifully" of his wife and child and how he longed to see them. He was in good spirits. The day before he had stood on Massanutten Mountain and seen how vulnerable was the enemy. A victory today could mean a visit to Milton. The last of the Second Corps had gone into position opposite Bowman's Ford and soon

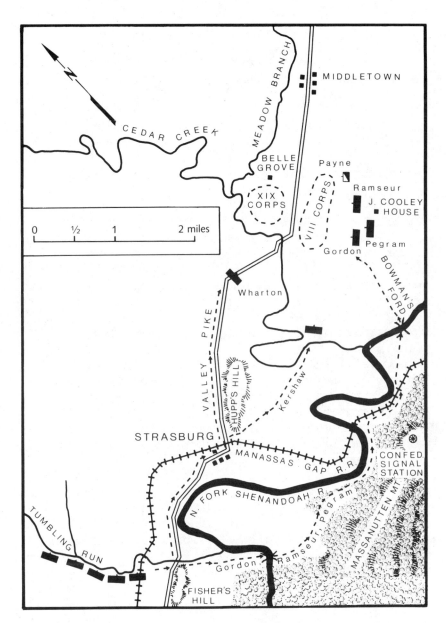

Confederate Deployment for the Battle of Cedar Creek, 19 October 1864

would be crossing the river. Rising to join his division, Ramseur said to Gordon, "Well, general, I shall get my furlough to-day."[46]

Light mist hung over the North Fork of the Shenandoah at four-thirty as Ramseur formed his division into two columns and started them across the river.[47] Battle's brigade splashed into the water first; those of Cox, Cook, and Grimes stretched out behind. In thirty minutes they were aligned near the Cooley house, facing northwest toward Belle Grove. The enemy's camps lay half a mile ahead, just east of the Valley Pike. Gordon's division, under Evans, was on Ramseur's left. Pegram's brigades formed a second line behind Evans.[48] Promptly at five o'clock, "as day was breaking and faint streaks of light appeared in the east," the Confederates rolled forward. The wave of cheering men hit George Crook's VIII Corps. Kershaw, at the sound of Gordon's attack, advanced on the Union flank to Gordon's left.[49]

Startled Federals, many of whom were asleep in their tents when the Second Corps raised the rebel yell, stumbled about in various states of undress, unable to concentrate their firepower. Some made a brief stand behind their works, but in the space of a few minutes all gave way and fled.[50] Sprinting through the camps of the VIII Corps, attackers swept up a hill below Belle Grove and routed William H. Emory's XIX Corps. Ramseur's brigades under Cox and Cook passed over the grounds of Belle Grove, while Battle and Grimes veered to the right. Smoke and fog clung to the ground along Cedar Creek and in hollows, defying the early morning rays of the sun. In a very short time and at small loss, the Confederates had driven from the battlefield two Federal corps, capturing eighteen pieces of artillery and 1,300 prisoners.[51]

Ramseur's mood was radiant. His demeanor in combat, described by General Robert Ransom as one of "great energy, brilliant dash (often amounting to impetuosity) and an enthusiasm which inspired those he led," had never been more exemplary. Mounted on a handsome bay and dressed with unusual care in full uniform, a flower in his lapel to honor his new child, he hastened from point to point along his lines urging his men on whenever the enemy showed signs of rallying. "His presence and manner," recalled one of his brigadiers, "was electrical."[52] As his soldiers pursued fleeing Federals, Ramseur encountered Kyd Douglas on the Valley Pike. "I went up to him with a message where I found him leading his men & driving the Enemy," wrote Douglas a month later. "He was greatly excited, pleased & laughingly cried 'Let's drive 'em D—— for I must get a furlough to see my little wife and new baby.'"[53]

Shortly after sunrise Ramseur dispatched skirmishers who cleared Union sharpshooters from Middletown. He then called for a battery and upon its arrival advanced against Federals clustered on a hill northwest of Belle

The battle of Cedar Creek—Confederate attack on the camps of the Federal XIX Corps.
(Battles and Leaders of the Civil War.)

Grove. The brigades of Grimes and Battle, together with a portion of Pegram's division, took six guns and many prisoners, but the enemy, members of Horatio Wright's well-respected VI Corps, "made a most stubborn resistance" and forced the attackers to withdraw.[54] When Ramseur and Pegram reported the presence of the VI Corps, Early directed Gabriel Wharton to bring his division into action on Pegram's right. The Federals repulsed Wharton also. Early then decided to dislodge them with artillery. At about eight o'clock, Colonel Tom Carter, who commanded the guns of the Second Corps, concentrated the fire of some twenty cannon and compelled the Federals to retire to a line directly west of Middletown. Ramseur occupied the hill they had abandoned. There, over the next hour, he reformed his division, much scattered in the morning's fighting, and replenished ammunition.[55]

Between nine and ten o'clock, harassed by Carter's artillery and outnumbered by Early's infantry, Wright's VI Corps fell back to a third position north of Middletown and west of the Valley Pike. The troops of Crook and Emory, virtually unengaged since their flight at dawn, went into line with Wright. By ten o'clock the Confederates were arrayed opposite the Federals. Extending east to west across the Valley Pike and passing through the northern edge of Middletown, the line began with Wharton on the right and continued through Pegram, Ramseur, and Kershaw to Gordon on the left.[56]

Jubal Early considered the battle won. To John Gordon, who rode up to him about this time, he remarked, "Well, Gordon, this is glory enough for one day. Precisely one month ago today we were going in the opposite direction." Gordon observed that the VI Corps remained on the field and explained that he had made preparations for a final assault. "No use in that," Early replied, "they will all go directly." Gordon demurred, asserting that the VI Corps would go only if pressed. Again Early stated that the enemy would pull back, ending the discussion.[57] The rest of the morning elapsed with no significant change in the opposing lines. Early began to worry. Substantial numbers of his men were reported leaving the front to plunder the Federal camps. In the open country above Middletown, Federal cavalry posed a threat to both Confederate flanks. While his officers waited to renew the attack, Early decided to "try and hold what had been gained" and ordered that captured artillery, wagons, and small arms be carried off. In early afternoon Gordon was allowed to advance, but when his skirmishers met stiff resistance Early concluded "that it would not do to press my troops further."[58]

Long hours of inaction dragged by, during which messages from the Confederate signalmen on Massanutten Mountain warned of a Federal buildup. Rosser reported the enemy increasing on the Confederate left. There was a gap between Gordon's right and Kershaw's left. Urgently Gordon requested support, but Early suggested only that Gordon extend his already weak line and bring up a battery. Three o'clock came—a full five hours had ticked by since the VI Corps retreated to its third position. Elation had given way to dread, as the southerners braced to receive an attack.[59]

About three-thirty the Federals struck.[60] Absent when Gordon surprised his sleeping soldiers that morning, Sheridan had hurried to the scene of battle, rallying dispirited troops along the way. Given time by Early's vacillation to organize an assault, he now had the XIX Corps hitting Gordon and Kershaw, the VI Corps, Ramseur and Pegram.[61] Ramseur watched as his skirmishers yielded ground, then pushed his four brigades forward a short distance and "handsomely repulsed" the enemy. The field in front of them was littered with arms and several battle flags dropped by the attackers. Given hope by their success, the Confederates set up a cheer.[62]

Before the cheering had stopped, however, it became evident that Gordon was in serious trouble on the left. The enemy had punctured his thin line, and Gordon's best efforts could not prevent the crumbling of his entire command. East of Gordon, Kershaw's troops also broke when they realized the brigades to their left had been overrun. Scarcely had the soldiers' victo-

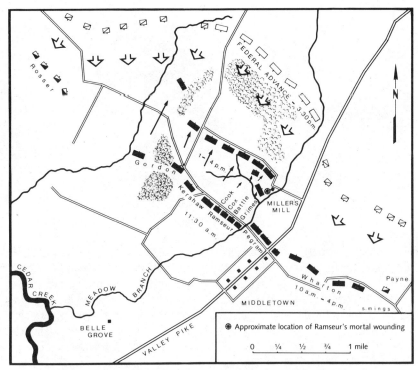

Battle of Cedar Creek, Late Morning to Midafternoon, 19 October 1864

rious yells died away when Ramseur heard the cry "We are flanked!" and saw many of his own men make for the rear. In an effort to keep his brigades in hand, he ordered them back 200 yards to a stone wall on a hill just southwest of Miller's Mill.[63]

Begun in orderly fashion, this withdrawal soon became a confused retreat, but Ramseur managed to rally a part of his division behind the wall.[64] With help from six guns of Wilfred E. Cutshaw's battalion and fragments of Kershaw's division, Ramseur's men held off the advancing Federals.[65] Ramseur galloped up and down his line with saber drawn, exhorting all to remain steady. By virtue of "his great popularity with his men & his own splendid conduct and bravery" he maintained control and was able to direct a constant and effective fire toward the enemy.[66] To the south Jubal Early, trying to stop the flight, pointed to "the gallant stand made by Ramseur with his small party." Often Ramseur had proved his courage and his capacity to lead, Early wrote soon after the battle, "but never did those qualities shine more conspicuously than on the afternoon of the 19th."[67]

The battle of Cedar Creek—counterattack of the Federal VI Corps.
(Courtesy Belle Grove, Inc.)

From four o'clock until well past five, Ramseur's force held fast. If Ramseur could keep them in place until nightfall, the Army of the Valley might be spared the ignominy of another complete rout. At about five o'clock he rode west to confer with Major G. B. Gerald of the Eighteenth Mississippi, who led the remnant of Benjamin G. Humphreys's brigade of Kershaw's division. Could Gerald hang on until dark? He could, answered the major, with sufficient ammunition. Ramseur promised to send some, after which, "in plain view of a long line of Yankees advancing and shooting like the mischief," he spurred back to his division.[68] Union troops were closing in from three sides. Earlier Ramseur had shaken off a slight wound; now, his bay took a bullet and went down. From one of William R. Cox's couriers Ramseur secured another horse. He had been in the saddle but a moment when that poor beast also was killed. Scanning the sloping ground west of the mill, he located a third animal and was in the process of mounting when a ball entered his right side, passed through both lungs, and lodged below his left arm.[69]

Major R. R. Hutchinson, Ramseur's assistant adjutant general, saw his chief fall, ran to him, and with help from others carried him to the rear. Caleb Richmond joined them and watched over his brother-in-law as Hutchinson went in search of an ambulance. With Ramseur out of action, the line began to disintegrate. Lest he be made a prisoner, Richmond and others from his staff lifted Ramseur onto one of their horses, and, with an officer running alongside to prevent his falling, moved him away from the firing. When Hutchinson returned with an ambulance, Ramseur was transferred to it and the driver headed up the Valley Pike.[70] Early's army was in full retreat now; the road was choked with wagons, artillery, other ambulances,

"The Mortal Wounding of General Stephen D. Ramseur on the Slope West of Miller's Mill." This dramatic portrayal mistakenly shows Ramseur mounted at the moment he received his mortal wound; he was actually preparing to mount when the fatal bullet struck. (James E. Taylor Sketchbook, Western Reserve Historical Society.)

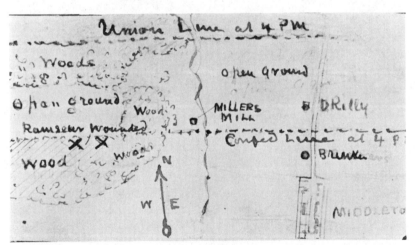

"Map of the Locality Where General Ramseur was Mortally Wounded." Caleb Richmond, Ramseur's brother-in-law and aide-de-camp, made this sketch several years after the war. (James E. Taylor Sketchbook, Western Reserve Historical Society.)

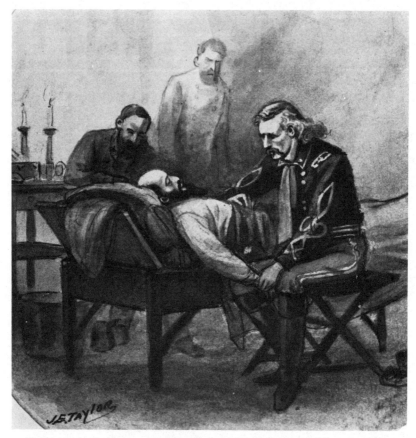

"Custer at the Dying Ramseur's Bedside in Belle Grove House." (James E. Taylor Sketchbook, Western Reserve Historical Society.)

and a horde of demoralized men. A bridge immediately above Strasburg broke down under the unusually heavy traffic, trapping Ramseur's vehicle and all others that had yet to cross. About dusk a northern voice asked the driver who was in the ambulance. Ramseur ordered him not to say, whereupon the slow-witted fellow replied, "The General says I must not tell." Upon hearing this, Federal cavalrymen who had caught up with the Confederates stranded below the bridge surrounded the ambulance and took Ramseur prisoner.[71]

Ramseur's captors escorted him to Sheridan's headquarters at Belle Grove, where the chief medical officer of the Union army and a captured Confederate surgeon conducted an examination and pronounced the wound mortal. R. R. Hutchinson, taken prisoner by the Federals while with the rear guard, learned of Ramseur's presence at Belle Grove and received permission to join him. Hutchinson found his commander in obvious pain, but "his hope in Christ led him to endure *all* patiently." Several old friends from West Point, now Union officers, visited Ramseur's bedside. Henry A. du Pont, who had roomed across the hall from Ramseur at the Academy, was deeply moved by this reunion. At one point du Pont seated himself "as quietly as possible on the side-rail of the bedstead," inadvertently sending "a thrill of pain" through Ramseur and prompting him to whisper, "Du Pont, you don't know how I suffer." George Custer and Wesley Merritt sat with Ramseur during the evening, perhaps recalling their farewell party at Benny Havens's tavern, and Sheridan "offered every assistance" in his power.[72]

Drifting in and out of consciousness, Ramseur lingered through the night. The doctors administered large quantities of laudanum, which made rest easier.[73] Whenever awake, Dodson spoke of friends and family. He asked that Robert Hoke, his friend since their childhood in Lincolnton and now a major general with Lee's army at Richmond, be told that he "died a Christian and had done his duty." Repeatedly he mentioned Nellie and their little child—how he wished he could see them once before he died. Near the end, he instructed Hutchinson to give his love to Nellie and to send her a lock of his hair. It was raw and windy outside on the morning of 20 October, a week short of a year after Dodson and Nellie had been married in Milton, when Hutchinson took up his pen to write a letter to Ellen Ramseur. "He died at 27 minutes past ten AM," noted the major, still seated at Ramseur's side. "He told me to tell you that he had a firm hope in Christ and trusted to meet you hereafter. He died as became a Confederate soldier and a firm believer."[74]

EPILOGUE

The crushing news of events at Cedar Creek reached Ramseur's father and sisters at Lincolnton on 22 October. Dodson had been the "idol of the family," a grief-stricken David Schenck recorded in his diary, and his death left relatives bowed down in grief.[1] Friends and neighbors gathered on 31 October to pay tribute, reviewing Ramseur's life in Lincolnton, his years at West Point, and his service to the southern cause. Proud of his military achievements, they felt a "pall of gloom . . . thrown over our whole Confederacy by the sudden fall of so valuable an officer in the midst of his brilliant career."[2]

Ramseur's remains were slow in reaching Lincolnton. Embalmed by the Confederate surgeon at Belle Grove, dressed in uniform with the flower still in the lapel, and placed in a mahogany casket, his body had been transported to the Peninsula for return to Confederate lines.[3] On 3 November Robert Hoke learned that a party of Federals was outside the southern works near Richmond with a flag of truce and Ramseur's coffin. Hoke accompanied the body to Richmond, where it lay in state at the capitol. Next morning, 4 November, Governor William "Extra Billy" Smith, who had fought with Ramseur in the Second Corps, provided a military escort to the depot, whence the remains left for North Carolina.[4]

About noon on Sunday, 6 November, the train bearing Ramseur's body pulled into Lincolnton. Waiting citizens placed the casket in a hearse filled with flowers, decorated with Confederate flags, and drawn by a span of black horses. Preceded by a muffled drum and a military guard with arms reversed, followed by a long line of mourners, the hearse moved from the depot to the courthouse and then to the Presbyterian church. Until two o'clock Monday afternoon the open coffin lay in the church for viewing. After the funeral services the body was taken to the Hoke family's vault, pending final disposition by the Ramseurs.[5]

Ellen Richmond Ramseur and her three-week-old daughter, Mary Dodson, were unable to make the trip to Lincolnton for the funeral. From Milton they sent a bouquet of flowers to be laid on the casket. Luly Ramseur wrote her sister-in-law on 8 November, assuring her that all in Lincolnton were praying for her and the child. Luly described her brother's features as "so

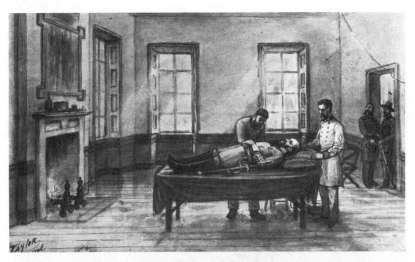

"Scene in the NE Chamber of Belle Grove House—Confederate Surgeon Embalming the Remains of General Stephen D. Ramseur, October 20th 1864." This room is actually the library, just off the main entry hall. (James E. Taylor Sketchbook, Western Reserve Historical Society.)

sweet, so peaceful, so natural, just as if he had fallen into a calm, sweet slumber" and wished Nellie had had the "sad, sweet privilege . . . of kissing his dear face once more." Physicians said the body could be preserved for several months, but Luly hoped Nellie would come as soon as possible. She enclosed the flowers that were on the body when it arrived in Lincolnton; Caleb would be bringing other "sad, sad relics," including the fatal bullet. "The whole country mourns his death, & every earthly honor is paid to him."[6]

Reaction from within the Army of Northern Virginia and elsewhere attested to the accuracy of Luly's statement. Upon receipt of Jubal Early's initial dispatch about Cedar Creek, Robert E. Lee informed Secretary of War Seddon that losses were slight but the "gallant General Ramseur was seriously wounded and fell into the hands of the enemy." Bryan Grimes spoke for the men of Ramseur's division when he wrote on 31 October that the "death of the brave and heroic soldier . . . is not only a loss to this division but to his State and the country at large. No truer or nobler spirit has been sacrificed in this . . . war."[7] On 25 October the Raleigh *Confederate* announced "his loss to our cause as a melancholy fact." W. W. Holden's *Standard*, so often criticized by Ramseur for its antiwar sentiment, proclaimed that "the gallant General Ramseur" had been tragically killed in the

An early view of the Ramseur monument on the Cedar Creek battlefield, with Belle Grove, where Ramseur died, in the background. Erected in 1920, the granite monument was unveiled by Ramseur's daughter, Mary Dodson. (Courtesy of Belle Grove, Inc.)

vain struggle against the North.[8] A Richmond paper spoke of Ramseur as the Chevalier Bayard of the Confederate army.[9]

Ramseur's soldierly qualities had been apparent from his days at West Point. Infused with a strong sense of Christian duty by his mother, and fascinated as a boy by the exploits of military figures, he had settled upon the army as the best place to begin a useful life. A staunch believer in southern rights, and in the superiority of what he perceived as the southern way of life, he easily transferred his loyalty, and with it his sense of duty, to the Confederacy.

Almost immediately his superiors marked him as a talented officer. As an artillerist on the Peninsula he impressed John B. Magruder; as a colonel at Malvern Hill he gained Lee's attention; as a brigadier he won praise from Jackson, Lee, and others. His brigade became known as one of the finest in

Grave of Stephen Dodson Ramseur, in the cemetery of the Episcopal church in Lincolnton, North Carolina. (Drawing by E. M. Sutherland.)

the army, and Lee came to rely upon him and his men. His reward was a major generalship at twenty-seven. While campaigning in the Shenandoah Valley and Maryland in summer and fall 1864 he gave promise of great success as a divisional commander.

Many factors contributed to Ramseur's rapid rise and excellent record as a soldier. By no means least were driving ambition and intense pride. In actively seeking command of the Forty-Ninth North Carolina, he cultivated the interest of influential politicians in Raleigh. Determined to make permanent his promotion to major general, he solicited David Schenck's help in again lining up political support. Sometimes he seemed more interested in the effect of a battle on his reputation and career than on the fortunes of the Confederacy. This was especially true after Stephenson's Depot, his worst failure as a combat leader. For that debacle he castigated his subordinates and soldiers, declining to accept any part of the blame. At other times, notably after Spotsylvania, he failed to give proper credit to other units and officers. He craved the approbation of superiors, and complained of unfair treatment from the press. No doubt these qualities reflected in part his youth and his slight acquaintanceship with adversity. Taken together, however, they constituted the least attractive aspect of his personality as a soldier.

Ramseur strove to reach his professional limits, and he expected no less from his men. A tough disciplinarian and drillmaster, he was unwavering in efforts to field a crack body of men that would do credit to the Confederacy and to himself. Knowing that health contributed to success on the battlefield, he insisted upon clean camps and did his best to see that his soldiers were well fed. His fearlessness in combat was "conspicuous throughout the army." Transformed by battle, he "absolutely reveled in the fierce joys of the strife, his whole being seemed to kindle and burn and glow amid the excitements of danger."[10] He never asked his men to do anything he would not attempt—a policy that resulted in his frequent wounds—and thereby won their trust. His attention to the physical well-being of his troops and his leadership by example produced a strong esprit de corps. An officer of the Second North Carolina wrote in 1864 that Ramseur was "universally beloved by every man in his brigade. No braver or better man lives than he is. He takes good care of his soldiers . . . fights hard and is very successful. His men like to fight under him."[11]

In battle Ramseur was aggressive, alert, and resolute. At Chancellorsville on 3 May he attacked with his brigade when others shrank back, bought precious time, and averted potential disaster. Anticipating the crisis in the salient at Spotsylvania, he had his regiments ready for action before the call came for them to advance. Though he had learned by mid-1863 the value of earthworks when confronting the usually more numerous Federals, the offensive was his forte. At Chancellorsville, Gettysburg, and Spotsylvania his troops delivered powerful assaults with telling effect. Ramseur's penchant for seizing the initiative, however, also contributed to his setbacks at Bethesda Church and Stephenson's Depot, where he moved forward without adequate preparation. His performances at Spotsylvania and in the Shenandoah Valley at Winchester and Cedar Creek showed that he also could defend skillfully against long odds. Indeed, as Jubal Early noted, Ramseur stood out in adverse circumstances, "a most gallant and energetic officer, whom no disaster appalled" and whose "courage and energy seemed to gain new strength in the midst of confusion and disorder."[12] A good eye for ground, as exhibited on Oak Hill at Gettysburg and during his slow withdrawal before Sheridan's divisions at Winchester, together with an artillerist's understanding of how best to use guns, enhanced his ability to function effectively in combat.

The Reverend E. H. Harding, an intimate friend during the last two years of Ramseur's life, admired his military prowess but thought his "greatest excellence was his *character as a man*."[13] He embodied virtues cherished by those of his class in the South who took seriously the concept of a gentleman.[14] Comrades lauded his personal attributes as warmly as his martial gifts. To Jubal Early he was a valued friend as well as an able lieutenant, "brave, chivalrous and capable." John B. Gordon, who considered Ramseur's record on the battlefield to be matched by "few in the Confederate army," spoke of him as "the chivalric soldier, the noble-hearted gentleman, the loving husband." Kyd Douglas declared that "aside from his ability and bravery he was one of the most attractive men in our army." Describing Ramseur as honest and gentle, Bryan Grimes termed him a "noble expression of God's handiwork."[15] Devoutly religious, loyal to friends, and devoted to his family, Ramseur displayed, in Harding's words, "all those qualities that excite the love and admiration of friends, and the respect of foes."[16] The tenderness with which Custer, du Pont, Merritt, and other Federals attended his deathbed underscored how highly men valued his friendship.

Soft-spoken and well-mannered, Ramseur delighted in the company of children and looked forward to the day when he and Nellie could raise their family in peace. He was ambivalent about a long-term career in the army, often expressing a desire to live out his life quietly as a small planter in western North Carolina. To Harding it seemed strange that "one so affectionate, so almost womanly in his feelings, should have been so completely at home amid the dreadful scenes of the battlefield."[17] Ramseur's love of the South, unquestioning support of slavery, and unwillingness to make his home under northern domination in a reunited nation dictated that he fight on. After Confederate reverses in the fall of 1864, he harbored no illusions about persuading the North to agree to an easy peace, but he believed to the last that with sacrifice the South could earn its nationhood. Willing to accept no less than independence, Ramseur gave his life in defense of a cause he believed was dedicated to ideals others saw exemplified in his own character.

NOTES

ABBREVIATIONS

Shortened titles of works found in the Bibliography and the following abbreviations are used in the notes.

BTHC — Barker Texas History Center, University of Texas, Austin.

DAB — Johnson, Allen, and Malone, Dumas, eds. *Dictionary of American Biography*. 20 vols. and index. New York, 1928–37.

DU — Duke University, William R. Perkins Library, Durham, N.C.

GDAH — Georgia Department of Archives and History, Atlanta, Ga.

NCC — North Carolina Collection, Wilson Library, University of North Carolina, Chapel Hill.

NCDAH — North Carolina Department of Archives and History, Raleigh.

OR — U.S. War Department. *The War of the Rebellion: A Compilation of the Official Records of the Union and Confederate Armies*. 127 vols., index, and atlas. Washington, D.C., 1880–1901.

Ramseur Papers SHC — Stephen Dodson Ramseur Papers, Southern Historical Collection, Wilson Library, University of North Carolina, Chapel Hill.

Schenck Diary — David Schenck Diary, David Schenck Papers, Southern Historical Collection, Wilson Library, University of North Carolina, Chapel Hill.

SHC — Southern Historical Collection, Wilson Library, University of North Carolina, Chapel Hill.

Smith Papers — William Alexander Smith Papers, William R. Perkins Library, Duke University.

PROLOGUE

1. Clark, "Address at Presentation of Portrait of Ramseur," p. 70; Wooster, *Secession Conventions of the South*, pp. 192–95; Raleigh *Register*, 22 May 1861; Warner and Yearns, *Biographical Register of the Confederate Congress*, pp. 63–64.

2. Holden, *Memoirs of W. W. Holden*, p. 17. Holden said the convention was made up of "about 70 Democrats and 50 Conservatives."

3. Clark, "Address at Presentation of Portrait of Ramseur," p. 70.

4. Raleigh *Register*, 22 May 1861.

CHAPTER 1

1. Clark and Saunders, *Colonial and State Records of North Carolina*, 8: 750–51; Sherrill, *Annals of Lincoln County*, pp. 8–9, 37, 42–43.

2. Sherrill, *Annals of Lincoln County*, pp. 36–40; DeMond, *Loyalists in North Carolina*, pp. 125–27; Graham, "The Battle of Ramsaur's Mill," pp. 20–22.

3. Sherrill, *Annals of Lincoln County*, pp. 24, 43, 68, 87, 107, 116–17, 123, 128; Clark and Saunders, *Colonial and State Records of North Carolina*, 22: 158–59; "John Wilfong, Esquire, with brief notice of the Wilfong Family," folder 11, Ramseur Papers SHC.

4. Jacob A. changed the name from Ramsour to Ramseur. Neither the date nor his reason is known.

5. Sherrill, *Annals of Lincoln County*, pp. 43, 231; genealogical data on the Dodson family compiled by, and in the possession of, Mrs. L. B. Satterfield of Milton, N.C.; Powell, *When the Past Refused to Die*; pp. xiii, 1, 118, 327, 362–64, 425, 499; Harding, "Sketch of Ramseur," p. 1.

6. Ramseur to David Schenck, 16 May 1856, folder 14, Ramseur Papers SHC. To Ramseur, then in his first year at West Point, the naming of streets sounded "*kinder* citylike."

7. Clark and Saunders, *Colonial and State Records of North Carolina*, 24: 778; Sherrill, *Annals of Lincoln County*, pp. 29, 436–43, 445, 448, 451–52; Cappon, "Iron-Making—A Forgotten Industry of North Carolina," pp. 337–38, 343, 345.

8. Cline, "The Youngest Major General: Stephen Dodson Ramseur," p. 2, among other studies, gives the number of children as six. However, the manuscript census returns for 1850 and 1860 list nine children—Mary, Stephen Dodson, David, Sallie, Lucy (nicknamed Luly), Fannie, Charles, Addie, and Harvey. All of the children except Mary lived to adulthood. U.S. Seventh Census, 1850, Schedule 1, Free Inhabitants; U.S. Eighth Census, 1860, Schedule 1, Free Inhabitants, BTHC. Lincolnton was the birthplace of three Confederate generals besides Ramseur, namely, Robert F. Hoke (born four days before Ramseur and his lifelong friend), William H. Forney, and Robert D. Johnston, and of two governors, William A. Graham of North Carolina and James Pinckney Henderson of Texas.

9. Harding, "Sketch of Ramseur," p. 1; Stedman, "Address at Unveiling Monument to Ramseur," p. 1, folder 11, Ramseur Papers SHC; Cox, *Address on Life and Charac-*

ter of Ramseur, pp. 12–13; Schenck, "Personal Recollections of General Ramseur," in *Sketches of Maj.-Gen. Stephen Dodson Ramseur*, p. 24. Schenck collected tributes, obituaries, newspaper articles, recollections, poems, and other material relating to Ramseur, had them bound as *Sketches*, and in 1892 presented the volume to Ramseur's widow. Schenck's short preface describes Ramseur as "my early companion in youth, my dearest friend in manhood, and connected with me by the strongest family tie, being my brother-in-law." The volume is in the North Carolina Collection, Wilson Library, University of North Carolina, Chapel Hill. (Hereafter abbreviated NCC.)

10. Harding, "Sketch of Ramseur," p. 9. The strong friendship between Ramseur and the Reverend Harding is discussed by Harding himself, by Stedman in his "Address at Unveiling Monument to Ramseur," Ramseur Papers SHC, and by Yarbrough in "Gen. Stephen Dodson Ramseur," NCC.

11. "Maj.-Gen. Stephen D. Ramseur," in Schenck, *Sketches*, p. 12.

12. Ibid., p. 15.

13. Schenck Diary, 23 July, 15 September, 2 October, 11, 16 November 1852, 2: 235, 237, 296, 311–13, 353, 357; 20 January, 2 May, 29 August 1853, 3: 14, 88, 178.

14. Ibid., 13, 23 July, 28 August 1852, 2: 227, 237, 278; 11 June, 25 August 1853, 3: 115, 174.

15. "Maj.-Gen. Stephen D. Ramseur," in Schenck, *Sketches*, p. 23.

16. Schenck Diary, 16 June, 7 July, 28 August, 11 September 1852, 2: 198, 221, 278, 292; 22 June 1853, 3: 125.

17. Sherrill, *Annals of Lincoln County*, pp. 284–85.

18. Schenck Diary, 28 July 1853, 3: 154.

19. Ibid., 28 December 1852, 2: 393; 6 January, 8 February 1853, 3: 4, 29.

20. "Maj.-Gen. Stephen D. Ramseur," in Schenck, *Sketches*, p. 23.

21. Ibid.

22. Harding, "Sketch of Ramseur," p. 10; Cox, *Address on Life and Character of Ramseur*, pp. 12–13.

23. *DAB*, s.v. "Ramseur, Stephen Dodson"; Schenck Diary, 6 May 1850, 1: 44; Sherrill, *Annals of Lincoln County*, pp. 451–53.

24. Schenck Diary, 15, 17, 22, 30 June, 11 September, 28 December 1852, 2: 196–97, 199, 204–5, 213, 289, 393.

25. Ramseur to Luly Ramseur, 13 February 1860, Ramseur to Ellen Richmond, 24 February 1860, folder 6, Ramseur Papers SHC.

26. Harding, "Sketch of Ramseur," p. 1; Cox, *Address on Life and Character of Ramseur*, p. 13; *DAB*, s.v. "Ramseur, Stephen Dodson."

27. Schenck Diary, 29 September 1853, 3: 198.

28. Shaw, *Davidson College*, pp. 67–70; Bridges, *Lee's Maverick General*, pp. 23–24.

29. Ramseur to Luly Ramseur, 17 October 1853, folder 6, Ramseur Papers SHC.

30. Shaw, *Davidson College*, p. 68; Ramseur to Lucy Dodson Ramseur, 27 June 1854, folder 6, Ramseur Papers SHC.

31. Ramseur to Luly Ramseur, 17 October 1853, folder 6, Ramseur Papers SHC.

32. Schenck Diary, 30 June 1854, 4: 22.

33. Ramseur to Lucy Dodson Ramseur, 24 July 1854, folder 6, Ramseur Papers SHC.

34. Ibid., 27 June 1854.

35. "Maj.-Gen. Stephen D. Ramseur," in Schenck, *Sketches*, pp. 13–14.

36. Schenck Diary, 26 February, 15 August, 22 December 1854, 11, 20 March 1855, 4: 9, 26, 56, 61–62.

37. Bridges, *Lee's Maverick General*, pp. 23–24; Ramseur to Lucy Dodson Ramseur, 27 June 1854, folder 6, Ramseur Papers SHC.

38. Stedman, "Address at Unveiling Monument to Ramseur," pp. 1–2, Ramseur Papers SHC; Cox, *Address on Life and Character of Ramseur*, p. 13. Lincoln County was in Craige's district, and he doubtless was mindful of the large Democratic majorities the county habitually voted. In 1853, when Craige was called an enemy of the Union for making southern rights an issue, Lincoln County had supported him. Sitterson, *The Secessionist Movement in North Carolina*, pp. 127, 175 n. 152, 176; Burnham, *Presidential Ballots 1836–1892*, pp. 205, 650, 658.

39. Ramseur to Schenck, 17 March 1855, folder 14, Ramseur Papers SHC.

CHAPTER 2

1. Ambrose, *Duty, Honor, Country*, pp. 87–89, 126–32. Ambrose quotes Cadet Cullen Bryant, who thought West Point covered more ground in one month than the ordinary college did in three, and Cadet Henry A. du Pont, who found the Academy at least twice as demanding as the University of Pennsylvania.

2. Ibid., p. 128; Schaff, *Spirit of Old West Point*, p. 38; *Centennial of United States Military Academy at West Point*, 1: 225–26, 228. (Hereafter cited as *Centennial History*.)

3. Wilson, *Under the Old Flag*, 1: 7.

4. Ambrose, *Duty, Honor, Country*, pp. 125, 145; "Report of the Commission . . . of June 21, 1860 to examine . . . West Point," pp. 56–57. (Hereafter cited as "Report of West Point Commission.")

5. Lucy Dodson Ramseur to Ramseur, 1 June 1855, Ramseur to Lucy Dodson Ramseur, 15 August 1855, folder 6, Ramseur Papers SHC.

6. Ambrose, *Duty, Honor, Country*, pp. 134, 141; *Centennial History*, 1: 229–30.

7. Ramseur to Schenck, 23 August 1855, folder 14, Ramseur Papers SHC.

8. Ibid., Ramseur to Lucy Dodson Ramseur, 15 August 1855, folder 6.

9. Ibid., Ramseur to Schenck, 23 August 1855, folder 14. The pressure to perform well in mathematics made life miserable for many cadets, one of whom, James J. Ewing, committed his views on the subject to the flyleaf of his calculus book: "God damn all mathematics to the lowest depths of hell!!" Forman, *West Point: A History*, p. 86.

10. Ramseur to Lucy Dodson Ramseur, 15 August 1855, Ramseur to Jacob A. Ramseur, 30 August 1855, folder 6, Ramseur Papers SHC.

11. Ibid., Ramseur to Schenck, 23 August 1855, Ramseur to Jacob A. Ramseur, 30 August 1855, folders 14, 6.

12. Ibid., Ramseur to Schenck, 27 October 1855, 19 January 1856, Ramseur to Lucy Dodson Ramseur, 30 September 1855.

13. Ibid., Ramseur to Jacob A. Ramseur, 2 February 1856, folder 6; Special Orders No. 20, 29 January 1856, included in summary of *Post Orders, 1856–1860* relating to Ramseur supplied by U.S. Military Academy Archives, West Point, N.Y. (Hereafter cited as *Post Orders*.)

14. Ramseur to Lucy Dodson Ramseur, 15 August 1855, folder 6, Ramseur Papers SHC.

15. Ibid., Ramseur to Schenck, 12 April, 16 May 1856, folder 14.

16. Ibid., 27 October 1855, Ramseur to Jacob A. Ramseur, 2 February 1856, folders 14, 6.

17. Ibid., Ramseur to Schenck, 27 October 1855, 12 April 1856, folder 14.

18. Ibid., 12 April 1856, folder 14; *Post Orders*, Special Orders No. 32, 1 March 1856.

19. Academic record for Ramseur's fifth-class year extracted from the *Official Registers, 1856–1860*, U.S. Military Academy Archives, West Point, N.Y. (Hereafter cited as "Extracts from *Official Registers*.")

20. Ramseur to Schenck, 16 May 1856, folder 14, Ramseur Papers SHC.

21. Ibid., 12 April 1856, folder 14; *Post Orders*, Special Orders No. 83, 12 June 1856.

22. Ambrose, "West Point in the Fifties," pp. 293–97, 299, 306; Hughes, *General William J. Hardee*, pp. 56–57.

23. Ramseur to Schenck, 2 May 1856, folder 14, Ramseur Papers SHC.

24. U.S. Sixth Census, 1840; U.S. Seventh Census, 1850, Schedule 2, Slave Inhabitants, BTHC.

25. Ramseur to Luly Ramseur, 17 October 1853, folder 6, Ramseur Papers SHC.

26. Ibid., Ramseur to Schenck, 22 July, 13 September 1856, folder 14.

27. Ibid., 8 November 1856, 9 November [1856].

28. Ibid., 8 November 1856.

29. Schaff, *Spirit of Old West Point*, p. 37; Ambrose, *Duty, Honor, Country*, p. 126; Ambrose, "West Point in the Fifties," p. 301.

30. Ramseur to Schenck, 8 November 1856, folder 14, Ramseur Papers SHC.

31. Ibid., 13 September 1856, 6 April 1857.

32. Schaff, *Spirit of Old West Point*, pp. 138–39; Wilson, *Under the Old Flag*, 1: 20–21; Longacre, *From Union Stars to Top Hat*, p. 33.

33. Ramseur to Schenck, 6 April 1857, Ramseur to Lucy Dodson Ramseur, 16 May 1857, folders 14, 6, Ramseur Papers SHC.

34. "Extracts from *Official Registers*" for Ramseur's fourth-class year; *Post Orders*, Special Orders, 16 June 1857.

35. *Post Orders*, Special Orders No. 119, 28 August 1857.

36. Ramseur to Schenck, 8 November 1857, folder 15, Ramseur Papers SHC.

37. "Extracts from *Official Registers*" for Ramseur's third-class year; Ramseur to Lucy Dodson Ramseur, 12 December 1856, folder 6, Ramseur Papers SHC.

38. Ramseur to Schenck, 28 February 1858, folder 15, Ramseur Papers SHC. Boredom was a common complaint among the cadets. Henry du Pont explained to

his mother in November 1856 that he wrote so little because "there is absolutely nothing unusual to tell you in this monotonous life." Ambrose, "West Point in the Fifties," p. 302.

39. Ambrose, *Duty, Honor, Country*, pp. 161–62; record of Ramseur's demerits extracted from the West Point *Register of Delinquency, 1856–1860*, U.S. Military Academy Archives, West Point, N.Y. (Hereafter cited as "Extracts from *Register of Delinquency*.") The use of tobacco was widespread at West Point. Ambrose quotes an ode to Lieutenant Cadmus Marcellus Wilcox, a member of the faculty who donned rubber-soled shoes to sneak up on unsuspecting cadets: "I hear the old rascal upon the stairs; / In spite of his rubbers, I hear him there. / He stole! He stole! He stole my pipe away!"

40. Ambrose, *Duty, Honor, Country*, pp. 162–64; Strode, *Jefferson Davis*, pp. 42–43.

41. Ramseur to Schenck, 12 April 1856, folder 14, Ramseur Papers SHC; Rowland, "Letters of a Virginia Cadet at West Point," *South Atlantic Quarterly* 14 (October 1915): 338.

42. Hughes, *General William J. Hardee*, pp. 57–58.

43. Ramseur to Schenck, 27 October 1855, folder 14, Ramseur Papers SHC.

44. Ambrose, *Duty, Honor, Country*, pp. 154–55, 163; "Report of the West Point Commission," pp. 110–11.

45. Ramseur to Luly Ramseur, 14 March 1858, Ramseur to Schenck, 24 May 1858, folders 6, 15, Ramseur Papers SHC.

46. Nearly all of Ramseur's letters touch on religion in some way. See for example Ramseur to Lucy Dodson Ramseur, 15 August 1855, and 30 September 1855, folder 6, Ramseur Papers SHC.

47. Ambrose, *Upton and the Army*, p. 7; Rowland, "Letters of a Virginia Cadet at West Point," *South Atlantic Quarterly* 15 (January 1916): 3; Ramseur to Schenck, 21 May 1857, folder 15, Ramseur Papers SHC.

48. Howard, *Autobiography of Oliver Otis Howard*, 1: 91–92; Schaff, *Spirit of Old West Point*, pp. 70–71.

49. Ramseur to Schenck, 24, 28 January, 27 March, 24 May 1858, folder 15, Ramseur Papers SHC.

50. Ibid., Ramseur to Schenck, 5 January 1859.

51. Ibid., Ramseur to Schenck, 8 November 1857, 24 January 1858. Jacob Ramseur's losses were substantial: the manuscript returns of the 1850 census list him as a merchant with twenty slaves and $14,000 in real property; the 1860 returns list him as a clerk in a cotton mill with eleven slaves and $2,500 in real property. U.S. Seventh and Eighth Census, 1850 and 1860, BTHC.

52. Ramseur to Schenck, 28 February, 27 March 1858, folder 15, Ramseur Papers SHC.

53. Ibid., 24 January 1858.

54. Ibid., 28 February, 27 March 1858, Ramseur to Luly Ramseur, 14 March 1858, folders 15, 6.

55. "Extracts from *Official Registers*" for Ramseur's third-class year.

56. *Post Orders*, Special Orders No. 81, 14 June 1858, Special Orders No. 118, 28 August 1858.

57. Schaff, *Spirit of Old West Point*, pp. 54–56; Wilson, *Under the Old Flag*, 1: 19–20.

58. Steiner, "Medical-Military Studies on the Civil War," pp. 1016–17. Steiner notes that Ramseur appears on the West Point sick list thirty-seven times. This number exceeded the average, but Steiner believes the diagnoses show a "concern with his health rather than poor health."

59. Ramseur to Schenck, 15 September, 20 November 1858, folder 15, Ramseur Papers SHC.

60. Ibid., 15 September 1858.

61. "Extracts from *Official Registers*" for Ramseur's second-class year.

62. Ramseur to Schenck, 2, 20 November 1858, 1 March 1859, folder 15, Ramseur Papers SHC. Although Ramseur's ranking at West Point was too low for him to enter the army engineers, Academy graduates of comparable standing often had successful careers as civil engineers or teachers.

63. Ibid., 15 September, 20 November 1858.

64. Ibid., Ramseur to Luly Ramseur, 14 November 1858, Ramseur to Schenck, 5 January 1859, folders 6, 15.

65. *Post Orders*, Special Orders No. 7, 17 January 1859. The other cadets involved were James H. Wilson, Horace Porter, Benjamin F. Sloan, and Alfred T. Smith.

66. Wilson, *Under the Old Flag*, 1: 10–11.

67. Ramseur to Schenck, 8 April 1859, folder 15, Ramseur Papers SHC; Schenck Diary, 12 April 1859, 4: 140–41.

68. Ramseur to Schenck, 29 April 1859, folder 15, Ramseur Papers SHC; Ambrose, *Duty, Honor, Country*, p. 141.

69. "Extracts from *Official Registers*" for Ramseur's second-class year; *Post Orders*, Special Orders No. 117, 11 July 1859.

70. *Post Orders*, Special Orders No. 109, 30 June 1859. On 27 July, Special Orders No. 132 canceled Ramseur's appointment as lieutenant because of absence without leave from the Academy. This is puzzling, for on 11 July Ramseur had received thirty days' furlough.

71. Schenck Diary, 25 August 1859, 4: 152–53.

72. *Post Orders*, Special Orders No. 147, 23 August 1859.

73. See du Pont, *Address of September 16, 1920*, pp. 2–4; Wesley Merritt to Mary Dodson Ramseur, 8 November [?], folder 3, Ramseur Papers SHC.

74. Schaff, *Spirit of Old West Point*, pp. 143–46.

75. Ramseur to Luly Ramseur, 10 October 1859, folder 6, Ramseur Papers SHC.

76. Schenck Diary, 25 November 1859, 4: 159; Ramseur to Ellen Richmond, 24 February 1860, folder 6, Ramseur Papers SHC.

77. Ramseur to Lucy Dodson Ramseur, 30 September 1855, folder 6, Ramseur Papers SHC.

78. Ibid., Ramseur to Schenck, 27 October 1855, 27 March 1858, folders 14, 15.

79. Ibid., Ramseur to Jacob A. Ramseur, 1 January 1860, Ramseur to Ellen Richmond, 24 February 1860, folder 6.

80. "Extracts from *Official Registers*" for Ramseur's first-class year.

81. Ramseur to Luly Ramseur, 13 February 1860, Ramseur to Ellen Richmond, 24 February 1860, folder 6, Ramseur Papers SHC.

82. Ibid., Ramseur to Luly Ramseur, 28 January, 13, 28 February 1860.

83. Certificate of membership in the Dialectic Society dated 1 January 1860, in Ramseur Papers NCDAH. See also Ambrose, *Duty, Honor, Country*, pp. 137–38. John Pelham of Alabama was president of the Dialectic Society at that time.

84. Zotos, "Class of 1861," pp. 9–11. This farewell party brought together a number of men who would make great reputations during the Civil War. Ramseur, Custer, Merritt, Rosser, and Ames rose to the rank of major general; Pelham, who left West Point in 1861 before graduating, became a renowned artillerist.

85. *Post Orders*, Orders No. 18, 14 June 1860.

86. "Extracts from *Official Registers*" for Ramseur's first-class year.

87. Cullum, *Biographical Register of West Point*, 2: 494–519; Schaff, *Spirit of Old West Point*, p. 129. Schaff calls the chapel the most admired building on the campus.

88. Benjamin Sloan to Mary Dodson Ramseur, 10 December 1898, folder 3, Ramseur Papers SHC.

89. Ibid., Ramseur to Luly Ramseur, 28 February 1860, folder 6.

90. Shepherd, "Gallant Sons of North Carolina," pp. 413–14; Henry E. Shepherd to Mary Dodson Ramseur, 15 March 1922, folder 11, Ramseur Papers SHC. In this letter Shepherd claimed that his recollection of Ramseur's face and form was "almost perfect." "If I were an artist," he wrote, "I could reproduce his features and expression from my boyish memory."

91. Ramseur to Luly Ramseur, 16 April 1860, folder 6, Ramseur Papers SHC.

92. Commission to date from 1 July 1860, signed by Secretary of War John B. Floyd on 2 July 1860, in Ramseur Papers NCDAH.

93. "Report of the West Point Commission," pp. 93–94.

94. Birkhimer, *Historical Sketch of the Artillery*, pp. 125–26.

95. "Maj.-Gen. Stephen D. Ramseur," in Schenck, *Sketches*, pp. 9–10.

96. Randall and Donald, *The Civil War and Reconstruction*, p. 184.

97. Ibid., p. 187.

98. Commission to date from 1 February 1861, signed by Abraham Lincoln and Secretary of War Simon Cameron on 19 March 1861, in Ramseur Papers NCDAH.

99. *DAB*, s.v. "Ramseur, Stephen Dodson."

100. Lorenzo Thomas to Abraham Lincoln, 8 April 1861, Ramseur Papers NCDAH. Ramseur was relieved of duty on 5 April and officially resigned 6 April.

101. Cox, *Address on Life and Character of Ramseur*, p. 14.

CHAPTER 3

1. Ellis, *Papers of John W. Ellis*, 2: 627.

2. Adjutant and Inspector General's Office, Montgomery, Ala., Special Orders No. 32, 22 April 1861, signed by Samuel Cooper, in Ramseur Papers NCDAH.

3. Ellis, *Papers of John W. Ellis*, 2: 664.

4. Ramsay, "Additional Sketch Tenth Regiment," p. 551.

5. Ellis, *Papers of John W. Ellis*, 1: 267.

6. Cox, *Address on Life and Character of Ramseur*, p. 14; Stedman, "Address at Unveiling Monument to Ramseur," p. 2, Ramseur Papers SHC.

7. Raleigh *Register*, 1 May 1861.

8. Cox, *Address on Life and Character of Ramseur*, pp. 14–16; Manarin, *North Carolina Troops*, 1: 40–41.

9. Commission as major in the Corps of Artillery and Engineers in the North Carolina State Troops to date from 16 May 1861, signed by P. Cowper and Henry T. Clark on 26 August 1861, in Ramseur Papers NCDAH.

10. Ramsay, "Additional Sketch Tenth Regiment," pp. 551–52; Manarin, *North Carolina Troops*, 1: 41.

11. Raleigh *Register*, 1 May, 17 July 1861.

12. "Maj.-Gen. Stephen D. Ramseur," in Schenck, *Sketches*, p. 10.

13. Edmondston, *"Journal of a Secesh Lady,"* p. 63. For a fuller account of this episode, see Prologue.

14. Ellis, *Papers of John W. Ellis*, 2: 887.

15. Raleigh *Register*, 17 July 1861.

16. Harding, "Sketch of Ramseur," p. 2.

17. Raleigh *Register*, 17 July 1861.

18. U.S. War Department, *War of the Rebellion*, ser. I, 2: 996–97. (Hereafter cited as *OR*; all citations are to series I.)

19. Schenck Diary, 27 July 1861, 5: 29; Raleigh *Register*, 31 July 1861.

20. Ramseur to Schenck, 7, [8] September 1861, folder 16, Ramseur Papers SHC; Cox, *Address on Life and Character of Ramseur*, p. 16; Harding, "Sketch of Ramseur," p. 2.

21. Harding, "Sketch of Ramseur," p. 3; Ramseur to Schenck, [8] September 1861, folder 16, Ramseur Papers SHC.

22. Stephen Dodson Richmond to Ellen Richmond, 25 September 1861, folder 6, Ramseur Papers SHC.

23. Pemberton, *Pemberton: Defender of Vicksburg*, p. 27; Smith, *Anson Guards*, p. 39.

24. Ramseur to Schenck, 11 March 1862, folder 16, Ramseur Papers SHC. Officially the *U.S.S. Merrimac* became the *C.S.S. Virginia*, but Ramseur and most other Confederates referred to the vessel by its original name.

25. Ramseur to Schenck, 7 September 1861, 11 March 1862, folder 16, Ramseur Papers SHC.

26. *OR*, 9: 44–45, 58–59; Settles, "The Military Career of Magruder," p. 188.

27. Ramseur to Schenck, 11 March 1862, folder 16, Ramseur Papers SHC.

28. Settles, "The Military Career of Magruder," pp. 189–90.

29. Ramseur to Schenck, 5 April 1862, folder 16, Ramseur Papers SHC.

30. "Maj.-Gen. Stephen D. Ramseur," in Schenck, *Sketches*, p. 10.

31. Settles, "The Military Career of Magruder," pp. 190–91.

32. Manarin, *North Carolina Troops*, 1: 41.

33. "Maj.-Gen. Stephen D. Ramseur," in Schenck, *Sketches*, p. 10; Ramseur to Schenck, 5 April 1862, folder 16, Ramseur Papers SHC. Allen B. Magruder, the staff officer who met the Ellis Light Artillery and commented on its appearance, wrote of his impressions in October 1864.

34. Settles, "The Military Career of Magruder," p. 194; Freeman, *R. E. Lee*, 2: 18.

35. Ramsay, "Additional Sketch Tenth Regiment," p. 552.

36. Ramseur to Schenck, 25 April 1862, folder 16, Ramseur Papers SHC.

37. Ibid., Stephen Dodson Richmond to "My Dear Brother," 24 March 1862, folder 6. "Cousin Dod started home last Saturday," wrote Richmond. "There is some probability of his being promoted while in N.C." If so, he would attach Stephen and another cousin, Caleb Richmond, to his command.

38. Ellis, *Papers of John W. Ellis*, 2: 802. Cox, *Address on Life and Character of Ramseur*, p. 17, and Stedman, "Address at Unveiling Monument to Ramseur," p. 2, Ramseur Papers SHC, mistakenly say Ramseur's election to a lieutenant colonelcy in the Third North Carolina came in May 1862.

39. Thomas Ruffin, Jr., to Ramseur, 26 March 1862, D. M. Barringer to Ramseur, 21 April 1862, Ramseur Papers NCDAH; Ramseur to Schenck, 5 April 1862, folder 16, Ramseur Papers SHC.

40. Schenck Diary, 27 April 1862, 4: 229; Commission to date from 12 April 1862, signed by P. Cowper and Henry T. Clark on 28 April 1862, in Ramseur Papers NCDAH.

41. Roulhac, "Forty-Ninth Regiment," pp. 125–26.

42. Ramseur to Schenck, 21 May 1862, folder 16, Ramseur Papers SHC.

43. Ibid.

44. Ibid., 1 June 1862.

45. Ibid., 5 June 1862.

46. Ibid., 11 June 1862. Butler's General Order No. 28, issued in New Orleans on 15 May 1862 and subsequently known as the "Woman Order," made him a great villain in the South. It stated that any southern woman who insulted a Federal officer would be "regarded and held liable to be treated as a woman of the town plying her avocation." Boatner, *Civil War Dictionary*, p. 945.

47. Ibid., 23 June 1862.

48. Dowdey, *Seven Days*, pp. 132, 159–60; *OR*, 11, pt. 2: 792.

49. On the southern side of the Seven Days' Campaign see, in addition to Dowdey, Freeman, *Lee's Lieutenants*, 1: 489–669.

50. *OR*, 11, pt. 2: 792.

51. Longstreet, *From Manassas to Appomattox*, p. 142; Hill, "McClellan's Change of Base and Malvern Hill," pp. 391–92.

52. For descriptions of the ground at Malvern Hill see *OR*, 11, pt. 2: 811–12; Freeman, *Lee's Lieutenants*, 2: 582–84; Dowdey, *Seven Days*, pp. 323–25.

53. Henderson, *Stonewall Jackson*, 2: 61; Hill, "McClellan's Change of Base and Malvern Hill," pp. 391–92; Dowdey, *Seven Days*, pp. 316–17.

54. *OR*, 11, pt. 2: 496.

55. Ibid.; Wise, *The Long Arm of Lee*, 1: 230–31.

56. *OR*, 11, pt. 2: 670, 643.

57. Fitz-John Porter, "The Battle of Malvern Hill," pp. 409, 417; Hill, "McClellan's Change of Base and Malvern Hill," p. 394.

58. *OR*, 11, pt. 2: 794–95. Cox, *Address on Life and Character of Ramseur*, p. 18, says that Ramseur sustained a "severe and disabling wound" in which the arm was broken. According to David Schenck's diary, 19 July 1862, 4: 238, the ball severed the "median nerve" and paralyzed the arm. Steiner, "Medical-Military Studies on the Civil War," p. 1017, believes that in this case the lay term "paralysis" probably "represents bone and soft part damage rather than a nerve injury."

59. Cox, *Address on Life and Character of Ramseur*, p. 18; Harding, "Sketch of Ramseur," p. 3. After Ramseur left the battlefield, a part of his regiment, "men of firm soul who were unwilling to accept defeat," attached themselves to Paul Semmes's brigade and again risked their lives on the slopes of Malvern Hill. At nine o'clock Semmes fell back, ending the struggle of 1 July. Hill, *Bethel to Sharpsburg*, 2: 174.

60. *OR*, 11, pt. 2: 795. Ramseur had 517 men fit for duty on 23 June and presumably about 500 at Malvern Hill. Ramseur to Schenck, 23 June 1862, folder 16, Ramseur Papers SHC.

61. Putnam, *Richmond During the Confederacy*, pp. 151–54.

62. Harding, "Sketch of Ramseur," p. 3.

63. Ramseur to Jacob A. Ramseur, [2] July 1862, folder 16, Ramseur Papers SHC. David Schenck had received from D. F. Chambers a dispatch dated 27 June 1862, sent 28 June 1862: "Rumor says Col. Ramseur of the forty-ninth N.C. is killed. It is not so he is well & all the members of his staff." Folder 16, Ramseur Papers SHC.

64. Special Orders No. 59, 10 July 1862, in Ramseur Papers NCDAH.

65. *OR*, 11, pt. 2: 795. Ransom's report is dated 11 July 1862.

66. Raleigh *Register*, 30 July 1862. This controversy arose during the gubernatorial contest between Zebulon Vance and William Johnston. W. W. Holden's *Standard*, supporting Vance, sought to magnify his role at Malvern Hill.

67. Schenck Diary, 19 July 1862, 4: 238.

68. Ramseur to Schenck, 21 May, 11, 23 June 1862, folder 16, Ramseur Papers SHC.

69. *OR*, 19, pt. 2: 683–84.

70. Ramseur to Schenck, 11 June 1862, folder 16, Ramseur Papers SHC.

71. Ibid., 27 October 1862; "Recollections of Ramseur," in Schenck, *Sketches*, p. 24.

72. Steiner, "Medical-Military Studies on the Civil War," p. 1017.

73. Harding, "Sketch of Ramseur," p. 4; Cox, *Address on Life and Character of Ramseur*, p. 18. According to Harding and Cox, Ramseur went to Richmond in October 1862 to make a decision about the offer of George B. Anderson's brigade. Actually, the known sequence is that Anderson died in Raleigh on 16 October; Ramseur

left Lincolnton 18 October, reaching Richmond on 25 October; and Lee sent his
name to the secretary of war 27 October. But Ramseur wrote Schenck at length on
27 October and did not mention promotion. It seems clear that he went to Richmond
for the purpose of seeing Dr. Gibson, learned in Richmond of Lee's action, and subsequently went to see the president.

74. Commission to date from 1 November 1862, in Ramseur Papers NCDAH; *OR*,
19, pt. 2: 698–99.

75. L. M. McAfee to Ramseur, 11 November 1862, John K. Ruffin to Ramseur, [?]
November 1862, J. W. Wilson to Ramseur, 10, 16 November 1862, Ramseur Papers
NCDAH.

76. Draft of thanks to Forty-Ninth North Carolina, [?] November 1862, Ramseur
Papers NCDAH.

77. Ramseur to Ellen Richmond, 25 December 1862, folder 6, Ramseur Papers
SHC.

78. Collier, *Representative Women of the South*, 2: 57.

79. Ramseur to Ellen Richmond, 25 December 1862, 1 January 1863, folders 6, 7,
Ramseur Papers SHC.

80. Grimes, *Extracts of Letters*, p. 27.

81. For an appraisal of Rodes's career prior to Chancellorsville, see Freeman,
Lee's Lieutenants, 1: 247–48.

82. "Maj.-Gen. Stephen D. Ramseur," in Schenck, *Sketches*, p. 7.

83. Ramseur to Ellen Richmond, 11 February 1863, folder 7, Ramseur Papers
SHC.

84. Ibid., 29 January 1863.

85. Manly, "Second Regiment," p. 169; Ramseur to Ellen Richmond, 12, 22 February 1863, folder 7, Ramseur Papers SHC.

86. Ramseur to Ellen Richmond, 21 March 1863, folder 7, Ramseur Papers SHC.

87. Bennett, "Fourteenth Regiment," pp. 713–14. For discussion of morale in the
Army of the Potomac at this time, see Adams, *Our Masters the Rebels*, pp. 139–40.

88. Ramseur to Ellen Richmond, 8, 11, 12, 17 February 1863, folder 7, Ramseur
Papers SHC.

89. Ibid., 28 February, 5, 11 April 1863.

90. Ibid., 8, 28 February 1863.

91. Ibid., 14 April 1863.

92. Ibid., Ramseur to Schenck, 29 April 1863, folder 16.

CHAPTER 4

1. Hotchkiss, *Make Me a Map*, pp. 135–36.
2. *OR*, 25, pt. 1: 939, 995.
3. Ibid., p. 796.
4. Lee, "Chancellorsville—Address," p. 561.
5. *OR*, 25, pt. 1, 796–97.

6. Livermore, *Numbers and Losses*, pp. 98–99.

7. Lee, "Chancellorsville—Address," p. 562.

8. Hotchkiss, *Make Me a Map*, p. 136.

9. Lee, "Chancellorsville—Address," p. 562; *OR*, 25, pt. 1: 797.

10. *OR*, 25, pt. 1: 995, 939.

11. Hotchkiss, *Make Me a Map*, pp. 136, 139.

12. Stiles, *Four Years Under Marse Robert*, pp. 166–69. Stiles was an artillery-man with McLaws's division. Ordered off the Plank Road to allow Jackson's infantry to pass, he thought he "had never seen anything equal to the swinging, silent stride with which they fairly devoured the ground."

13. *OR*, 25, pt. 1: 939.

14. Bigelow, *Campaign of Chancellorsville*, p. 347; Catton, *Glory Road*, p. 166. George Gordon Meade, who commanded Hooker's V Corps, was pleased with Hooker's progress on 30 April but impatient "to get into the open country beyond" Chancellorsville. He and the other Union generals felt uncomfortable in the gloomy woods of the Wilderness. Cleaves, *Meade of Gettysburg*, pp. 105–6.

15. *OR*, 25, pt. 1: 796–97.

16. Ibid., pp. 797, 940.

17. Ibid., p. 995; Smith, "Stonewall Jackson's Last Battle," p. 204.

18. *OR*, 25, pt. 1: 940; Hotchkiss, *Make Me a Map*, p. 137; Parker, "Thirtieth Regiment," p. 500; Grimes, *Extracts of Letters*, p. 29.

19. *OR*, 25, pt. 1: 995; Raleigh *Register*, 16 May 1863.

20. McLendon, "Reminiscences," 1 May, Smith Papers DU. W. A. Smith used Mc-Lendon's reminiscences in writing *The Anson Guards*, cited several times herein.

21. *OR*, 25, pt. 1: 995; Bigelow, *Campaign of Chancellorsville*, p. 256, map 15.

22. Caldwell, *History of McGowan's Brigade*, p. 74.

23. Manly, "Second Regiment," p. 169; *OR*, 25, pt. 2: 328; Raleigh *Register*, 16 May 1863.

24. Lee, "Chancellorsville—Address," pp. 567–68; Henderson, *Stonewall Jackson*, 2: 429–32; Talcott, "General Lee's Strategy at Chancellorsville," pp. 9–10, 16–17.

25. *OR*, 25, pt. 1: 940, 995, 798.

26. Hotchkiss, *Make Me a Map*, p. 139; Bennett, "Fourteenth Regiment," p. 715; Casler, *Four Years in the Stonewall Brigade*, pp. 142–43; Caldwell, *History of Mc-Gowan's Brigade*, p. 76; McLendon, "Reminiscences," 2 May, Smith Papers DU.

27. *OR*, 25, pt. 1: 798; Henderson, *Stonewall Jackson*, 2: 434–35.

28. Lee, "Chancellorsville—Address," pp. 571–72.

29. *OR*, 25, pt. 1: 940–41, 995, 798; Smith, "Stonewall Jackson's Last Battle," p. 208. Melzi Chancellor's place was also known as Dowdall's Tavern.

30. *OR*, 25, pt. 1: 941–42, 798, 885; Lee, "Chancellorsville—Address," pp. 573–74.

31. *OR*, 25, pt. 1: 995; Bigelow, *Campaign of Chancellorsville*, pp. 298, 308.

32. Hotchkiss, *Virginia*, pp. 385–86; Freeman, *Lee's Lieutenants*, 2: 567, 570; *OR*, 25, pt. 1: 942–43, 887, 792.

33. Bigelow, *Campaign of Chancellorsville*, pp. 317, 328, 344, map 24.

34. Hotchkiss, *Make Me a Map*, p. 140.

35. *OR*, 25, pt. 1: 887, 943, 995; Bigelow, *Campaign of Chancellorsville*, map 24.

36. *OR*, 25, pt. 1: 887, 943, 995; Bigelow, *Campaign of Chancellorsville*, pp. 346–56.

37. Wise, *Long Arm of Lee*, 2: 508–9.

38. *OR*, 25, pt. 1: 943; Freeman, *Lee's Lieutenants*, 2: 594.

39. Grimes, *Extracts of Letters*, pp. 32–33; Lane, "History of Lane's Brigade," p. 496.

40. *OR*, 25, pt. 1: 995–96; Ramseur to J. H. S. Funk, 22 May 1863, Ramseur Papers NCDAH.

41. Manly, "Second Regiment," p. 170; Stedman, "Address at Unveiling Monument to Ramseur," p. 3, Ramseur Papers SHC; Osborne, "Fourth Regiment," p. 251.

42. Grimes, *Extracts of Letters*, p. 32.

43. *OR*, 25, pt. 1: 1013, 996; Raleigh *Register*, 16 May 1863; Bennett, "Fourteenth Regiment," p. 716; Osborne, "Fourth Regiment," p. 251.

44. *OR*, 25, pt. 1: 996, 944.

45. Smith, *Anson Guards*, p. 182; McIntosh, "Campaign of Chancellorsville," p. 89.

46. *OR*, 25, pt. 1: 944, 1017, 966; Terry, "Stonewall Brigade," p. 366; Parker, "Thirtieth Regiment," p. 501. Ramseur's official report did not credit the Stonewall Brigade with helping the Thirtieth North Carolina cover his right flank. Freeman's suggestion (*Lee's Lieutenants*, 2: 597 n. 72) that Ramseur did not know of the Virginians' contribution can hardly be right, for he had corresponded with Funk before he wrote his report. Almost certainly Ramseur was unwilling to share credit for holding the Confederate line, and he probably was influenced by two beliefs about the Virginia troops, namely, that they received excessively generous treatment in the press, and that a portion of the Stonewall Brigade was among the skulkers behind Slocum's works.

47. *OR*, 25, pt. 1: 996.

48. North Carolina (Raleigh) *Standard*, 19 May 1863; Raleigh *Register*, 16 May 1863.

49. Ledford, *Reminiscences*, pp. 75–76; *OR*, 25, pt. 1: 996–97.

50. *OR*, 25, pt. 1: 945, 997.

51. Ibid., pp. 947, 997–98; Manly, "Second Regiment," pp. 170–71; Steiner, "Medical-Military Studies on the Civil War," p. 1018; Ramseur to Schenck, 10 [May] 1863, folder 16, Ramseur Papers SHC. In the 20 May 1863 Raleigh *Register*, Ramseur's casualty list takes up three full columns. According to Fox, *Regimental Losses*, p. 558, only three brigades in Lee's army ever were harder hit in a single battle.

52. *OR*, 25, pt. 1: 997, 886.

53. Ramseur to Schenck, 10 [May] 1863, folder 16, Ramseur Papers SHC; *OR*, 25, pt. 1: 889, 946, 944, 997, *OR*, 27, pt. 3: 871–72. Secretary of War James A. Seddon sent a similar letter to Vance and directed the Conscript Bureau to assign conscripts to Ramseur's brigade until its strength equaled the average of the other North Carolina brigades. Seddon wrote Lee that he hoped by this means to bring new recruits under "the inspiring influence" of the "valor and discipline" of Ramseur's brigade (ibid., pp. 874–75).

54. *OR*, 25, pt. 1: 997–98.

55. Steiner, "Medical-Military Studies on the Civil War," p. 1018.

56. Ramseur to Schenck, 10 [May] 1863, Ramseur to Ellen Richmond, 17 May 1863, folders 16, 7, Ramseur Papers SHC; Ramseur to J. H. S. Funk, 22 May 1863, Ramseur Papers NCDAH.

57. J. H. S. Funk to Ramseur, 9 May 1863, Ramseur Papers NCDAH. Funk, colonel of the Fifth Virginia, had assumed command of the Stonewall Brigade upon the death of General Elisha F. Paxton the morning of 3 May.

58. Ramseur to J. H. S. Funk, 22 May 1863, Ramseur Papers NCDAH.

59. *OR*, 25, pt. 1: 996. On 19 May the Richmond *Enquirer* absolved the Stonewall Brigade of all guilt. Four days later a friend wrote Ramseur from Charlotte that he had drafted a piece for circulation among Carolina newspapers in which he "attempted to place you and your brigade right as I learned it from many Sources." M. F. Young to Ramseur, 23 May 1863, Ramseur Papers NCDAH. The North Carolina (Raleigh) *Standard* asserted on 3 June 1863 that Ramseur's brigade "executed a movement at Chancellorsville which even the famous Stonewall Brigade had failed to perform." A controversy over the behavior of the Stonewall Brigade dragged on for years. See *OR*, 25, pt. 1: 1015–16; Terry, "Stonewall Brigade"; Smith, *Anson Guards*, p. 182; and Osborne, "Fourth Regiment," p. 251. The best modern treatment of the role of the Stonewall Brigade in the battle is Robertson, *The Stonewall Brigade*.

60. Ramseur to Schenck, 22 May 1863, folder 16, Ramseur Papers SHC.

61. Ibid., 10 [May], 22 May 1863. The North Carolina newspapers had in fact praised Ramseur and his brigade highly. See for example the *Register*, 13, 16 May 1863, and the *Standard*, 3 June 1863.

62. *OR*, 25, pt. 2: 810, 840. The *Standard*, 3 June 1863, condemned the appointment of Harry Heth to command a newly created division in Hill's Third Corps. Ramseur had turned the tide of battle at Chancellorsville, but Heth had been promoted. Why? Heth was "one of the pets, and we believe, a relation of the President." Actually, Heth was not kin to Jefferson Davis, but he was a Virginian, and thus an easy target in North Carolina.

63. Ramseur to Ellen Richmond, 29 May 1863, folder 7, Ramseur Papers SHC.

64. Pender, *The General to His Lady*, p. 238; Smith, *Anson Guards*, pp. 191–92.

65. Freeman, *R. E. Lee*, 3: 18–19.

66. *OR*, 25, pt. 2: 835, 852–53; ibid., 51, pt. 2: 720.

67. Hotchkiss, *Make Me a Map*, pp. 145–46; Moore, *Story of a Cannoneer*, p. 184; Ramseur to Ellen Richmond, 29 May 1863, folder 7, Ramseur Papers SHC.

68. Ramseur to Ellen Richmond, 17, 29 May, 3 June 1863, folder 7, Ramseur Papers SHC.

69. *OR*, 27, pt. 2: 545–46; Hotchkiss, *Make Me a Map*, pp. 147–49; Hale and Phillips, *History of Forty-Ninth Virginia*, pp. 67–68.

70. *OR*, 27, pt. 2: 546; Osborne, "Fourth Regiment," p. 253; Bennett, "Fourteenth Regiment," p. 717; Hotchkiss, *Make Me a Map*, p. 150; Smith, *Anson Guards*, pp. 197–98.

71. *OR*, 27, pt. 2: 546–49, 592; Bennett, "Fourteenth Regiment," p. 718; Nye, *Here Come the Rebels!*, pp. 132–34.

72. *OR*, 27, pt. 2: 549–50; Nye, *Here Come the Rebels!*, pp. 146–47; Smith, *Anson Guards*, p. 199.

73. *OR*, 27, pt. 2: 551.

74. Stikeleather, "Recollections of the Civil War," p. 36, J. Bryan Grimes Papers, SHC; Smith, *Anson Guards*, p. 200; Casler, *Stonewall Brigade*, pp. 168, 170; Osborne, "Fourth Regiment," p. 253. Rodes commented that the deportment of his soldiers "challenged the admiration of their commanding officers, while it astonished the people along the line of march." *OR*, 27, pt. 2: 551.

75. Ramseur to Ellen Richmond, 23, 28 June 1863, folder 7, Ramseur Papers SHC.

76. Hotchkiss, *Make Me a Map*, pp. 155–56; Bennett, "Fourteenth Regiment," p. 718; Ramseur to Ellen Richmond, 28 June 1863, folder 7, Ramseur Papers SHC.

77. *OR*, 27, pt. 2: 551–52; Thomas, *History of the Doles–Cook Brigade*, pp. 73, 745.

78. *OR*, 27, pt. 2: 552–54, 587.

79. Ibid., p. 554; Tucker, *High Tide at Gettysburg*, pp. 129–31.

80. *OR*, 27, pt. 2: 554, 587; May, "Reminiscences of the War Between the States," p. 5, GDAH; Fred. Phillips to David Schenck, 27 October 1891, typescript in Ramseur Papers NCDAH; Turner and Wall, "Twenty-Third Regiment," p. 237.

81. F. M. Parker to Fred. Phillips, 29 May 1891, typescript in Ramseur Papers NCDAH; *OR*, 27, pt. 2: 587, 589–90, 595, 554; R. T. Bennett to Fred. Phillips, 28 May 1891, typescript in Ramseur Papers NCDAH.

82. Raleigh *Register*, 19 August 1863.

83. *OR*, 27, pt. 2: 445, 554–55, 587; "First Confederates to Enter Gettysburg," p. 620. During the pursuit of the Federals, remembered one soldier, Ramseur turned to a courier and said, "D—— it, tell them to send me a battery! I have sent for one half a dozen times!" Scarcely had he finished giving the order when, according to this witness, Ramseur "threw up both arms and, looking up, said: 'God Almighty, forgive me for that oath.'" Hufham, "Gettysburg," pp. 455–56.

84. Norman, *Portion of My Life*, p. 185; Cox, *Address on Life and Character of Ramseur*, p. 28; and Grimes, "Gettysburg," p. 3, and Stikeleather, "Recollections of the Civil War," p. 43, both in J. Bryan Grimes Papers, SHC; McLendon, "Reminiscences," 1 July, Smith Papers DU.

85. *OR*, 27, pt. 2: 445.

86. *OR*, 27, pt. 2: 349; McIntosh, "Review of the Gettysburg Campaign," p. 119.

87. *OR*, 27, pt. 2: 555.

88. Ibid., pp. 587, 556; Norman, *Portion of My Life*, p. 186.

89. Ramseur to Ellen Richmond, 3 July 1863, folder 7, Ramseur Papers SHC.

90. Norman, *Portion of My Life*, p. 187.

91. *OR*, 27, pt. 2: 558.

92. Ramseur to Ellen Richmond, 8 July 1863, folder 7, Ramseur Papers SHC.

93. *OR*, 27, pt. 2: 558; Hotchkiss, *Make Me a Map*, p. 161.

94. Ramseur to Ellen Richmond, [19?], 29 July 1863, folder 7, Ramseur Papers SHC.

95. *OR*, 27, pt. 2: 562; Ramseur to Ellen Richmond, 3 August 1863, folder 7, Ramseur Papers SHC.

96. Ramseur to Ellen Richmond, 29 July 1863, folder 7, Ramseur Papers SHC; Warner, *Generals in Gray*, pp. 162–63.

97. Reported in the Raleigh *Register*, 9 September 1863.

98. Freeman, *Lee's Lieutenants*, 3: 217–19; Barrett, *The Civil War in North Carolina*, pp. 171–72; Schenck Diary, 11 September 1863, 4: 264–65; Ramseur to Schenck, n.d., folder 16, Ramseur Papers SHC; Park, "War Diary," p. 18.

99. Ramseur to Ellen Richmond, 2, 7, 8 September 1863, folder 8, Ramseur Papers SHC.

100. When Bragg's Army of Tennessee won a victory at Chickamauga on 19–20 September, Ramseur credited the "brave fellows from the Army of N. Va. who have beaten the Yanks on so many fields." Ramseur to Ellen Ramseur, n.d., folder 10, Ramseur Papers SHC.

101. Hairston to "My Darling Fanny," 20 September 1863, folder 33, Peter W. Hairston Papers, SHC; Chambers, *Diary of Captain Chambers*, p. 138. Chambers, a captain in the Forty-Ninth North Carolina, noted in his diary on 21 September 1863 that "Col. McAfee, Capt. Durham, . . . and Capt. Davis . . . started to Gen. S. D. Ramseur's wedding this evening." Apparently, Ramseur was not able to notify all those invited to the wedding that it had been postponed.

102. Ramseur to Ellen Richmond, 17, 27 September 1863, folder 8, Ramseur Papers SHC.

103. A. S. Pendleton to Ramseur, 8 October 1863, Ramseur Papers NCDAH.

104. Mary Dodson Ramseur note in folder 1, Ramseur Papers SHC.

CHAPTER 5

1. Ramseur to Ellen Ramseur, 24 November 1863, folder 8, Ramseur Papers SHC; *OR*, 29, pt. 1: 631–33.

2. Ramseur to Ellen Ramseur, 26 November 1863, folder 8, Ramseur Papers SHC.

3. *OR*, 29, pt. 1: 830, 876.

4. Ibid., p. 886; Hotchkiss, *Make Me a Map*, p. 185.

5. *OR*, 29, pt. 1: 831–33, 876–77, 886; Early, *War Memoirs*, pp. 320–21.

6. Hotchkiss, *Make Me a Map*, pp. 185–86; Lee, *Forget-Me-Nots of the Civil War*, p. 101. More than one-third of Lee's book consists of letters written by two of her brothers in the Fourth North Carolina.

7. Early, *War Memoirs*, pp. 322–23; *OR*, 29, pt. 1: 834–35, 878, 886; McLendon, "Reminiscences," 28–30 November 1863, Smith Papers DU.

8. Lee, *Forget-Me-Nots of the Civil War*, p. 101.

9. Early, *War Memoirs*, p. 324; *OR*, 29, pt. 1: 835, 878, 887; Ramseur to Schenck, 8 December 1863, folder 16, Ramseur Papers SHC.

10. Smith, *Anson Guards*, p. 219; McLendon, "Reminiscences," 2 December 1863, Smith Papers DU.

11. Ramseur to Ellen Ramseur, 3 December 1863, Ramseur to Schenck, 12 December 1863, folders 8, 16, Ramseur Papers SHC.

12. Smith, *Anson Guards*, pp. 219–20; Early, *War Memoirs*, pp. 324–25; *OR*, 29, pt. 1: 835.

13. Ramseur to Schenck, 8 December 1863, folder 16, Ramseur Papers SHC. For Robert E. Lee's reaction to the campaign see *OR*, 29, pt. 1: 820.

14. Goff, *Confederate Supply*, pp. 197–201.

15. Freeman, *R. E. Lee*, 3: 247.

16. Ramseur to Schenck, 12, 28 December 1864, folder 17, Ramseur Papers SHC.

17. Lee, *Forget-Me-Nots of the Civil War*, pp. 96, 103–4, 110–11; Smith, *Anson Guards*, p. 222.

18. Ramseur to Schenck, 12, 28 January, 30 April 1864, Ramseur to Ellen Ramseur, 15 April 1864, folders 17, 9, Ramseur Papers SHC.

19. Bardolph, "Inconstant Rebels," pp. 165, 168; Martin, *Desertion of Alabama Troops*, pp. 28–33. Martin estimates 40 percent of the army was absent without leave at the end of December 1863. In "A Test Case of the 'Crying Evil': Desertion among North Carolina Troops," Richard Reid questions the long-held assumptions that North Carolinians deserted in larger numbers than soldiers from other states, and that there was a link between antiwar activities in North Carolina and desertions in the Army of Northern Virginia.

20. Bardolph, "Inconstant Rebels," pp. 175, 183–86; Tatum, *Disloyalty in the Confederacy*, p. 127.

21. Ramseur to Schenck, [August–September 1863], 16 February 1864, folders 16, 17, Ramseur Papers SHC; Bardolph, "Inconstant Rebels," p. 184.

22. Bennett, "Fourteenth Regiment," p. 721.

23. Bardolph, "Inconstant Rebels," p. 185; Ramseur to Ellen Ramseur, 28 April 1864, folder 9, Ramseur Papers SHC.

24. Tucker, *Zeb Vance*, pp. 337–38.

25. Lee, *Forget-Me-Nots of the Civil War*, p. 109; Leon, *Diary of a Tar Heel*, p. 58.

26. Bennett, "Fourteenth Regiment," p. 721.

27. Leon, *Diary of a Tar Heel*, p. 58; Lee, *Forget-Me-Nots of the Civil War*, pp. 109–10.

28. Tucker, *Zeb Vance*, pp. 338–40.

29. Ramseur to Ellen Ramseur, 24 November, 9, 17 December 1863, folder 8, Ramseur Papers SHC. Ella Lonn argues that attention to camp routine, and especially to cleanliness and exercise in winter quarters, were much neglected in the Confederate armies, and that morale dropped accordingly. Lonn, *Desertion During the Civil War*, p. 11.

30. Ramseur to Ellen Ramseur, 9, 17 December 1863, 15, 28 April 1864, folders 8, 9, Ramseur Papers SHC.

31. Lee, *Forget-Me-Nots of the Civil War*, pp. 106–8; Bennett, "Fourteenth Regiment," p. 720; Smith, *Anson Guards*, pp. 225–26.

32. Ramseur to Schenck, 28 January 1864, folder 16, Ramseur Papers SHC.

33. *OR*, 33: 1144–45, 1150.

34. Ramseur to Schenck, 16 February 1864, folder 17, Ramseur Papers SHC.

35. Ibid., 28 January, 16 February 1864, folders 16, 17.

36. Ibid., Ramseur to Ellen Ramseur, 17 December 1863, folder 8. On the abolition of substitution and the difficulties of compelling those who had furnished sub-

stitutes to enter service themselves see Moore, *Conscription and Conflict in the Confederacy*, pp. 44–47.

37. Ramseur to Schenck, 16 February 1864, folder 17, Ramseur Papers SHC.

38. Ibid., exemption for David Schenck dated 29 March 1864, Ramseur to Schenck, 28 January, 16 February 1864, folders 9, 17.

39. Ibid., Ramseur to Schenck, 12, 16 February 1864, folder 17.

40. Smith, *Anson Guards*, pp. 225, 228 29; Lee, *Forget-Me-Nots of the Civil War*, pp. 111–12.

41. Bennett, "Fourteenth Regiment," pp. 720–21; Smith, *Anson Guards*, p. 225; Ramseur to Ellen Ramseur, 28, 30 April 1864, folder 9, Ramseur Papers SHC. In the latter part of 1863 the Chaplains' Association of the Second and Third Army Corps had numbered Ramseur's brigade among those units in which "God was working wonderfully." Jones, *Christ in the Camp*, pp. 325, 351.

42. Hopkins, "The Hard-Fought Battle," pp. 55–58.

43. Ramseur to Ellen Ramseur, 24 November, 3, 9, 17 December 1863, Ramseur to Schenck, 8 December 1863, folders 8, 16, Ramseur Papers SHC. In the letter of 9 December Dodson expressed sympathy for those among his men who were separated from their families. Some had not seen their wives and children for more than two years.

44. Ramseur to Ellen Ramseur, 7, 12, 15, 17 December 1863, Ramseur to Schenck, 12 January 1864, folders 8, 17, Ramseur Papers SHC.

45. Ibid., Ramseur to Schenck, 12, 28 January, 12, 16 February, 13 March 1864, folder 17.

46. Ibid., 16 February 1864, folder 17.

47. Ibid., 13 March, Ramseur to Ellen Ramseur, 15, 16 April 1864, folders 17, 9.

48. Ibid., Ramseur to Schenck, 13 March 1864, folder 17.

49. Ibid., Ramseur to Ellen Ramseur, 24, 28, 30 April 1864, folder 9.

CHAPTER 6

1. Ramseur to Ellen Ramseur, 2, 3 May 1864, 12 December 1863, folders 9, 8, Ramseur Papers SHC.

2. Ibid., 3 May 1864, folder 9; Howard, *Recollections of a Maryland Confederate Soldier*, pp. 268–69.

3. Alexander, *Military Memoirs of a Confederate*, pp. 496–97; Longstreet, *From Manassas to Appomattox*, p. 552.

4. *OR*, 36, pt. 1: 1070, 1054, 1081.

5. Henderson, "Campaign in the Wilderness of Virginia," p. 265; Early, *War Memoirs*, p. 344.

6. *OR*, 51, pt. 2: 890; ibid., 36, pt. 1: 1081.

7. Ibid., p. 1070; Grant, *Personal Memoirs*, 2: 192–93; Alexander, *Military Memoirs of a Confederate*, p. 501; *OR*, 36, pt. 2: 952.

8. *OR*, 36, pt. 2: 952; ibid., pt. 1: 1071, 1081.

9. Steere, *Wilderness Campaign*, pp. 257–58, 292, map 17.

10. R.C.———, "Gen. Lee at the Wilderness," p. 483; Hotchkiss, *Make Me a Map*, p. 202.

11. Steere, *Wilderness Campaign*, pp. 319–22, 324–25, 340, map 19.

12. *OR*, 36, pt. 1: 1071.

13. Steere, *Wilderness Campaign*, pp. 323–24; Webb, "Through the Wilderness," pp. 158–59.

14. *OR*, 36, pt. 1: 1081.

15. Bennett, "Fourteenth Regiment," pp. 721–22; Smith, *Anson Guards*, p. 235.

16. *OR*, 36, pt. 1: 1081; Steere, *Wilderness Campaign*, p. 324.

17. *OR*, 36, pt. 1: 1081; Alexander, *Military Memoirs of a Confederate*, pp. 505–8.

18. Gordon, *Reminiscences of the Civil War*, pp. 266–67.

19. Livermore, *Numbers and Losses*, pp. 110–11; Freeman, *Lee's Lieutenants*, 3: 372.

20. Hotchkiss, *Make Me a Map*, p. 202.

21. Early, *War Memoirs*, p. 350.

22. *OR*, 36, pt. 2: 969–70.

23. Freeman, *Lee's Lieutenants*, 3: 378.

24. *OR*, 36, pt. 1: 1041.

25. Ibid.; Walker, *Life of Anderson*, p. 162.

26. Wainwright, *Diary of Battle*, p. 355.

27. Caldwell, *History of McGowan's Brigade*, pp. 135–36.

28. *OR*, 36, pt. 1: 1081, 1071; Caldwell, *History of McGowan's Brigade*, p. 138.

29. Lee, *Forget-Me-Nots of the Civil War*, p. 114; *OR*, 36, pt. 1: 1056, 1071.

30. *OR*, 36, pt. 1: 1071; Osborne, "Fourth Regiment," p. 255.

31. *OR*, 36, pt. 1: 1081, 1082–83, 1071.

32. Hotchkiss, *Make Me a Map*, p. 202.

33. *OR*, 36, pt. 1: 1071–72; Dowdey, *Lee's Last Campaign*, pp. 195–97. Dowdey's maps on p. 196 show the positions of each of the Confederate divisions.

34. Hotchkiss, *Virginia*, p. 447; Old, "Trees Whittled Down at Horse Shoe," pp. 20–21; *OR*, 36, pt. 1: 1071–72. Confederate officers in the salient, acutely aware of the threat of enfilading fire, ordered their men to protect themselves by constructing traverses—"short breastworks some twelve or fifteen feet long running back . . . from the front [of the principal works] and about the same distance apart and open to the rear." Brown, "Battle of the Bloody Angle," pp. 94–95.

35. *OR*, 36, pt. 1: 1072, 1089; Hotchkiss, *Make Me a Map*, p. 203; Grant, *Personal Memoirs*, 2: 224.

36. *OR*, 36, pt. 1: 1072, 1044, 1086.

37. Howard, *Recollections of a Maryland Confederate Soldier*, pp. 293–94; *OR*, 36, pt. 1: 1072, 1086.

38. *OR*, 36, pt. 1: 1082.

39. Hotchkiss, *Make Me a Map*, p. 203; Gordon, *Reminiscences of the Civil War*, pp. 274–75; Stikeleather, "Recollections of the Civil War," p. 65, J. Bryan Grimes Papers, SHC.

40. *OR*, 36, pt. 1: 1082.

41. Ibid., p. 1072; Walker, "The Bloody Angle," pp. 235–36.

42. *OR*, 36, pt. 1: 336; Venable, "Wilderness to Petersburg," pp. 529–30.

43. *OR*, 36, pt. 1: 1072.

44. Ibid., p. 1082; Bone, "Civil War Reminiscences," p. 31, Lowry Shuford Collection, NCDAH; Lee, *Forget-Me-Nots of the Civil War*, pp. 115, 118.

45. *OR*, 36, pt. 1: 1082; Osborne, "Fourth Regiment," p. 257.

46. Watson, "Forty-Fifth Regiment," p. 51.

47. Ramseur to Ellen Ramseur, 16, 19 May, 4 June 1864, folder 9, Ramseur Papers SHC.

48. Grimes, *Extracts of Letters*, pp. 53–54; Stikeleather, "Recollections of the Civil War," pp. 65–67, J. Bryan Grimes Papers, SHC; Bennett, "Fourteenth Regiment," p. 723; Lee, *Forget-Me-Nots of the Civil War*, p. 115.

49. Colonel Edwin A. Osborne of Bryan Grimes's Fourth North Carolina asserted that after Ramseur was hit Grimes led the brigade until the end of the battle. But Ramseur's testimony and that of others make it clear that Ramseur remained in control. Ewell's report noted that "General Ramseur [was] severely wounded early in the day, but . . . refused to leave the field." Ramseur's own report, Colonel Bennett's account of his regiment's activities in the northwest corner of the salient later in the day, and a letter written on 17 May 1864 by Walter Lee of the Fourth North Carolina indicate that Ramseur not only remained in command, but also was present at the front with his regiments. Osborne, "Fourth Regiment," p. 256; *OR*, 36, pt. 1: 1073 (Ewell), 1083 (Ramseur); Bennett, "Fourteenth Regiment," p. 724; Lee, *Forget-Me-Nots of the Civil War*, p. 118; Ramseur to Ellen Ramseur, 19 May, 4 June 1864, folder 9, Ramseur Papers SHC. See also Hendrix, "That Bloody Angle Battle," p. 438.

50. Osborne, "Fourth Regiment," p. 257; Smith, *Anson Guards*, p. 261; *OR*, 36, pt. 1: 1072; Manly, "Second Regiment," p. 172.

51. *OR*, 36, pt. 1: 1082, 1072–73, 1092–94; Charles S. Venable to N. H. Harris, 24 November 1871, quoted in "General Lee to the Rear," p. 107; Harris, *Movements of the Confederate Army*, p. 27.

52. *OR*, 36, pt. 1: 1082; Lee, *Forget-Me-Nots of the Civil War*, p. 107; Bennett, "Fourteenth Regiment," pp. 723–24.

53. Gordon, *Reminiscences of the Civil War*, pp. 282–85; *OR*, 36, pt. 1: 1073; Caldwell, *History of McGowan's Brigade*, p. 143.

54. Graphic accounts of the fighting along the northern bend of the salient abound. They are nearly unanimous in terming it the most desperate fighting of the war and invoke many images in attempting to describe the sounds made by the minié balls that seemed to fill the air. One of Ramseur's soldiers likened the noise to "some musical instrument," "wounded men crying," "humming of bees," and "cats in the depth of the night." Lee, *Forget-Me-Nots of the Civil War*, p. 116.

55. Bennett, "Fourteenth Regiment," p. 724; Galloway, "Hand-to-Hand Fighting at Spotsylvania," pp. 172–73. A portion of the oak tree is preserved in the Smithsonian Institution.

56. Lee, *Forget-Me-Nots of the Civil War*, p. 118; Bennett, "Fourteenth Regiment," p. 723; Smith, *Anson Guards*, pp. 240–41; Ramseur to Ellen Ramseur, 4 June 1864, folder 9, Ramseur Papers SHC.

57. Wainwright, *Diary of Battle*, p. 368; Caldwell, *History of McGowan's Brigade*, p. 143.

58. Gordon, *Reminiscences of the Civil War*, p. 285.

59. *OR*, 36, pt. 1: 1073, 1082; Caldwell, *History of McGowan's Brigade*, p. 143; Lee, *Forget-Me-Nots of the Civil War*, p. 116.

60. Manly, "Second Regiment," pp. 171–72; Bennett, "Fourteenth Regiment," p. 723; Lee, *Forget-Me-Nots of the Civil War*, pp. 116–17.

61. *OR*, 36, pt. 1: 1082; Ramseur to Ellen Ramseur, 30 May, 4 June 1864, folder 9, Ramseur Papers SHC. Bryan Grimes wrote his wife that "Gen. Lee rode down in person to thank the Brigade for its gallantry, saying, 'we deserved the thanks of the country, we had saved his army.'" Grimes, *Extracts of Letters*, p. 54. But Ramseur said only that Lee called him to army headquarters to thank him, and no other account mentions a visit from Lee.

62. Osborne, "Fourth Regiment," p. 257; Venable, "Wilderness to Petersburg," pp. 532–33; Ramseur to Ellen Ramseur, 30 May 1864, folder 9, Ramseur Papers SHC; Freeman, *Lee's Lieutenants*, 3: 448.

63. Ramseur to Ellen Ramseur, 16 May 1864, folder 9, Ramseur Papers SHC.

64. Ibid., 30 May, 4 June 1864. The account by the British correspondent, widely quoted in postbellum sketches of Ramseur, is reproduced in part in Stedman, "Address at Unveiling Monument to Ramseur," p. 5, Ramseur Papers SHC.

65. Hotchkiss, *Make Me a Map*, pp. 204–5; *OR*, 36, pt. 1: 1057; Gordon, *Reminiscences of the Civil War*, p. 289.

66. Cutshaw, "Battle Near Spotsylvania Court-House," pp. 332–33; Ramseur to Ellen Ramseur, 19 May 1864, folder 9, Ramseur Papers SHC.

67. *OR*, 36, pt. 1: 1073, 1082; Bennett, "Fourteenth Regiment," p. 726.

68. Caldwell, *History of McGowan's Brigade*, p. 151; *OR*, 36, pt. 1: 1073. The careful Porter Alexander puts Ewell's strength on 20 April at 17,079. The disaster in the salient at Spotsylvania on 12 May was responsible for a good percentage of his heavy loss. Alexander, *Military Memoirs of a Confederate*, p. 497.

69. *OR*, 36, pt. 1: 1082–83.

70. Ibid., p. 1083.

71. Lee, *Forget-Me-Nots of the Civil War*, pp. 119–20.

72. *OR*, 36, pt. 1: 1073, 1083; Ramseur to Ellen Ramseur, 20, 30 May, 4 June 1864, folder 9, Ramseur Papers SHC. In his letter to Nellie of 30 May, Ramseur said that, after Gordon broke, he himself was ordered to retreat but protested and declared that "I could & would hold the enemy in check. The order was revoked the Yankee advance repulsed & our corps saved from heavy loss." Criticism of the giver of the order to retreat, whether Ewell or Rodes, is implicit in this passage. Ramseur's official report contains no such language.

73. "Opposing Forces at the Beginning of Grant's Campaign Against Richmond," p. 182; Livermore, *Numbers and Losses*, pp. 112–13; Blackford and Blackford, *Letters From Lee's Army*, p. 249.

74. Freeman, *Lee's Lieutenants*, 3: 496; Early, *War Memoirs*, p. 359.

75. Hotchkiss, *Make Me a Map*, p. 206.

76. Early, *War Memoirs*, pp. 359–61; *OR*, 36, pt. 1: 1058, 1074, 1083.

77. Early, *War Memoirs*, pp. 361–62; *OR*, 36, pt. 1: 1083; Hotchkiss, *Make Me a Map*, p. 208.

78. Hotchkiss, *Make Me a Map*, p. 208.

79. Ramseur to Ellen Ramseur, 30 May 1864, folder 9, Ramseur Papers SHC; *OR*, 36, pt. 3: 851, 854.

80. Hotchkiss, *Make Me a Map*, p. 208.

81. Early, *War Memoirs*, p. 362; Alexander, *Military Memoirs of a Confederate*, p. 534; Christian, "Bethesda Church," pp. 237–38.

82. Christian, "Bethesda Church," p. 238; Peyton, "Record of Pegram's Brigade," 30 May 1864, Chancellorsville Battlefield Park, Va.; Hale and Phillips, *History of Forty-Ninth Virginia*, pp. 135–36.

83. Peyton, "Record of Pegram's Brigade," 30 May 1864, Chancellorsville Battlefield Park, Va.

84. Ramseur to Ellen Ramseur, 31 May 1864, folder 9, Ramseur Papers SHC; *OR*, 51, pt. 2: 974–75. Freeman does not mention Ramseur, but states that Early attacked "head on, without proper reconnaissance or co-ordination with the First Corps." *Lee's Lieutenants*, 3: 502. In truth, Ramseur and Early should share the blame. The former apparently suggested that the assault be made, and the latter gave the order.

85. Ramseur to Ellen Ramseur, 31 May 1864, folder 9, Ramseur Papers SHC.

86. *OR*, 36, pt. 1: 1059; Hotchkiss, *Make Me a Map*, pp. 208–9.

87. McMahon, "Cold Harbor," p. 217.

88. Ibid., pp. 217–18; Venable, "Wilderness to Petersburg," p. 536; *OR*, 36, pt. 1: 1059; Ramseur to Ellen Ramseur, 4 June 1864, folder 9, Ramseur Papers SHC.

89. Beall, "Twenty-First Regiment," pp. 140–41; Ramseur to Ellen Ramseur, 4 June 1864, folder 9, Ramseur Papers SHC.

90. Nevins, *War for the Union*, p. 45; Freeman, *Lee's Lieutenants*, 3: 512–13.

91. Ramseur to Ellen Ramseur, 4 June 1864, folder 9, Ramseur Papers SHC.

92. Commission in Ramseur Papers, NCDAH.

93. *OR*, 36, pt. 3: 873–74. By this same order, William R. Cox was made brigadier general and given Ramseur's brigade, and Bryan Grimes made brigadier general and given the brigade of Junius Daniel, mortally wounded at Spotsylvania.

94. Parker, "Thirtieth Regiment," p. 503; Ledford, *Reminiscences*, pp. 78–79; "Personal Recollections of General Ramseur," in Schenck, *Sketches*, p. 24; James W. Wilson to Miss Richmond, 7 July 1863, folder 1, Ramseur Papers SHC; Smith, *Anson Guards*, p. 260; Harding, "Sketch of Ramseur," p. 6. When with his sharpshooters, Ramseur occasionally displayed his skill as a marksman. He related to David Schenck an incident in which a Federal scout was observing the Confederate line at a seemingly safe distance. After watching his men try in vain to hit the man, Ramseur, "with some irritation, called for a sharpshooter's rifle and brought down the scout the first fire, and then rode out and took his Burnside rifle from him." Ramseur sent the rifle to Schenck as a trophy. "Personal Recollections of General Ramseur," in Schenck, *Sketches*, p. 24.

95. Ramseur to Ellen Ramseur, 28 April 1864, folder 9, Ramseur Papers SHC.

CHAPTER 7

1. Ramseur to Ellen Ramseur, 4, 7, 9, 11 June 1864, folder 9, Ramseur Papers SHC.

2. Ibid., 9, 11 June 1864.

3. Ibid., Ramseur to Schenck, 20 August 1864, folder 17.

4. *OR*, 43, pt. 1: 1003; Johnston, "Garland–Iverson–Johnston Brigade," p. 523; Beall, "Hoke–Godwin–Lewis Brigade," pp. 525–26. Freeman, citing *OR*, 36, pt. 3: 873, states that Lewis commanded Pegram's brigade while Pegram recovered from his wound, but Ramseur's letters make clear that Lewis had Hoke's brigade and Lilley had Pegram's. Ramseur to Schenck, 1, 20 August 1864, folder 17, Ramseur Papers SHC.

5. This number is approximate. Ramseur wrote that he had 1,800 effectives in a battle near Winchester on 20 July 1864. Inspection reports of 20 August 1864 place the number at just over 2,000. Ramseur to Schenck, 1 August 1864, folder 17, Ramseur Papers SHC; *OR*, 43, pt. 1: 1002.

6. Hotchkiss, *Make Me a Map*, p. 211; Worsham, *Jackson's Foot Cavalry*, p. 146; Park, "Diary," p. 373.

7. *OR*, 37, pt. 1: 346; Early, *War Memoirs*, pp. 371–72.

8. Hotchkiss, *Make Me a Map*, p. 211; Worsham, *Jackson's Foot Cavalry*, p. 147; Park, "Diary," p. 373.

9. Early, *War Memoirs*, p. 373; Blackford, "Battle of Lynchburg," pp. 287–88.

10. Early, *War Memoirs*, p. 373; Worsham, *Jackson's Foot Cavalry*, p. 147; Blackford, "Battle of Lynchburg," p. 288.

11. Moore, "General Hunter's Raid," p. 189; Blackford, "Battle of Lynchburg," pp. 288–89.

12. Vandiver, *Jubal's Raid*, pp. 7, 45; Early, *War Memoirs*, p. 375; Hotchkiss, *Make Me a Map*, p. 212.

13. Early, *War Memoirs*, pp. 375–76; *OR*, 37, pt. 1: 766.

14. Hotchkiss, *Make Me a Map*, p. 212; Douglas, *I Rode With Stonewall*, p. 290.

15. Early, *War Memoirs*, pp. 377–79; Douglas, *I Rode With Stonewall*, p. 291; Hotchkiss, *Make Me a Map*, pp. 212–13; *OR*, 43, pt. 1: 602.

16. Hotchkiss, *Make Me a Map*, p. 213.

17. *OR*, 37, pt. 1: 766–67; Early, *War Memoirs*, p. 380.

18. Peyton, "Record of Pegram's Brigade," 24 June 1864, Chancellorsville Battlefield Park, Va.

19. Worsham, *Jackson's Foot Cavalry*, p. 149; Brown, "First Regiment," pp. 153–54; Douglas, *I Rode With Stonewall*, p. 292; *OR*, 43, pt. 1: 602.

20. Berkeley, *Four Years*, p. 84; Douglas, *I Rode With Stonewall*, p. 290. For a Union view on the destruction at the Virginia Military Institute, see du Pont, *Campaign of 1864*, pp. 68–69; du Pont was a classmate of Ramseur's at West Point and an officer in Hunter's army.

21. Worsham, *Jackson's Foot Cavalry*, p. 149; Ramseur to Ellen Ramseur, 27 June 1864, folder 9, Ramseur Papers SHC.

22. Park, "Diary," pp. 375–76; Douglas, *I Rode With Stonewall*, p. 293.

23. Early, *War Memoirs*, p. 382; Park, "Diary," p. 375; Worsham, *Jackson's Foot Cavalry*, p. 149.

24. *OR*, 51, pt. 2: 1028–29; Ramseur to Ellen Ramseur, 30 June 1864, folder 9, Ramseur Papers SHC.

25. Douglas, *I Rode With Stonewall*, p. 292; Hotchkiss, *Make Me a Map*, p. 213; Early, *War Memoirs*, p. 384.

26. Hotchkiss, *Make Me a Map*, p. 214; Early, *War Memoirs*, p. 384.

27. Douglas, *I Rode With Stonewall*, pp. 292–93; Park, "Diary," p. 378; Ramseur to Ellen Ramseur, 7 July 1864, folder 9, Ramseur Papers SHC.

28. Early, *War Memoirs*, pp. 385–86.

29. Worthington, *Battle that Saved Washington*, p. 107.

30. Worsham, *Jackson's Foot Cavalry*, p. 151; Ray, "Sixth Regiment," p. 324; Early, *War Memoirs*, p. 386.

31. Worthington, *Battle that Saved Washington*, pp. 89–92; Early, *War Memoirs*, p. 387; Hotchkiss, *Make Me a Map*, pp. 214–15.

32. Worthington, *Battle that Saved Washington*, pp. 107–9, 128.

33. Early, *War Memoirs*, pp. 387–88; Turner and Wall, "Twenty-Third Regiment," pp. 245–46.

34. Worthington, *Battle that Saved Washington*, pp. 134–35, 152; Worsham, *Jackson's Foot Cavalry*, p. 154; Early, *War Memoirs*, pp. 387–88.

35. *OR*, 37, pt. 1: 202, 348; Early, *War Memoirs*, p. 388; Park, "Diary," p. 379.

36. Hotchkiss, *Make Me a Map*, p. 215.

37. *OR*, 37, pt. 1: 388; Vandiver, *Jubal's Raid*, p. 121; Douglas, *I Rode With Stonewall*, p. 294.

38. *OR*, 37, pt. 1: 348; London, "Thirty-Second Regiment," p. 531.

39. Early, *War Memoirs*, p. 389; Warner, *Generals in Gray*, p. 79; Cooling, *Defending Washington*, p. 195, map.

40. Early, *War Memoirs*, p. 390; Toon, "Twentieth Regiment," p. 122.

41. Park, "Diary," p. 379; Cramer, *Lincoln Under Enemy Fire*, p. 17; *OR*, 37, pt. 1: 348; Cooling, *Defending Washington*, p. 195, map. T. F. Toon, in command of Robert Johnston's brigade of Ramseur's division, thought that he "could have taken everything in my front if I had been allowed to continue my advance." Toon, "Twentieth Regiment," p. 122.

42. Worsham, *Jackson's Foot Cavalry*, p. 156.

43. Douglas, *I Rode With Stonewall*, pp. 294–95; Gordon, *Reminiscences of the Civil War*, pp. 314–15.

44. Early, *War Memoirs*, p. 392.

45. Ibid.; *OR*, 37, pt. 1: 348.

46. Hotchkiss, *Make Me a Map*, pp. 215–16; Early, *War Memoirs*, p. 396.

47. Ramseur to Ellen Ramseur, 27 June, 15 July 1864, Ramseur to Schenck, 1 August 1864, folders 9, 17, Ramseur Papers SHC.

48. Ibid., Ramseur to Schenck, 1 August 1864, folder 17.

49. Ibid., Ramseur to Ellen Ramseur, 23 July 1864, folder 9.

50. *OR*, 37, pt. 1: 346; Douglas, *I Rode With Stonewall*, pp. 295–96. Though the Confederates did not know it, Lincoln had watched the skirmishing from Fort Stevens on 11–12 July.

51. Ramseur to Schenck, 1, 20 August 1864, Ramseur to Ellen Ramseur, 23 July 1864, folders 17, 9, Ramseur Papers SHC. Each of these letters contains a detailed account of the action on 20 July; together, they constitute far and away the fullest narrative by Ramseur of any of his battles. Ramseur's figure of 250 killed, wounded, and missing appears in the Confederate reports. W. W. Averell, the Federal commander, puts the southern loss at 73 killed, 130 wounded, and 267 captured, and his own at 53 killed, 155 wounded, and 6 missing. *OR*, 37, pt. 2: 599–600 (Confederate); *OR*, 37, pt. 1: 327 (Averell).

52. Ramseur to Schenck, 1, 20 August 1864, folder 17, Ramseur Papers SHC.

53. Ibid., Ramseur to Ellen Ramseur, 23 July (two letters) 1864, folder 9. In *Attack and Die*, McWhiney and Jamieson cite Ramseur's criticism of his men in these letters to Ellen Ramseur to support their thesis that southern generals, who were products of a Celtic culture "that rejected careful calculation and patience" (p. xv), were slavishly devoted to wild frontal attacks. Ramseur (whose lineage was Teutonic rather than Celtic) was, it is true, not averse to mounting assaults, particularly if conditions seemed as favorable as Vaughn's reports indicated at Stephenson's Depot. But Ramseur's anger over Stephenson's Depot focused on Lewis's and Lilley's failure to hold their ground—his own soldiers' willingness to attack was not an issue. Moreover, Ramseur's letters beginning with the Mine Run campaign make it clear that he thought entrenchments could help offset the northern advantage in numbers.

54. Ramseur to Schenck, 1, 20 August 1864, Ramseur to Ellen Ramseur, 10 August 1864, folders 17, 9, Ramseur Papers SHC.

55. Raleigh *Confederate*, 30 July 1864. The *Confederate* printed the *Enquirer*'s articles. General Lewis, widely quoted as believing that Ramseur failed to take proper precautions before advancing, wrote after the war that "Ramseur was not altogether responsible for the mistake that occurred, for he had every reason to suppose that the information furnished by Vaughn was correct." Cox, *Address on Life and Character of Ramseur*, p. 36.

56. Ramseur to Schenck, 1 August 1864, folder 17, Ramseur Papers SHC.

57. Peyton, "Record of Pegram's Brigade," 20 July 1864, Chancellorsville Battlefield Park, Va. Captain Samuel D. Buck, like Peyton a member of the Thirteenth Virginia, wrote in his postwar memoirs that "Gen. Ramseur was a most gallant officer but was in some way misled and walked into the enemy as though they were friends." *With the Old Confeds*, p. 108. Henry Robinson Berkeley, a member of the battery that lost its guns at Stephenson's Depot, merely observed that Ramseur "ran into an ambush the Yanks had set for us." *Four Years*, p. 89.

58. Early, *Memoir of the Last Year*, p. 64; *OR*, 37, pt. 1: 347.

59. Ramseur to Ellen Ramseur, 10 August 1864, folder 9, Ramseur Papers SHC.

60. *OR*, 37, pt. 1: 353–54. On 10 August Ramseur, in forwarding to Ewell a report of his brigade's activities in May 1864, had closed his letter of transmittal with

a plaintive reference to Stephenson's Depot: "After my disaster of the 20th ultimo (which I have asked Major New to explain to you in person), I need all the encouragement you can give me." New was a member of Ramseur's staff. *OR*, 36, pt. 1: 1081.

61. Ellen Ramseur to Ramseur, 3 August 1864, folder 9, Ramseur Papers SHC.

62. Ibid., Ramseur to Schenck, 20 August, 17 [September] 1864, folder 17. John Pegram was probably the unnamed Virginian Ramseur considered his rival for divisional command.

63. Ibid., 20 August 1864, Ramseur to Ellen Ramseur, 10, 15 August 1864, folders 17, 9.

64. Ibid., Ramseur to Ellen Ramseur, 23 July, 15, 28, 29 August 1864, folders 9, 10.

65. Ibid., 30, 31 August 1864, folder 10.

66. Ibid., 6, 10, 12 [?] September, Ramseur to Schenck, 17 [September] 1864, folders 10, 17.

67. Ibid., Ramseur to Ellen Ramseur, 6 September 1864, folder 10. The key Democratic plank asserted that "after four years of failure to restore the Union by the experiment of war, . . . justice, humanity, liberty and the public welfare demand that immediate efforts be made for a cessation of hostilities." Certainly this was language to give southerners hope. But the Democrats went on to urge a "convention of the States, or other peaceable means, to the end that at the earliest practicable moment peace may be restored on the basis of the Federal Union of the States"— terms that were not acceptable to any southerner still devoted to independence. Zornow, *Lincoln & Party Divided*, pp. 132–33.

68. Ramseur to Ellen Ramseur, 16 September 1864, folder 10, Ramseur Papers SHC. McClellan's letter stated flatly that "Union is the one condition of peace—we ask no more." Zornow, *Lincoln & Party Divided*, p. 136.

69. Ramseur to Ellen Ramseur, 14, 17 September 1864, folder 10, Ramseur Papers SHC.

70. Ibid., 29 August 1864; Gordon, *Reminiscences of the Civil War*, p. 317.

71. Grant, *Personal Memoirs*, 2: 316–21; Sheridan, *Personal Memoirs*, 1: 462–66; *OR*, 37, pt. 1: 347. On 30 July the Raleigh *Confederate* called the action at Kernstown a victory in which the "troops under Gen. Ramseur more than retrieved their character." Ramseur wrote Nellie that the Confederates "paid 'em back" on 24 July, but his subsequent letters made clear that he did not think Kernstown completely erased the stigma of Stephenson's Depot. Ramseur to Ellen Ramseur, 28 July 1864, folder 9, Ramseur Papers SHC.

72. Ramseur to Ellen Ramseur, 10, 15, 28, 29 August, 6, [12?] September 1864, folder 10, Ramseur Papers SHC.

73. Ibid., [12?] September 1864.

74. Ibid., [12?], 16, 17 September 1864.

75. Ibid., [12?], 16 September 1864.

76. Ibid., 15, 28 August, 14 September 1864.

77. Ibid., 10, 11, 14 September 1864.

78. Douglas, *I Rode With Stonewall*, p. 308.

79. Ramseur to Ellen Ramseur, 28 July, 10 August, 6 September 1864, folders 9, 10, Ramseur Papers SHC.

80. Ibid., 14 September 1864, folder 10.

81. Ibid., 6, 10, 11, [12?] September 1864.

82. Ibid., Ramseur to Schenck, 8 December 1863, 28 January 1864, folders 16, 17.

83. Ibid., Ramseur to Ellen Ramseur, 7, 19, 23 July, 17, 30 September 1864, folders 9, 10.

84. "Personal Recollections of General Ramseur," in Schenck, *Sketches*, p. 25; Ramseur to Schenck, 11 June 1862, 8 December 1863, 17 [September] 1864, folders 16, 17, Ramseur Papers SHC.

85. Ibid., Ramseur to Ellen Ramseur, 30 August 1864, folder 10. The railroad involved was the Virginia Central, which for a time in 1864 refused to carry the mails. Public outcry and, more importantly, government concessions ended the dispute. Black, *Railroads of Confederacy*, pp. 226–27.

86. Ramseur to Ellen Ramseur, 6, 14, 17, 30 September 1864, folder 10, Ramseur Papers SHC.

87. Early, *War Memoirs*, p. 414.

88. Hotchkiss, *Make Me a Map*, p. 228.

89. Ramseur to Ellen Ramseur, 17 September 1864, folder 10, Ramseur Papers SHC.

90. Early, *War Memoirs*, p. 415; *OR*, 43, pt. 1: 554. Sheridan's caution stemmed not from personality but from orders. Grant thought Early's army numbered 40,000, and he instructed Sheridan in early August to remain on the defensive until the Union army around Harpers Ferry was large enough to overmatch the Confederates. *OR*, 43, pt. 1: 43.

91. Ramseur to Ellen Ramseur, [12?] September 1864, folder 10, Ramseur Papers SHC; Douglas, *I Rode With Stonewall*, pp. 308–9. Robert Rodes also thought Early should refrain from splitting his small command with Sheridan so close. He had told Early as much, Rodes said to William R. Cox, adding with some irritation that he could not get Early to believe him. Cox, *Address on Life and Character of Ramseur*, p. 39.

92. Turner and Wall, "Twenty-Third Regiment," p. 251; Douglas, *I Rode With Stonewall*, p. 309.

93. Douglas, *I Rode With Stonewall*, p. 309; Turner and Wall, "Twenty-Third Regiment," pp. 251–53.

94. Turner and Wall, "Twenty-Third Regiment," p. 252.

95. Early, *War Memoirs*, pp. 420–21; Douglas, *I Rode With Stonewall*, p. 309.

96. Ramseur to Schenck, 10 October 1864, folder 17, Ramseur Papers SHC.

97. Douglas, *I Rode With Stonewall*, p. 309.

98. Early, *War Memoirs*, p. 420; *OR*, 43, pt. 1: 554.

99. Ramseur to Schenck, 10 October 1864, folder 17, Ramseur Papers SHC; Early, *War Memoirs*, p. 421; Gordon, *Reminiscences of the Civil War*, p. 320.

100. Gordon, *Reminiscences of the Civil War*, p. 321; Early, *War Memoirs*, pp. 421–22.

101. Early, *War Memoirs*, pp. 422–24; Worsham, *Jackson's Foot Cavalry*, p. 168; *OR*, 43, pt. 1: 555.

102. *OR*, 43, pt. 1: 555; Early, *War Memoirs*, p. 425; Ramseur to Schenck, 10 October 1864, folder 17, Ramseur Papers SHC.

103. Early, *War Memoirs*, pp. 425–26; Ramseur to Schenck, 10 October 1864, folder 17, Ramseur Papers SHC. Ramseur wrote that Rodes's division "came off in tolerable order" while Gordon's panicked.

104. *OR*, 43, pt. 1: 555; Livermore, *Numbers and Losses*, p. 127.

105. *OR*, 43, pt. 1: 552, 555; Ramseur to Ellen Ramseur, 30 September 1864, folder 10, Ramseur Papers SHC; Warner, *Generals in Gray*, p. 108.

106. Early, *War Memoirs*, pp. 426–28; *OR*, 43, pt. 1: 555.

107. Ramseur to Schenck, 10 October 1864, folder 17, Ramseur Papers SHC.

108. Douglas, *I Rode With Stonewall*, pp.309–10.

109. Toon, "Twentieth Regiment," p. 123; Turner and Wall, "Twenty-Third Regiment," p. 253; Beall, "Twenty-First Regiment," p. 141; Herring, "General Rodes at Winchester," p. 184.

110. Freeman, *Lee's Lieutenants*, 3: 582; Douglas, *I Rode With Stonewall*, p. 310.

111. Ramseur to Schenck, 10 October 1864, folder 17, Ramseur Papers SHC.

112. Ibid., Ramseur to Ellen Ramseur, 25 September 1864, folder 10.

CHAPTER 8

1. Early, *War Memoirs*, p. 429.

2. *OR*, 43, pt. 1: 556; ibid., pt. 2: 877; Johnston, "Sketches," p. 323.

3. *OR*, 43, pt. 1: 556; "The Cavalry at Fisher's Hill," pp. 51–52; *OR Atlas*, plate 82, map 11; Early, *War Memoirs*, p. 429.

4. Hotchkiss, *Make Me a Map*, p. 230; Lane, "Battle of Fisher's Hill," p. 290.

5. Garnett, "Diary," p. 8.

6. Allan, "Reminiscences," p. 143; Hotchkiss, *Make Me a Map*, p. 230.

7. Lane, "Battle of Fisher's Hill," pp. 291–92; Hotchkiss, *Make Me a Map*, p. 230.

8. Lane, "Battle of Fisher's Hill," p. 292; Grimes, *Extracts of Letters*, pp. 71–72; Hotchkiss, *Make Me a Map*, p. 230.

9. Cox, *Address on Life and Character of Ramseur*, p. 43; Grimes, *Extracts of Letters*, pp. 71–72; P. J. Rast, "Fisher's Hill," pp. 123–24.

10. Early, *War Memoirs*, p. 430; Hotchkiss, *Make Me a Map*, pp. 230–31.

11. Hotchkiss, *Make Me a Map*, p. 231; Garnett, "Diary," p. 9; Beall, "That Stampede at Fisher's Hill," p. 26; Early, *War Memoirs*, p. 430.

12. Hotchkiss, *Make Me a Map*, pp. 231–32; *OR*, 43, pt. 1: 556; Early, *War Memoirs*, pp. 430–32.

13. *OR*, 43, pt. 2: 878.

14. Garnett, "Diary," pp. 9–10.

15. Early, *War Memoirs*, pp. 432–35; Hotchkiss, *Make Me a Map*, pp. 232–33.

16. *OR*, 43, pt. 1: 556; ibid., pt. 2: 880–81.

17. Ramseur to Ellen Ramseur, 30 September 1864, Ramseur to Schenck, 10 October 1864, folders 10, 17, Ramseur Papers SHC.

18. Ibid., Ramseur to Ellen Ramseur, 2, 5, 10, 15 October 1864, Ramseur to Schenck, 10 October 1864, folders 10, 17.

19. Gordon, *Reminiscences of the Civil War*, p. 327.

20. Ramseur to Ellen Ramseur, 10, 15 October 1864, Ramseur to Schenck, 10 October 1864, folders 10, 17, Ramseur Papers SHC.

21. Ibid., Ramseur to Ellen Ramseur, 25, 30 September, 2 October 1864, folder 10.

22. Ibid., Ramseur to Schenck, 10 October 1864, folder 17.

23. Ibid., Ramseur to Ellen Ramseur, 5 October 1864, folder 10.

24. *OR*, 43, pt. 2: 882.

25. Cox, *Address on Life and Character of Ramseur*, p. 43; Garnett, "Diary," p. 7; Grimes, *Extracts of Letters*, p. 68; Lane, "Battle of Fisher's Hill," p. 290. A fuse-cutter in J. L. Massie's battery of William Nelson's battalion of artillery, Lane observed that "General Ramseur was as brave a man as ever drew a sword in defence of the South" but lacked "those qualities which could estimate the numbers or penetrate the designs of the enemy"—an apparent reference to Stephenson's Depot and, perhaps, Bethesda Church. R. A. Brock, one of the editors of the *Southern Historical Society Papers*, noted at the bottom of Lane's text that he did not share this critical view of Ramseur.

26. Ramseur to Schenck, 10 October 1864, folder 17, Ramseur Papers SHC. Ramseur did not name the generals he thought might receive permanent command of his division.

27. Ibid., Ramseur to Ellen Ramseur, 5, 10, 15 October 1864, folder 10.

28. Ibid., 5 October 1864.

29. Grimes, *Extracts of Letters*, pp. 75–76; Hotchkiss, *Make Me a Map*, pp. 234–35.

30. *OR*, 43, pt. 2: 880–81.

31. Early, *War Memoirs*, p. 437; *OR*, 43, pt. 1: 561.

32. Hotchkiss, *Make Me a Map*, p. 237; Early, *War Memoirs*, pp. 437–38.

33. Ramseur to Ellen Ramseur, 15 October 1864, folder 10, Ramseur Papers SHC.

34. Hotchkiss, *Make Me a Map*, pp. 237–38; Early, *War Memoirs*, pp. 437–38; *OR*, 43, pt. 1: 561.

35. Hotchkiss, *Make Me a Map*, pp. 237–38; Early, *War Memoirs*, pp. 438–39; Gordon, *Reminiscences of the Civil War*, pp. 333–35.

36. Ramseur to Ellen Ramseur, 17 October 1864, folder 10, Ramseur Papers SHC.

37. Ibid., Bryan Grimes to Ellen Ramseur, 27 June 1873, folder 3. At the northern terminus of the Massanutten range are three promontories called Three Top Mountain. Signal Knob, the one closest to Strasburg, was used extensively by Confederates and Federals to observe their opponent's movements. The Confederate signal

corps flashed messages from Signal Knob to a station on Fort Mountain opposite Seven Fountains, thence to Stony Man south of Luray, and from Stony Man to eastern Virginia. The news from Nellie made this trip in reverse. Hale, *Four Valiant Years*, p. 449.

38. Ramseur to Ellen Ramseur, 17 October 1864, folder 10, Ramseur Papers SHC.

39. Will dated 18 October 1864, folder 10, Ramseur Papers SHC. Ramseur had sent an earlier will (content unknown) to David Schenck only eight days previously. Ramseur to Schenck, 10 October 1864, folder 17. The will of 18 October left all of his personal property and half of his real property to Nellie; the other half of his real property was to be divided among his sisters Lucy, Fannie, and Addie Ramseur. At their deaths or marriages the property was to go to Nellie.

40. Hotchkiss, *Make Me a Map*, p. 238; Early, *War Memoirs*, pp. 440–42.

41. *OR*, 43, pt. 2: 882; Early, *War Memoirs*, pp. 435, 452. According to Early's estimates Kershaw had 2,700; Ramseur, 2,100; Gordon, 1,700; Pegram, 1,200; and Wharton, 1,100.

42. Hotchkiss, *Make Me a Map*, p. 238.

43. Abel H. Crawford to Dora, 21 October 1864, Abel H. Crawford Papers, DU; Gordon, *Reminiscences of the Civil War*, p. 336.

44. *OR*, 43, pt. 1: 598.

45. Hale and Phillips, *History of Forty-Ninth Virginia*, p. 168; C. S. M., "Battle of Cedar Creek," p. 444; Gordon, *Reminiscences of the Civil War*, p. 335.

46. Gordon, *Reminiscences of the Civil War*, pp. 64, 338. Gordon, misinterpreting the comment, thought Ramseur was predicting his own death.

47. Hotchkiss, *Make Me a Map*, p. 239.

48. *OR*, 43, pt. 1: 598; *OR Atlas*, plate 82, map 9.

49. C. S. M., "Battle of Cedar Creek," p. 444; Hotchkiss, *Make Me a Map*, p. 239.

50. Abel H. Crawford to Dora, 21 October 1864, Abel H. Crawford Papers, DU; Gordon, *Reminiscences of the Civil War*, p. 339.

51. *OR*, 43, pt. 1: 561, 598–99; Gordon, *Reminiscences of the Civil War*, pp. 339–40.

52. Cox, *Address on Life and Character of Ramseur*, pp. 46, 52.

53. Henry Kyd Douglas to Miss Tippie, 20 November 1864, Henry Kyd Douglas Papers, DU. Douglas explained that the D—— did not "stand for cuss words but for my name. Gen R was a member of the church." A somewhat different version of this incident appears in Douglas, *I Rode With Stonewall*, p. 317.

54. *OR*, 43, pt. 1: 599.

55. Ibid.; Early, *War Memoirs*, pp. 444–46.

56. Hotchkiss, *Make Me a Map*, p. 239; *OR Atlas*, plate 82, map 9.

57. Gordon, *Reminiscences of the Civil War*, pp. 341–42.

58. *OR*, 43, pt. 1: 562; *OR Atlas*, plate 82, map 9; Early, *War Memoirs*, pp. 447–48.

59. Gordon, *Reminiscences of the Civil War*, pp. 342, 346; Hotchkiss, *Make Me a Map*, p. 239.

60. Estimates of the time of the Federal attack vary from three o'clock to four-

thirty. Hotchkiss (*Make Me a Map*, p. 239) gives the latter hour; Grimes (*OR*, 43, pt. 1: 599), who wrote the official report for Ramseur's division at Cedar Creek, puts the time at three-thirty; Cox (*Address on Life and Character of Ramseur*, p. 47) at about three; du Pont (*Address of September 16, 1920*, p. 7), who took part in the northern attack, at three-thirty to four.

61. Merritt, "Sheridan in Shenandoah," pp. 517–19.

62. *OR*, 43, pt. 1: 599; Early, *War Memoirs*, p. 448.

63. *OR*, 43, pt. 1: 599–600; Watkins, "Reminiscences 1864–1865," pp. 197–99, Smith Papers DU.

64. Early, *War Memoirs*, pp. 448–49, states that Ramseur "succeeded in retaining with him two or three hundred men of his division." Grimes, *OR*, 43, pt. 1: 600, and Cox, *Address on Life and Character of Ramseur*, pp. 48–49, suggest that a far larger number of Confederates rallied.

65. Early, *War Memoirs*, p. 449.

66. Ellen Richmond to David Schenck, 1 February 1884, folder 18, Ramseur Papers SHC, quoting a letter of unknown date from Caleb Richmond to her.

67. Harding, "Sketch of Ramseur," p. 7.

68. Early, *War Memoirs*, p. 449; Gerald, "Notes on Battle of Cedar Creek," p. 391; Benson, "Battle of Cedar Creek," pp. 390–91.

69. R. R. Hutchinson to Ellen Ramseur, 20 October 1864, Ramseur Papers NCDAH; Cox, *Address on Life and Character of Ramseur*, p. 47; "Personal Recollections of General Ramseur," in Schenck, *Sketches*, p. 22. A map of the locality where Ramseur was wounded may be found in a manuscript entitled "With Sheridan up the Shenandoah Valley in 1864: Leaves from a Special Artist's Sketch Book and Diary," by James E. Taylor in the collections of the Western Reserve Historical Society, Cleveland, Ohio. Taylor, artist for *Frank Leslie's Illustrated Newspaper*, kept a diary amplified after the war into this 568-page handwritten book illustrated with hundreds of his drawings. For a profile of Taylor, see Skoch, "James Taylor's Diary and Sketchbook," pp. 36–43.

While working on several drawings that featured Ramseur, Taylor corresponded with David Schenck (Taylor to Schenck, 9 January 1884, Ramseur Papers NCDAH). Schenck sent Taylor's questions on to Ellen Ramseur, who used letters from her brother Caleb Richmond to supply answers (Ellen Ramseur to Schenck, 4 February 1884, folder 18, Ramseur Papers SHC). Taylor credited "Major Winston" with executing the map, but the accompanying text, supposedly written by Winston, is an excerpt from Caleb Richmond's letter to Ellen Ramseur cited in note 66 above. Taylor used more of the letter elsewhere, attributing these passages to "Ramseur's Brother In Law—Caleb Schenck." Penciled above the map is David Schenck's name. The map, it seems reasonable to assume, was drawn by Caleb Richmond and passed from Ellen Ramseur through David Schenck to Taylor.

70. R. R. Hutchinson to Ellen Ramseur, 20 October 1864, Ramseur Papers NCDAH.

71. C. S. M., "Battle of Cedar Creek," pp. 445–46; Early, *War Memoirs*, pp. 449–50.

72. R. R. Hutchinson to Ellen Ramseur, 20 October 1864, Ramseur Papers

NCDAH; du Pont, *Address of September 16, 1920*, pp. 9–13 (du Pont's account, the fullest of Ramseur's last hours, should be used with caution except where du Pont was a direct participant).

73. See du Pont, *Address of September 16, 1920*, pp. 13–14.

74. R. R. Hutchinson to Ellen Ramseur, 20 October 1864, Ramseur Papers NCDAH.

EPILOGUE

1. Schenck Diary, 22 October 1864, 6: 25–26.

2. "Maj.-Gen. Stephen D. Ramseur," in Schenck, *Sketches*, p. 7.

3. Ibid., "Personal Recollections of General Ramseur," p. 22.

4. Ibid., "Maj.-Gen. Stephen D. Ramseur," p. 4.

5. Ibid., pp. 1–3. Although Ramseur was a Presbyterian, his remains subsequently were buried in the cemetery of the Episcopal church in Lincolnton.

6. Luly Ramseur to Ellen Ramseur, 11 November 1864, folder 10, Ramseur Papers SHC. Ellen Richmond Ramseur wore the clothing of deep mourning for the rest of her life. She was buried beside her husband in 1900. Their daughter, Mary Dodson Ramseur, who never married, died in 1935. In 1869 the town of Columbia, North Carolina, was renamed Ramseur in honor of the general.

7. *OR*, 43, pt. 1: 553, 600. Given command of Ramseur's division following Cedar Creek, Bryan Grimes ably led it for the remainder of the war.

8. Raleigh *Confederate*, 28 October 1864; North Carolina (Raleigh) *Standard*, 28 October 1864.

9. Harding, "Sketch of Ramseur," p. 9.

10. Bryan Grimes to Ellen Ramseur, 27 June 1873, folder 3, Ramseur Papers SHC; Harding, "Sketch of Ramseur," p. 9.

11. Norman, *Portion of My Life*, p. 183.

12. Early, *War Memoirs*, p. 450.

13. Harding, "Sketch of Ramseur," p. 9.

14. In his interesting quantitative study *Goodmen*, Michael Barton isolates five key character terms with which southerners were more concerned than northerners—"kind," "noble," "gentleman," "brave," and "gallant." Each of these appears frequently in estimates of Ramseur by his contemporaries.

15. Harding, "Sketch of Ramseur," p. 7; Gordon, *Reminiscences of the Civil War*, pp. 64–65; Douglas, *I Rode With Stonewall*, p. 317; Bryan Grimes to Ellen Ramseur, 27 June 1873, folder 3, Ramseur Papers SHC.

16. Harding, "Sketch of Ramseur," p. 9.

17. Ibid.

BIBLIOGRAPHY

MANUSCRIPTS

Atlanta, Ga.
  Georgia Department of Archives and History
    W. H. May. "Reminiscences of the War Between the States." Typescript dated
      1886, in UDC bound typescripts, vol. 10.
Austin, Tex.
  Barker Texas History Center, University of Texas
    U.S. Eighth Census, 1860, manuscript returns of Schedule 1, Free Inhabitants,
      and Schedule 2, Slave Inhabitants, for Caswell County and Lincoln County,
      North Carolina. Microfilm copies of originals in Record Group No. 29, Na-
      tional Archives.
    U.S. Seventh Census, 1850, manuscript returns of Schedule 1, Free Inhabi-
      tants, and Schedule 2, Slave Inhabitants, for Caswell County and Lincoln
      County, North Carolina. Microfilm copies of originals in Record Group No.
      29, National Archives.
    U.S. Sixth Census, 1840, manuscript returns for Caswell County and Lincoln
      County, North Carolina. Microfilm copies of originals in Record Group No.
      29, National Archives.
Chancellorsville, Va.
  Chancellorsville Battlefield Park
    George Q. Peyton. "Record of Pegram's Brigade 1864." Typescript.
Chapel Hill, N.C.
  North Carolina Collection, Wilson Library, University of North Carolina
    David Schenck, comp. *Sketches of Maj.-Gen. Stephen Dodson Ramseur*. N.p.,
      1892.
    Mrs. J. A. Yarbrough. "Gen. Stephen Dodson Ramseur." Typescript.
  Southern Historical Collection, Wilson Library, University of North Carolina
    J. Bryan Grimes. "Gettysburg." Manuscript dated 29 July 1911, in J. Bryan
      Grimes Papers, series 2, vol. 39.
    Peter W. Hairston Papers.
    Stephen Dodson Ramseur Papers.
    David Schenck. Diary. Original and 12-volume typed transcript in David
      Schenck Papers (typed transcript was used in preparation of this study).
    Charles Stedman. "Address at Unveiling of Monument to Major General S. D.
      Ramseur Near Middletown, Va., Sept. 16th, 1920." Typescript in folder 11,
      Stephen Dodson Ramseur Papers.
    J. A. Stikeleather. "Recollections of the Civil War in the United States." Manu-
      script dated 27 May 1909, in J. Bryan Grimes Papers, series 2, vol. 36.

Cleveland, Ohio
  Western Reserve Historical Society
    James E. Taylor. Sketchbook.
Durham, N.C.
  William R. Perkins Library, Manuscript Department, Duke University
    Abel H. Crawford Papers.
    Henry Kyd Douglas Papers.
    John L. McLendon. "Reminiscences 1862–1863." In William Alexander Smith
      Papers.
    Thomas J. Watkins. "Reminiscences 1864–1865." Manuscript in William Alex-
      ander Smith Papers.
Milton, N.C.
  Genealogical data on Stephen Dodson family compiled by and in the possession of
    Mrs. L. B. Satterfield.
Raleigh, N.C.
  North Carolina Department of Archives and History
    J. W. Bone. "Civil War Reminiscences." Manuscript dated 1904, in Civil War and
      Confederate Material, Lowry Shuford Collection, 1862–1919.
    Stephen Dodson Ramseur Papers.
West Point, N.Y.
  U.S. Military Academy Archives
    Official Registers, 1856–1860 (printed); *Post Orders, 1856–1860*; *Register of
      Delinquency, 1856–1860*. Used through extracts and summaries relating to
      Ramseur supplied by Chief of Archives, U.S. Military Academy.

PRINTED SOURCES

A. Books

Alexander, Edward Porter. *Military Memoirs of a Confederate*. 1907. Reprint. Bloom-
  ington, Ind., 1962.
Berkeley, Henry Robinson. *Four Years in the Confederate Artillery: The Diary of Pri-
  vate Henry Robinson Berkeley*. Edited by William H. Runge. Chapel Hill, N.C.,
  1961.
Betts, Alexander Davis. *Experiences of a Confederate Chaplain, 1861–1864, by Rev.
  A. D. Betts, Chaplain 30th N.C. Troops*. Edited by W. A. Betts. N.p., n.d.
Blackford, Susan Leigh, and Blackford, Charles Minor III, comps. and eds. *Letters
  from Lee's Army*. New York, 1947.
Buck, Samuel D. *With the Old Confeds, Actual Experiences of a Captain in the Line*.
  1925. Reprint. Gaithersburg, Md., 1983.
Caldwell, J. F. J. *The History of a Brigade of South Carolinians, Known First as
  "Gregg's," and Subsequently as "McGowan's Brigade."* 1866. Reprint. Dayton, Ohio,
  1974.
Casler, John O. *Four Years in the Stonewall Brigade*. Second edition 1906. Reprint.
  Marietta, Ga., 1951.

Chambers, Henry A. *Diary of Captain Henry A. Chambers*. Edited by T. H. Pearce. Wendell, N.C., 1983.

Clark, Walter, ed. *Histories of the Several Regiments and Battalions from North Carolina in the Great War 1861–1865*. 5 vols. Raleigh, N.C., 1901.

———, and Saunders, William L., eds. *Colonial and State Records of North Carolina*. 30 vols. Raleigh and Goldsboro, N.C., 1886–1914.

Cox, William R. *Address on the Life and Character of Maj. Gen. Stephen D. Ramseur Before the Ladies' Memorial Association of Raleigh, N.C., May 10th, 1891*. Raleigh, N.C., 1891.

Douglas, Henry Kyd. *I Rode With Stonewall: The War Experiences of the Youngest Member of Jackson's Staff*. Chapel Hill, N.C., 1940.

du Pont, Henry A. *Address of September 16, 1920, at the Unveiling of the Monument Erected to the Memory of Major General Stephen D. Ramseur, on the Cedar Creek Battlefield, Near Middletown, Virginia*. Winterthur, Del., 1920.

———. *The Campaign of 1864 in the Valley of Virginia and the Expedition to Lynchburg*. New York, 1925.

Early, Jubal A. *A Memoir of the Last Year of the War for Independence in the Confederate States of America*. Lynchburg, Va., 1867.

———. *War Memoirs: Autobiographical Sketch and Narrative of the War Between the States*. 1912. Reprint. Bloomington, Ind., 1960.

Edmondston, Catherine Ann Devereux. *"Journal of a Secesh Lady": The Diary of Catherine Ann Devereux Edmondston, 1860–1866*. Edited by Beth Gilbert Crabtree and James W. Patton. Raleigh, N.C., 1979.

Ellis, John W. *The Papers of John W. Ellis*. Edited by Noble J. Tolbert. 2 vols. Raleigh, N.C., 1964.

Gordon, John B. *Reminiscences of the Civil War*. New York, 1903.

Grant, Ulysses S. *Personal Memoirs*. 2 vols. New York, 1886.

Grimes, Bryan. *Extracts of Letters of Major-Gen'l Bryan Grimes, to his Wife, Written While in Active Service in the Army of Northern Virginia*. Edited by Pulaski Cowper. Raleigh, N.C., 1884.

Harris, Nat. H. *Movements of the Confederate Army in Virginia. And the Part Taken Therein by the Nineteenth Mississippi Regiment . . . From the Diary of Gen. Nat H. Harris*. Compiled by W. M. Harris. Duncansby, Miss., 1901.

Holden, W. W. *Memoirs of W. W. Holden*. Edited by William K. Boyd. Durham, N.C., 1911.

Hotchkiss, Jedediah. *Make Me a Map of the Valley: The Civil War Journal of Stonewall Jackson's Topographer*. Edited by Archie P. McDonald. Dallas, 1973.

Howard, McHenry. *Recollections of a Maryland Confederate Soldier and Staff Officer Under Johnston, Jackson, and Lee*. 1914. Reprint. Dayton, Ohio, 1974.

Howard, Oliver Otis. *Autobiography of Oliver Otis Howard, Major General United States Army*. 2 vols. New York, 1908.

Johnson, Robert Underwood, and Buel, Clarence Clough, eds. *Battles and Leaders of the Civil War*. 4 vols. New York, 1887.

Jones, J. William. *Christ in the Camp; or, Religion in Lee's Army*. Richmond, 1887.

———, and others, eds. *Southern Historical Society Papers*. 52 vols. and 2-vol. index. 1876–1959. Reprint. New York, 1977–80.

Ketchey, John A. *Life, Adventures and Suffering of J. A. Ketchey, Written by Himself.* Salisbury, N.C., 1874.

Ledford, P. L. *Reminiscences of the Civil War 1861–1865.* Thomasville, N.C., 1909.

Lee, Laura Elizabeth, ed. *Forget-Me-Nots of the Civil War.* St. Louis, 1909.

Leon, L. *Diary of a Tar Heel Confederate Soldier.* Charlotte, N.C., 1913.

Longstreet, James. *From Manassas to Appomattox.* 1896. Reprint. Bloomington, Ind., 1960.

Moore, E. A. *The Story of a Cannoneer Under Stonewall Jackson.* Lynchburg, Va., 1910.

Norman, William M. *A Portion of My Life: Being a Short & Imperfect History written while a prisoner of war on Johnson's Island 1864.* Winston-Salem, N.C., 1959.

Pender, William Dorsey. *The General to His Lady: The Civil War Letters of William Dorsey Pender to Fanny Pender.* Edited by William Woods Hassler. Chapel Hill, N.C., 1965.

Putnam, Sallie A. *In Richmond During the Confederacy.* 1867. Reprint. New York, 1961.

Shaffner, John Francis. *Diary of Dr. J. F. Shaffner, Sr., Commencing September 13, 1863, Ending February 5, 1865.* N.p., [1936].

Sheridan, Philip H. *Personal Memoirs.* 2 vols. New York, 1888.

Smith, William Alexander. *The Anson Guards, Company C, Fourteenth Regiment North Carolina Volunteers 1861–1865.* 1914. Reprint. Wendell, N.C., 1978.

Stiles, Robert. *Four Years Under Marse Robert.* 1903. Reprint. Dayton, Ohio, 1977.

Thomas, Henry W. *History of the Doles–Cook Brigade Army of Northern Virginia.* 1903. Reprint. Dayton, Ohio, 1981.

U.S. War Department. *The War of the Rebellion: A Compilation of the Official Records of the Union and Confederate Armies.* 127 vols., index, and atlas. Washington, D.C., 1880–1901.

Wainwright, Charles S. *A Diary of Battle: The Personal Journals of Charles S. Wainwright, 1861–1865.* Edited by Allan Nevins. New York, 1962.

Wilson, James Harrison. *Under the Old Flag.* 2 vols. New York, 1912.

Worsham, John H. *One of Jackson's Foot Cavalry.* 1912. Reprint. Jackson, Tenn., 1964.

B. Articles and Parts of Books

Allan, William. "Reminiscences of Field Ordnance Service with the Army of Northern Virginia—1863–'5." In *Southern Historical Society Papers*, edited by J. William Jones and others. 14: 137–46.

Ambrose, Stephen E., ed. "West Point in the Fifties: The Letters of Henry A. du Pont." *Civil War History* 10 (September 1964): 291–308.

Beall, James F. "The Hoke–Godwin–Lewis Brigade." In *Histories of the Several Regiments and Battalions from North Carolina in the Great War 1861–1865*, edited by Walter Clark. 4: 525–26.

———. "Twenty-First Regiment." In *Histories of the Several Regiments and Battalions from North Carolina in the Great War 1861–1865*, edited by Walter Clark. 2: 129–46.

Beall, T. S. "That Stampede at Fisher's Hill." *Confederate Veteran* 5 (January 1897): 26.

Bennett, R. T. "Fourteenth Regiment." In *Histories of the Several Regiments and Battalions from North Carolina in the Great War 1861–1865*, edited by Walter Clark. 1: 705–32.

Benson, Captain. "Battle of Cedar Creek, Va." *Confederate Veteran* 27 (October 1919): 390–91.

Blackford, Charles M. "The Campaign and Battle of Lynchburg." In *Southern Historical Society Papers*, edited by J. William Jones and others. 30: 279–332.

Brown, Hamilton A. "First Regiment." In *Histories of the Several Regiments and Battalions from North Carolina in the Great War 1861–1865*, edited by Walter Clark. 1: 134–56.

Brown, Joseph Newton. "The Battle of the Bloody Angle, Spotsylvania, May 12, 1864." In *A Colonel at Gettysburg and Spotsylvania*, edited by Varina D. Brown. Columbia, S.C., 1931.

"The Cavalry at Fisher's Hill." *Confederate Veteran* 3 (February 1895): 51–52.

Christian, C. B. "The Battle at Bethesda Church." In *Southern Historical Society Papers*, edited by J. William Jones and others. 37: 236–42.

C. S. M. "The Battle of Cedar Creek." In *Southern Historical Society Papers*, edited by J. William Jones and others. 16: 443–46.

Cutshaw, W. E. "The Battle Near Spotsylvania Court-House on May 18, 1864." In *Southern Historical Society Papers*, edited by J. William Jones and others. 33: 320–34.

"First Confederates to Enter Gettysburg." *Confederate Veteran* 5 (December 1897): 620.

Galloway, G. Norton. "Hand-to-Hand Fighting at Spotsylvania." In *Battles and Leaders of the Civil War*, edited by Robert Underwood Johnson and Clarence Clough Buel. 4: 170–74.

Garnett, James M. "Diary of Captain James M. Garnett, Ordnance Officer Rodes's Division, 2d Corps, Army of Northern Virginia." In *Southern Historical Society Papers*, edited by J. William Jones and others. 27: 1–16.

—. " 'General Lee to the Rear'—The Incident with Harris' Mississippi Brigade." In *Southern Historical Society Papers*, edited by J. William Jones and others. 8: 105–10.

Gerald, G. B. "Notes on the Battle of Cedar Creek." In *Southern Historical Society Papers*, edited by J. William Jones and others. 16: 391–92.

[Harding, E. H.] "Sketch of Major General S. D. Ramseur." *The Land We Love* 5 (May 1868): 1–10.

Henderson, G. F. R. "The Campaign in the Wilderness of Virginia, 1864." In *The Civil War: A Soldier's View*, edited by Jay Luvaas. Chicago, 1958.

Hendrix, D. I. "That Bloody Angle Battle." *Confederate Veteran* 17 (September 1909): 438.

Herring, Marcus D. "General Rodes at Winchester." *Confederate Veteran* 28 (May 1920): 184.

Hill, Daniel Harvey. "McClellan's Change of Base and Malvern Hill." In *Battles and*

Leaders of the Civil War, edited by Robert Underwood Johnson and Clarence Clough Buel. 2: 383–95.

Hopkins, A. C. "The Hard-Fought Battle and Bloodless Victory in Orange County, Va., March 23, 1864." In *Camp Fires of the Confederacy*, edited by Ben LaBree. Louisville, Ky., 1898.

Hufham, James Dunn, Jr. "Gettysburg (Being an account of the experiences of a veteran, told by himself)." *The Wake Forest Student* 16 (April 1897): 451–56.

Johnston, James F. "The Garland–Iverson–Johnston Brigade." In *Histories of the Several Regiments and Battalions from North Carolina in the Great War 1861–1865*, edited by Walter Clark. 4: 521–24.

Johnston, J. Stoddard. "Sketches of Operations of General John C. Breckinridge; No. 2." In *Southern Historical Society Papers*, edited by J. William Jones and others. 7: 317–23.

Lane, James H. "History of Lane's North Carolina Brigade." In *Southern Historical Society Papers*, edited by J. William Jones and others. 8: 97–104.

Lane, John H. "The Battle of Fisher's Hill." In *Southern Historical Society Papers*, edited by J. William Jones and others. 19: 289–95.

Lee, Fitzhugh. "Chancellorsville—Address of General Fitzhugh Lee Before the Virginia Division, A.N.V. Association, October 29, 1879." In *Southern Historical Society Papers*, edited by J. William Jones and others. 7: 545–85.

London, Henry A. "Thirty-Second Regiment." In *Histories of the Several Regiments and Battalions from North Carolina in the Great War 1861–1865*, edited by Walter Clark. 2: 521–36.

McIntosh, David Gregg. "The Campaign of Chancellorsville." In *Southern Historical Society Papers*, edited by J. William Jones and others. 40: 44–100.

———. "Review of the Gettysburg Campaign, By One Who Participated There." In *Southern Historical Society Papers*, edited by J. William Jones and others. 37: 74–143.

McMahon, Martin T. "Cold Harbor." In *Battles and Leaders of the Civil War*, edited by Robert Underwood Johnson and Clarence Clough Buel. 4: 213–20.

Manly, Matt. "Second Regiment." In *Histories of the Several Regiments and Battalions from North Carolina in the Great War 1861–1865*, edited by Walter Clark. 1: 157–76.

Merritt, Wesley. "Sheridan in the Shenandoah Valley." In *Battles and Leaders of the Civil War*, edited by Robert Underwood Johnson and Clarence Clough Buel. 4: 500–521.

Moore, J. Scott. "General Hunter's Raid." In *Southern Historical Society Papers*, edited by J. William Jones and others. 27: 179–91.

Old, W. W. "Trees Whittled Down at Horse Shoe." In *Southern Historical Society Papers*, edited by J. William Jones and others. 33: 16–24.

"Opposing Forces at the Beginning of Grant's Campaign Against Richmond." In *Battles and Leaders of the Civil War*, edited by Robert Underwood Johnson and Clarence Clough Buel. 4: 179–84.

Osborne, E. A. "Fourth Regiment." In *Histories of the Several Regiments and Battalions from North Carolina in the Great War 1861–1865*, edited by Walter Clark. 1: 229–80.

Park, Robert E. "Diary" [6 June–17 August 1864]. In *Southern Historical Society Papers*, edited by J. William Jones and others. 1: 370–86.

————. "War Diary . . . January 28th, 1863–January 27th, 1864." In *Southern Historical Society Papers*, edited by J. William Jones and others. 26: 1–31.

Parker, F. M. "Thirtieth Regiment." In *Histories of the Several Regiments and Battalions from North Carolina in the Great War 1861–1865*, edited by Walter Clark. 2: 495–505.

Porter, Fitz-John. "The Battle of Malvern Hill." In *Battles and Leaders of the Civil War*, edited by Robert Underwood Johnson and Clarence Clough Buel. 2: 406–27.

Ramsay, John A. "Additional Sketch Tenth Regiment." In *Histories of the Several Regiments and Battalions from North Carolina in the Great War 1861–1865*, edited by Walter Clark. 1: 551–82.

Rast, P. J. "Fisher's Hill." In *Confederate Veteran* 23 (March 1915): 123–24.

Ray, Neill W. "Sixth Regiment." In *Histories of the Several Regiments and Battalions from North Carolina in the Great War 1861–1865*, edited by Walter Clark. 1: 293–336.

R. C. ————. "Gen. Lee at the 'Wilderness.'" *The Land We Love* 5 (October 1868): 481–86.

"Report of the Commission Appointed under the eighth section of the act of Congress of June 21, 1860, to examine into the organization, system of discipline, and course of instruction of the United States Military Academy at West Point." 36th Congress, 2nd Session, 1861. Senate Misc. Doc. 3.

Roulhac, Thomas R. "Forty-Ninth Regiment." In *Histories of the Several Regiments and Battalions from North Carolina in the Great War 1861–1865*, edited by Walter Clark. 3: 125–49.

Rowland, Kate Mason, ed. "Letters of a Virginia Cadet at West Point, 1859–1861." *South Atlantic Quarterly* 14 (October 1915): 330–47.

————. "Letters of a Virginia Cadet at West Point, 1859–1861." *South Atlantic Quarterly* 15 (January 1916): 1–17.

Smith, James Power. "Stonewall Jackson's Last Battle." In *Battles and Leaders of the Civil War*, edited by Robert Underwood Johnson and Clarence Clough Buel. 3: 203–14.

Talcott, T. M. R. "General Lee's Strategy at the Battle of Chancellorsville: A Paper Read by Request Before R. E. Lee Camp, No. 1, C.V., May 20th, 1906." In *Southern Historical Society Papers*, edited by J. William Jones and others. 34: 1–27.

Terry, William. "The 'Stonewall Brigade' at Chancellorsville." In *Southern Historical Society Papers*, edited by J. William Jones and others. 14: 364–70.

Toon, Thomas F. "Twentieth Regiment." In *Histories of the Several Regiments and Battalions from North Carolina in the Great War 1861–1865*, edited by Walter Clark. 2: 111–27.

Turner, V. E., and Wall, H. C. "Twenty-Third Regiment." In *Histories of the Several Regiments and Battalions from North Carolina in the Great War 1861–1865*, edited by Walter Clark. 2: 181–268.

Venable, Charles S. "The Campaign from the Wilderness to Petersburg." In *Southern Historical Society Papers*, edited by J. William Jones and others. 14: 522–42.

Walker, James A. " 'The Bloody Angle': The Confederate Disaster at Spotsylvania

Court-House, May 12, 1864, by which the 'Stonewall Brigade' was annihilated."
In *Southern Historical Society Papers*, edited by J. William Jones and others. 21:
229–38.

Watson, Cyrus Barksdale. "Forty-Fifth Regiment." In *Histories of the Several Regiments and Battalions from North Carolina in the Great War 1861–1865*, edited by
Walter Clark. 3: 35–61.

Webb, Alexander S. "Through the Wilderness." In *Battles and Leaders of the Civil War*, edited by Robert Underwood Johnson and Clarence Clough Buel. 4: 152–69.

C. Newspapers

North Carolina (Raleigh) *Standard*. 1861–1864
Raleigh *Confederate*. 1861–1864
Raleigh *Register*. 1861–1864

SECONDARY WORKS

A. Books

Adams, Michael C. C. *Our Masters the Rebels: A Speculation on Union Military Failure in the East, 1861–1865*. Cambridge, Mass., 1978.

Ambrose, Stephen E. *Duty, Honor, Country: A History of West Point*. Baltimore,
1966.

——. *Upton and the Army*. Baton Rouge, La., 1964.

Barrett, John G. *The Civil War in North Carolina*. Chapel Hill, N.C., 1963.

Barton, Michael. *Goodmen: The Character of Civil War Soldiers*. University Park,
Pa., 1981.

Bigelow, John. *The Campaign of Chancellorsville: A Strategic and Tactical Study*. New
Haven, Conn., 1910.

Birkhimer, William E. *Historical Sketch of the Organization, Administration, Materiel and Tactics of the Artillery, United States Army*. 1884. Reprint. New York, 1968.

Black, Robert C. *The Railroads of the Confederacy*. Chapel Hill, N.C., 1952.

Boatner, Mark M., III. *The Civil War Dictionary*. New York, 1959.

Bridges, Hal. *Lee's Maverick General: Daniel Harvey Hill*. New York, 1961.

Burnham, W. Dean. *Presidential Ballots 1836–1892*. Baltimore, 1955.

Catton, Bruce. *Glory Road*. Garden City, N.Y., 1952.

The Centennial of the United States Military Academy at West Point, New York 1802–1902. 2 vols. 1904. Reprint. New York, 1969.

Cleaves, Freeman. *Meade of Gettysburg*. Norman, Okla., 1960.

Cline, Joseph Frederick, Jr. "The Youngest Major General: Stephen Dodson Ramseur." M.A. thesis, University of North Carolina, 1968.

Coddington, Edwin B. *The Gettysburg Campaign: A Study in Command*. New York,
1968.

Collier, Mrs. Bryan Wells [Margaret W.]. *Representative Women of the South*. 2 vols.
N.p., n.d.

Cooling, B. Franklin. *Symbol, Sword & Shield: Defending Washington during the Civil War*. Hamden, Conn., 1975.
Coulter, E. Merton. *The Confederate States of America 1861–1865*. Baton Rouge, La., 1950.
Cramer, John H. *Lincoln Under Enemy Fire*. Baton Rouge, La., 1948.
Cullum, George W. *Biographical Register of the Officers and Graduates of the U.S. Military Academy at West Point*. 3 vols. with additions. New York, 1868.
DeMond, Robert O. *The Loyalists in North Carolina During the Revolution*. Durham, N.C., 1940.
Dowdey, Clifford. *Lee's Last Campaign: The Story of Lee and His Men Against Grant—1864*. Boston, 1960.
_____. *The Seven Days: The Emergence of Lee*. Boston, 1964.
Forman, Sidney. *West Point: A History of the United States Military Academy*. New York, 1950.
Fox, William F. *Regimental Losses in the American Civil War 1861–1865*. Albany, N.Y., 1889.
Freeman, Douglas Southall. *Lee's Lieutenants*. 3 vols. New York, 1942–44.
_____. *R. E. Lee*. 4 vols. New York, 1934, 1936.
Goff, Richard D. *Confederate Supply*. Durham, N.C., 1969.
Hale, Laura Virginia. *Four Valiant Years in the Lower Shenandoah Valley*. Strasburg, Va., 1968.
_____, and Phillips, Stanley S. *History of the Forty-Ninth Virginia Infantry C.S.A.: "Extra Billy Smith's Boys."* Lanham, Md., 1981.
Henderson, G. F. R. *Stonewall Jackson and the American Civil War*. 2 vols. 1898. Reprint. London, 1911.
Hill, Daniel Harvey. *Bethel to Sharpsburg*. 2 vols. Raleigh, N.C., 1926.
Hotchkiss, Jedediah. *Virginia*. Vol. 3 of *Confederate Military History*, edited by Clement A. Evans. 12 vols. 1899. Reprint. New York, 1962.
Hughes, Nathaniel Cheairs, Jr. *General William J. Hardee: Old Reliable*. Baton Rouge, La., 1965.
Livermore, Thomas L. *Numbers and Losses in the Civil War in America: 1861–1865*. 1900. Reprint. Bloomington, Ind., 1957.
Long, E. B. *The Civil War Day by Day: An Almanac 1861–1865*. Garden City, N.Y., 1971.
Longacre, Edward G. *From Union Stars to Top Hat: A Biography of the Extraordinary General James Harrison Wilson*. Harrisburg, Pa., 1972.
Lonn, Ella. *Desertion During the Civil War*. New York, 1928.
McWhiney, Grady, and Jamieson, Perry D. *Attack and Die: Civil War Military Tactics and the Southern Heritage*. University, Ala., 1982.
Manarin, Louis H., comp. *North Carolina Troops 1861–1865: A Roster*. 8 vols. to date. Raleigh, N.C., 1966–81.
Martin, Bessie. *Desertion of Alabama Troops from the Confederate Army: A Study in Sectionalism*. New York, 1932.
Miers, Earl Schenck. *The Last Campaign: Grant Saves the Union*. Philadelphia, 1972.
Miller, Francis Trevelyan, ed. *The Photographic History of the Civil War*. 10 vols. New York, 1911.

Moore, Albert Burton. *Conscription and Conflict in the Confederacy*. New York, 1924.

Nevins, Allan. *The War for the Union: The Organized War to Victory 1864–1865*. New York, 1971.

Nye, Wilbur Sturtevant. *Here Come the Rebels!* Baton Rouge, La., 1965.

Pemberton, John C. *Pemberton: Defender of Vicksburg*. Chapel Hill, N.C., 1942.

Powell, William S. *When the Past Refused to Die: A History of Caswell County, North Carolina 1777–1977*. Durham, N.C., 1977.

Randall, James G., and Donald, David. *The Civil War and Reconstruction*. Lexington, Mass., 1969.

Robertson, James I., Jr. *The Stonewall Brigade*. Baton Rouge, La., 1963.

Schaff, Morris. *The Spirit of Old West Point*. New York, 1907.

Settles, Thomas M. "The Military Career of John Bankhead Magruder." Ph.D. dissertation, Texas Christian University, 1972.

Shaw, Cornelia. *Davidson College*. New York, 1923.

Sherrill, William L. *Annals of Lincoln County North Carolina*. 1937. Reprint. Baltimore, 1972.

Sitterson, Joseph Carlyle. *The Secessionist Movement in North Carolina*. Chapel Hill, N.C., 1939.

Stackpole, Edward J. *Sheridan in the Shenandoah: Jubal Early's Nemesis*. Harrisburg, Pa., 1961.

Steere, Edward. *The Wilderness Campaign*. Harrisburg, Pa., 1960.

Strode, Hudson. *Jefferson Davis, American Patriot 1808–1861*. New York, 1955.

Tatum, Georgia Lee. *Disloyalty in the Confederacy*. Chapel Hill, N.C., 1934.

Tucker, Glenn. *High Tide at Gettysburg*. Indianapolis, 1958.

———. *Zeb Vance: Champion of Personal Freedom*. Indianapolis, 1965.

Vandiver, Frank E. *Jubal's Raid: General Early's Famous Attack on Washington in 1864*. New York, 1960.

Walker, C. Irvine. *The Life of Lieutenant-General Richard Heron Anderson*. Charleston, S.C., 1917.

Warner, Ezra J. *Generals in Gray*. Baton Rouge, La., 1959.

———, and Yearns, Wilfred Buck. *Biographical Register of the Confederate Congress*. Baton Rouge, La., 1975.

Wise, Jennings C. *The Long Arm of Lee*. 2 vols. Lynchburg, Va., 1915.

Wooster, Ralph A. *The Secession Conventions of the South*. Princeton, N.J., 1962.

Worthington, Glenn H. *Fighting for Time, or, The Battle that Saved Washington and Mayhap the Union*. Baltimore, 1932.

Zornow, William F. *Lincoln & the Party Divided*. Norman, Okla., 1954.

B. Articles

Bardolph, Richard. "Inconstant Rebels: Desertion of North Carolina Troops in the Civil War." *North Carolina Historical Review* 41 (April 1964): 163–89.

Cappon, Lester J. "Iron-Making—A Forgotten Industry of North Carolina." *North Carolina Historical Review* 9 (October 1932): 331–48.

Clark, Walter. "An Address Delivered at the Presentation of the Portrait of Major

General Stephen D. Ramseur." *The North Carolina Booklet* 16 (October 1916): 69–75.

Graham, William A. "The Battle of Ramsaur's Mill, June 20, 1780." *The North Carolina Booklet* 4 (June 1904): 5–23.

Reid, Richard. "A Test Case of the 'Crying Evil': Desertion among North Carolina Troops during the Civil War." *North Carolina Historical Review* 58 (July 1981): 234–62.

Shepherd, Henry E. "Gallant Sons of North Carolina." *Confederate Veteran* 27 (November 1919): 413–14.

Skoch, George F., ed. "With a Special in the Shenandoah: From James Taylor's Diary and Sketchbook." *Civil War Times Illustrated* 21 (April 1982): 36–43.

Stedman, Charles M. "Gen. Stephen Dodson Ramseur." *Confederate Veteran* 28 (December 1920): 453–57.

Steiner, Paul E. "Medical-Military Studies on the Civil War, VII: Major General Stephen D. Ramseur, C.S.A." *Military Medicine* 130 (October 1965): 1016–22.

Zotos, Helen. "Class of 1861." *American Weekly* 3 (September 1961): 8–13.

INDEX